KIERKEGAARD AND CHRISTENDOM

JOHN W. ELROD

Kierkegaard and Christendom

PRINCETON UNIVERSITY PRESS
PRINCETON, N.J.

Copyright © 1981 by Princeton University Press
Published by Princeton University Press, Princeton, New Jersey
IN THE UNITED KINGDOM:
Princeton University Press, Guildford, Surrey

All Rights Reserved
Library of Congress Cataloging in Publication Data will be
found on the last printed page of this book

Publication of this book was assisted
by a grant from the Publications Program of the
National Endowment for the Humanities

This book has been composed in Linotype Baskerville

Clothbound editions of Princeton University Press books
are printed on acid-free paper, and binding materials are
chosen for strength and durability

Printed in the United States of America by
Princeton University Press, Princeton, New Jersey

For my parents,
　John Charles Elrod
　Carolyn Barnette Elrod

CONTENTS

ACKNOWLEDGMENTS

I WISH to express my sincerest appreciation to Professor Howard V. Hong and Professor Robert L. Perkins for their critical readings of the entire manuscript. To my colleagues and friends, Paul W. Hollenbach, Joseph H. Kupfer, and Richard J. Van Iten, I am most grateful for the many conversations in which they helped me to work through many difficult points in the writing of this book. My editors at Princeton, Mr. Sanford Thatcher and Ms. Gretchen Oberfranc, have also been enormously helpful in preparing the manuscript for publication, and to them I also owe a special debt of thanks. I also want to express my indebtedness to Iowa State University, the National Endowment for the Humanities, and the American Philosophical Society for providing grants that made the writing of the book possible. Finally, to my wife, Mimi, I am deeply grateful for doing more than her share during those long months of research and writing.

. . . the commandment is that you *shall* love, but when you understand life and yourself, then it is as if you should not need to be commanded, because to love human beings is the only thing worth living for; without this love you really do not live; to love human beings is also the only salutary consolation for both time and eternity, and to love human beings is the only true sign that you are a "Christian." . . .

Works of Love

People think that the world needs a republic, and they think that it needs a new social order and a new religion—but it never occurs to anybody that what the world now needs, confused as it is by much knowing, is a Socrates.

The Sickness unto Death

THIS BOOK attempts to provide an interpretation of Søren Kierkegaard's second literature.[1] This literature comprises those published and unpublished writings that were composed after the publication of *Concluding Unscientific Postscript* in 1846. These writings have been traditionally referred to as Kierkegaard's religious writings, as opposed to the more philosophically oriented pseudonymous works published between 1840 and 1846. Unlike the pseudonymous works, which generated the existentialist and neo-orthodox traditions in philosophy and theology, the second literature has neither received sustained scholarly attention nor enjoyed the broad-ranging philosophical and theological influence of the earlier pseudonymous writings. It is true, of course, that individual works—*Two Ages*, the two books published under the Anti-Climacus pseudonym, *Training in Christianity* and *The Sickness unto Death*, as well as the polemical articles written against "Christendom" in the last months of Kierkegaard's life—have received scholarly analyses and exercised influence in the fields of theology and social criticism. But little, if any, serious effort has been made to read and interpret these later writings as a whole. The reasons for this neglect are not altogether clear, although it seems obvious that, lacking any interesting and compelling twentieth-century corollary such as existentialism or neo-orthodox theology, there simply has not been sufficient motivation to study this second literature with the precision and care that characterize many of the studies of the earlier pseudonymous books.

It is true that Kierkegaard's second literature reflects a spiritual turn from the aesthetic orientation of the earlier

[1] I am indebted to Professor Robert Perkins for this term.

pseudonyms to a consistent preoccupation with exploring and developing that ethical-religious mode of existence that some of his earlier pseudonyms described and appreciated but did not existentially adopt. This spiritual turn, which Kierkegaard began slowly to make in 1846, involves a change in his conception of himself as an author. Whereas Kierkegaard, through the pseudonyms, had taken an aesthetic stance with the intention of leading his reader *to choose* the life of duty and faith, as opposed to the life of pleasure, he sought in his second literature *to cultivate* that ethical-religious subjectivity within his reader. Rather than simply presenting his reader with the existential options open to him, Kierkegaard came to understand his vocation as an author to be one of communicating with his reader in such a way as to enable him to cultivate the ethical-religious mode of existence made possible by Christianity. The second literature is devoted to enabling his reader to understand that the essence of Christianity is to love one's neighbor as one loves oneself. And the form of this literature is intended to be Socratic in the sense that, like Socrates, Kierkegaard hoped to seduce the reader into an awareness that his Christianity is not at all Christian and that he as an individual must himself change if he is to actualize the essentially loving character of the gospel of Jesus Christ.

As are the preceding pseudonymous writings, the second literature is therapeutic in nature in that it seeks to cultivate an existential change in the reader. The pseudonyms sought to rescue the individual from the objectifying mentality of Hegelian metaphysics by employing a variety of devices to enable the reader to discover that the subjective life could not be expressed, understood, or fulfilled in any abstract system of thought. The purpose of the second literature is also to change the reader; however, its motivation is not opposition to Hegelian philosophy but to the political, economic, and cultural changes rapidly transforming Denmark from a feudalistic to a modern nation state. Writing under his own name, Kierkegaard sought to rescue the individual from the illusion that his spirit was being improved by his participation in the modernization of Denmark.

Modernization began in earnest in Denmark in the eighteenth century and achieved full momentum in the nineteenth. During the late eighteenth and nineteenth centuries, the country experienced a surge of growth and change that transformed it from a backward, feudal, and agrarian state into a modern, liberal democracy. Its transition into a modern nation state was rapid, relatively smooth, and without bloodshed. This period witnessed fundamental changes in almost every dimension of public and private life. Economic reform in both the rural and urban sectors of Denmark led the way toward the emergence of the new state. In the second half of the eighteenth century, the practice of communal farming in small villages and on large estates gave way to private ownership of land and individual farming for profit. The profit motive kindled economic change within the cities as well. The old guild systems gave way to a competitive labor market. Industry, especially in textiles, began to flourish once the principles and practices of free enterprise were adopted by Danish businessmen. Investments in the textile and beer industries, the new railroad transportation system, farm land, and amusement park fueled the economy's return to health after its virtual collapse in 1813, the year of Kierkegaard's birth.

These economic and social changes were accompanied by equally significant developments within other sectors of Danish life. A free press appeared, making possible for the first time in Danish history the wide circulation of a plurality of political and cultural ideas and criticisms of governmental policies and practices. The nobility and the clergy quietly lost their influence with the king in establishing governmental policy and were replaced by their more knowledgable colleagues in the university. The University of Copenhagen became a center of influence, first, on the king before the establishment of the constitutional monarchy in 1848 and, later, on the elected assembly that was given the constitutional authority to govern the country. In addition to exercising its new-found influence, the university also aided the coming of experimental science to Denmark. Cartesianism had been firmly replaced by Newtonian physics by 1800. The publication of Darwin's *Origin of the Species* in 1859 found immediate and enthusiastic acceptance among Danish academics who were themselves already at work both empirically and speculatively on an evolutionary accounting of the emergence of the species.

Denmark's many economic and cultural developments were complemented by an equally significant change in its form of government. The benevolence of Denmark's kings was undoubtedly responsible in part for delaying the appearance of a democratic form of government. But in 1848, under pressure from both within and outside the university, King Frederik VII signed a constitutional monarchy into law, and for the first time in Danish history the individual Dane could choose his own government. With this royal act, Denmark became a modern state. It rested politically on the principles of democratic liberalism, economically on the principles of laissez-faire capitalism, scientifically on the principles of experimental science, and academically and culturally on the principles of free inquiry and uncensored expression and dissemination of ideas. It is in these senses that we can speak of the late eighteenth and nineteenth centuries as the period of Denmark's modernization.

The philosophical principle at work in most of these changes is the principle of individualism as it is developed in liberal political theory. The social-political philosophy that developed from Thomas Hobbes through John Locke to John Stuart Mill, Adam Smith, and David Ricardo provided the philosophical basis for the modernization of Denmark. Certainly, the substance of this social-political philosophy is not a single, monolithic view of self and society that is etched in stone and transferred from one philosopher to the next without significant change. Nevertheless, the following points appear to be ones to which liberal theorists would generally subscribe. First, the essence of human nature is identified as freedom from dependence upon the will of others. Second, being free in this sense means that the individual is free from any relations with others except those he voluntarily enters into with a view to his own interest. Third, the individual is the proprietor of his own person and capacities and for this reason owes nothing to society. Fourth, each individual's freedom can rightfully be limited only by those obligations and rules that protect the freedom of others. Fifth, political society is a human contrivance for the protection of each individual's property in both his person and goods and for the maintenance of orderly relations between free persons.[2] This theory of liberalism tended to force such concepts as freedom, rights, obligation, equality, justice, labor, society, and God to conform to this individualistic philosophy. Central to this doctrine is the concept of the individual as a being who is endowed with certain natural rights that are protected by political and judicial authority. To be a member of a society means both to have these rights protected and to be free to pursue what is in one's interest so long as the rights of others are not violated. The pursuit of what one perceives to be in one's own interest is the meaning of freedom, and the maximization of one's interest requires the other only in a negative sense, that is, as one who acknowledges and does not infringe upon these natural rights.

It would be mistaken to suggest that Kierkegaard's second literature addresses the emergence of the modern liberal state in this theoretical form, for it clearly does not. Readers of Kierkegaard's published works will search in vain for anything resembling a full and critical discussion of Danish modernization in just these terms. There are indeed certain journal entries that deal with liberalism, but even here his

[2] C. B. MacPherson, *The Political Theory of Possessive Individualism* (London: Oxford University Press, 1975), pp. 263ff.

discussion of social and political philosophical issues takes an almost aphoristic form.[3] It is simply not Kierkegaard's style as a thinker to address these sorts of problems in the standard theoretical, abstract, and objective fashion in which they were confronted in modern philosophy. In this sense, Kierkegaard continued the philosophical style initiated with his pseudonyms. One only need read *Either/Or* to discover that Hegelian philosophy is to be criticized not theoretically but in terms of concrete life situations. Kierkegaard allows his reader to encounter Hegel critically by presenting aspects of his philosophy in the form of human character and existential situations involving psychological, ethical, and religious dimensions. In this manner, the reader is led to see the existential inadequacies of Hegel's philosophical position. This pedagogical style also characterizes Kierkegaard's second literature in that he chose to deal primarily with the modern liberal state not in social scientific and philosophical terms but as it concretely formed and shaped the individual's spirit as he lived through its development in Denmark.

Kierkegaard, then, confronted the issue of modernization as it molded the lives of Danes who eagerly participated in Denmark's coming of age. This style required Kierkegaard to write his books in such a manner that they addressed the reader whose way of life was being shaped by the economic, political, and social changes occurring in Denmark during this period. For Kierkegaard, these fundamental institutional changes in the fabric of society were problematic precisely because of the profoundly formative impact they exercised on the individuals who lived through them. Kierkegaard, then, both confronts and critically addresses the modern liberal Danish state as it forms and shapes the individual's style of life. Neither his confrontation with nor his response to this powerful event is theoretical and abstract. In Kierkegaard's view, the human spirit, not books, is the proper locus for addressing this phenomenon.

[3] *JP*, IV, 4060-4242.

What appeared to trouble him most about the emergence of the modern liberal state is that it nurtured an egotistical mode of subjectivity. By uncritically existing within and embracing this new social order, individuals became egotistical in their relations to one another. The construction of a society predicated on the priority of the individual and his right to pursue his own best interests as he perceived them sets individuals in an uncompromising opposition to one another. This opposition encourages the establishment of subtle mechanisms within the political, economic, and social dimensions of life that enable both individuals and groups to advance their interests at the expense of others. We shall see that in Kierkegaard's view the individual is by nature a subjective being who is essentially motivated by the desire to acquire an identity. Kierkegaard's way of making this crucial point in *Works of Love* is to claim that the individual cannot avoid loving himself. Self-love, which is the desire for a publicly recognizable and valued identity, sets the individual on a collision course with all others who seek the same end. As Kierkegaard saw it, the modern liberal state is simply a subtle conduit for this basic impulse in human selves. The new society coming into being in his Denmark accomplished nothing less than providing social, political, and economic structures in which this conflict could be civilly conducted.

This problem was compounded by the cultural endorsement given to this aspect of modernization by both the arts and religion. Though somewhat distinct from the individualism of the liberalism, the versions of individualism celebrated and affirmed in the artistic and religious sectors were not incompatible with the egotism being cultivated by institutional developments within the social, political, and economic dimensions of society. Kierkegaard believed that contemporary Danish literature, and especially contemporary religion, provided the cultural legitimation that any major social upheaval requires. Quite unwittingly, according to Kierkegaard, the religion of Denmark contributed to the cultivation of this egotistical subjectivity. An informal alliance between religion on the one hand and political and social developments on the other conspired to bring into being an aesthetic mode of subjectivity, which Kierkegaard identified as egotism.

It is in this sense that Kierkegaard referred to his modern Denmark as Christendom. Kierkegaard did not intend for the term to signify the segregated sacred dimension of Danish life but, rather, the modern Danish state. Kierkegaard believed that to live in Christendom involves nothing less than living in a religiously legitimated social order that cultivates and nurtures egotistical relations among its citizens. The works that constitute the second literature, then, are addressed to the reader who is unwittingly caught up in this social and religious experiment. Kierkegaard viewed his task as the Socratic one of awakening his reader from three illusions: his ignorance about himself as a being who egotistically loves himself and desires to achieve a publicly recognizable and valued identity; his self-deception that he is a Christian; and his belief that Denmark is a Christian state. Moreover, the Socratic task includes not only awakening the reader to a self-knowledge but also encouraging him to choose the good, which Kierkegaard conceived of as loving one's neighbor as one loves oneself. Kierkegaard believed that only by loving one's neighbor could egotistical self-love be transformed into a nonegotistical form. It is in this sense that Kierkegaard will be identified as an ethicist, for he viewed his vocation as one of attacking Christendom socratically by leading his reader to love his neighbor as he already loves himself.

In the following chapters, I attempt to show that one can reasonably interpret Kierkegaard's second literature as an ethical-religious attack on Christendom. Toward this end, the first chapter attempts briefly to provide analyses of the major social, economic, political, and cultural trends of development in Denmark in the late eighteenth and nineteenth centuries. The prospect of becoming familiar with a host of obscure and, from the standpoint of major trends in European history, irrelevant figures who fashioned Danish modernization might seem less appealing than an effort at linking Kierkegaard with the more familiar lines of modernization in France, Germany, and England and the key figures in their development. But even though it would be both interesting and useful to compare Kierkegaard's views on modernization with, for example, those of Hegel and Marx, it would be a serious mistake to begin a study of Kierkegaard's views on this matter with this sort of comparison. As we know, few writers are more socratically oriented than Kierkegaard; therefore, in his writings he does not address himself to a general public about an equally general and abstract phenomenon called modernization. Kierkegaard's books possess a decidedly pamphleteering quality in that they directly confront both specific issues and movements and the concrete impact that these are exerting on individual human beings. It is precisely because Kierkegaard pays such close attention to the uniquely Danish contours of modernization and its all-encompassing impact on the lives of individuals that we cannot without great peril to our understanding of Kierkegaard ignore the historical situation in which he developed his second literature.

In the second chapter, Kierkegaard's social criticism is organized in such a way as to give the reader an awareness of the main lines of his criticisms of Danish modernization. The remaining five chapters attempt to illuminate the ethical-religious basis of those criticisms. Ethics and religion are schematically separated for the purpose of analyzing both the content of each and the relations between them. In the third and fourth chapters, we shall investigate Kierkegaard's critical analysis of Christendom, as well as the ethical response that he believed was required. The third chapter explores, first, Kierkegaard's conception of the "natural man" as one who egotistically loves himself and, then, the way in which the processes of modernization institutionalize this egotistical self-love. The fourth chapter attempts to show that Kierkegaard based his ethics on the view of the other as a neighbor whom one is obliged to love as one loves onself. In this chapter, Kierkegaard's claim that proper self-love and love for one's neighbor are mutually inclusive is analyzed, and I argue that in this notion Kierkegaard offered his own ethical alternative to the political conception of human relations and society that is implicit in the institutional structures of modernization. In the fifth and sixth chapters, I explore the manner in which Kierkegaard attempted to provide a religious grounding of this ethical conception of human relations and community.

The final chapter is not directly concerned with the content of Kierkegaard's ethical-religious attack on Christendom but delineates the manner of its communication. Just as the pseudonymous authorship cannot be fully grasped without paying serious attention to the pseudonymous method of communicating its content, so in turning to Kierkegaard's second literature it is crucial to study the method of communicating its content as well. To read Kierkegaard's second literature as an ethical-religious diagnosis of Christendom leads one to focus on the substance of Kierkegaard's criticisms of modernization. In this sense, one can read Kierkegaard's second literature on a theoretical level much as one reads Marx's writings. But to read Kierkegaard exclusively in this manner is to complete only a portion of one's task when writing and reading about him. For it is equally important to see that his works not only diagnostically inform the reader that the central problem within Christendom is his egotistical self-love but also seek to change him in such a manner that his egotistical self-love becomes a proper self-love.

Kierkegaard is more than a social critic. In the final analysis, he is a religious author who is essentially motivated to help his reader find his way along the ethical-religious path toward acquiring a pure heart. Kierkegaard addresses his individual reader with the religious assumption that his life is an ethical-religious pilgrimage. This assumption is never more clearly apparent than in the form of his communication with each individual reader. To ignore Kierkegaard's style of communication would represent a failure to penetrate fully his second literature and, perhaps more fundamentally, to take ourselves seriously as readers of Kierkegaard.

ABBREVIATIONS OF
KIERKEGAARD'S WORKS

THE following presses have kindly granted me permission to quote from books to which they hold the copyright: Harper and Row, Publishers, Inc.; Indiana University Press; Oxford University Press; Princeton University Press.

AC   *Attack upon "Christendom."* Translated with an introduction by Walter Lowrie. With a supplementary introduction by Howard A. Johnson. Princeton: Princeton University Press, 1968.

ANOL   *Armed Neutrality and An Open Letter.* Translated and edited by Howard V. Hong and Edna H. Hong. With an introduction by Gregor Malantschuk. Bloomington: Indiana University Press, 1968.

AR   *On Authority and Revelation.* Translated with an introduction and notes by Walter Lowrie. Harper Torchbook, The Cloister Library. New York: Harper and Row, 1966.

CD   *Christian Discourses.* Translated with an introduction by Walter Lowrie. London: Oxford University Press, 1952.

CDR   *The Concept of Dread.* Translated with an introduction by Walter Lowrie. 2d ed. Princeton: Princeton University Press, 1957.

CLA   *Crisis in the Life of an Actress.* Translated with an introduction and notes by Stephen Crites. Harper Torchbook. New York: Harper and Row, 1967.

CUP   *Concluding Unscientific Postscript.* Translated by Walter Lowrie and David Swenson. With an introduction by Walter Lowrie. Princeton: Princeton University Press, 1941.

DODE   *De Omnibus Dubitandum Est.* Translated by T. H. Croxall. Stanford: Stanford University Press, 1958.

xxii

ED   *Edifying Discourses.* Translated by David F. Swenson and Lillian Marvin Swenson. 4 vols. Minneapolis: Augsburg Publishing House, 1943-46.

E/O   *Either/Or.* Translated by David F. Swenson and Lillian Marvin Swenson. With revisions and a forward by Howard A. Johnson. 2 vols. Princeton: Princeton University Press, 1972.

FSE   *For Self-Examination and Judge for Yourselves.* Translated with an introduction and notes by Walter Lowrie. Princeton: Princeton University Press, 1944.

GS   *The Gospel of Our Suffering.* Translated by A. S. Aldworth and W. S. Ferrie. Grand Rapids: William B. Eerdmans Publishing Company, 1964.

JFY   *Judge for Yourselves.*

JP   *Søren Kierkegaard's Journals and Papers.* Translated and edited by Howard V. Hong and Edna H. Hong. 7 vols. Bloomington: Indiana University Press, 1967-78.

PA   *The Present Age.* Translated by Alexander Dru. With an introduction by Walter Kaufmann. Harper Torchbook, The Cloister Library. New York: Harper and Row, 1962.

PF   *Philosophical Fragments.* Translated by David F. Swenson. Revised by Howard V. Hong. With an introduction by Niels Thulstrup and commentary by Niels Thulstrup and Howard V. Hong. Princeton: Princeton University Press, 1962.

PH   *Purity of Heart Is to Will One Thing.* Translated with an introduction by Douglas V. Steere. Harper Torchbook, The Cloister Library. New York: Harper and Row, 1966.

POV   *The Point of View of My Work as an Author.* Translated with an introduction and notes by Walter Lowrie. Harper Torchbook, The Cloister Library. New York: Harper and Row, 1962.

SKJ   *The Journals of Søren Kierkegaard.* Translated and edited by Alexander Dru. Oxford: Oxford University Press, 1951.

SKP   *Søren Kierkegaards Papirer.* Edited by P. A. Heiberg, V. Kuhr, and E. Torsting. 20 vols. Copenhagen: Glyendal, 1909-48.

SUD   *The Sickness unto Death.* Translated with an introduction and notes by Walter Lowrie. Princeton: Princeton University Press, 1941.

TC   *Training in Christianity.* Translated with an introduction and notes by Walter Lowrie. Princeton: Princeton University Press, 1944.

WL   *Works of Love.* Translated with an introduction by Howard V. Hong and Edna H. Hong. New York: Harper and Row, 1962.

KIERKEGAARD AND CHRISTENDOM

CHAPTER ONE

The Modernization of Denmark

SØREN KIERKEGAARD could hardly have lived through a more significant and dramatic period in Danish history. His lifetime, 1813-1855, measures a period of great upheaval and change in practically every dimension of Danish life. These internal transitions followed Denmark's loss of prestige in Europe as a result of its loss of Norway in 1814 and of the duchies of Schleswig and Holstein in 1864. Both events were occasioned by humiliating military defeats, by the British in 1813 and by Prussia in 1864. This period saw the final transformation of Denmark from a medium-sized European power into a small, weak, and poverty-stricken nation, one so small and helpless that it was almost absorbed into the German Confederation. Added to the military humiliation of 1813 was economic collapse caused by the rampant inflation that accompanied the Napoleonic wars. Despite efforts to stem inflation by increasing taxes and printing more money, the currency had dropped to one-fourteenth of its face value by 1812. On 5 January 1813 King Frederik VI proclaimed the state bankrupt. The nation's bank, the Kurantbank, closed, and money was revalued at about one-tenth of its face value.[1]

Kierkegaard was born into a nation racked by severe economic and foreign-policy crises, which themselves

[1] Kierkegaard provides a sardonic autobiographical interpretation of this Danish misfortune: "I was born in 1813, in that bad fiscal year when so many other bad banknotes were put in circulation, and my life seems most comparable to one of them. There is a suggestion of greatness in me, but because of the bad conditions of the times I am not worth very much. A banknote like that sometimes becomes a family's misfortune" (*JP*, V, 5725).

marked the beginning of internal reform and change on a scale so all-encompassing that we may speak of this period as marking the birth of modern Denmark. Indeed, Kierkegaard lived through the transition of Denmark from a state operating according to feudalistic principles in agriculture and industry and presided over by an absolute monarch to a state exceeded only by England in its commitment to the principles of democratic and economic liberalism. Accompanying these radical and swift political and economic changes were the advent of experimental science, the flowering of Denmark's golden age of literature (1802-1830), the emergence of a strong spirit of nationalism, and the beginning of ecclesiastical reform.

ECONOMIC AND POLITICAL CHANGE

Prince Christian Frederik, later Christian VIII of Denmark, observed in 1814 that through commercial trade the lower classes "lose their simplicity and their plainness of thought; they talk politics; in short, they are no longer peasants."[2] His observation was well-founded, for since the middle of the eighteenth century, efforts had been made to replace centuries-old feudalistic agricultural policies. Under the leadership of village patriarchs, agricultural policies were established and heavy fines and penalties levied against individuals who refused to cooperate. This agricultural policy was aimed not at production of surpluses for purposes of trade but at production of only those supplies necessary to sustain the village.

This collectivist policy lasted through the eighteenth century, though it began to come under reevaluation and criticism in the last half of that century. Most criticism and agitation for reform came from professors of economics at the University of Copenhagen, who emphasized the importance of private property, profit and investment of

[2] B. J. Hovde, *The Scandinavian Countries, 1720-1865: The Rise of the Middle Class*, 2 vols. (Boston: Chapman and Grimes, 1943), II, 520.

profit, and use of technology in order to increase yields and profits. The *Danmarks og Norges Oeconomiske Magazin* offered a medal in 1760 for the best answer to the question: "What are the most considerable obstacles to the abolition of common holdings in land, and by what means can they most easily and certainly be overcome, without prejudice to those concerned?" Only one economist in all of Denmark favored retention of the old communal system. There was practically unanimous agreement among the academics, the king, and large landowners that agriculture would be enormously stimulated by placing it on a profit basis. Common lands were consolidated and divided; large estates, once the owners saw the profit to be made from rising land values, were voluntarily divided into small farms and rented or sold to farmers who were freed to operate them independently. The most important objective in the government's program was to stimulate peasant ownership or hereditary tenure. To this end, the king made low-interest loans available for the purchase of small farms; where outright ownership was not possible, farmers were encouraged to rent and lease land. In addition, peasants were granted freedom from compulsory labor and freedom to move throughout the country. All the government legislation necessary for this transformation of farm policy had been approved by the king by the turn of the century, and by 1865 the communalistic structure of agriculture had been completely replaced by a capitalistic one.

It is no wonder that in 1814 Prince Christian Frederik could observe that increased political activity accompanied the demise of the peasantry and communal and estate farming. The establishment of individual ownership of farms and of individual enterprise as the cornerstones of nineteenth-century agriculture resulted inevitably in democratic political activity in rural districts. Small landowners slowly established themselves as a political force with which the king and later the democratically elected parliament had to contend. They worked for equalization of the burdens of taxation and military conscription, which previously was confined to the peasant class. Aggressive and enterprising members of the class discovered the possibility of upward mobility by means of economic success in farming, business, or industry.

The placing of agriculture on a capitalistic base was accompanied by an equally radical transformation of the urban economy. By 1814 the principles of laissez-faire economics had been accepted by economists in Denmark. In any case, change in the direction of capitalism was already under way by the time the thought of Adam Smith, Thomas Malthus, and David Ricardo reached Denmark. Agricultural reform, population increase, and industrialization, which created new trades and products not covered by the guilds, were all influential in the breakdown of the old feudalistic guild system by the turn of the century. The ideas of the liberal economists merely fueled the drive toward its complete dismantling.

Proponents of the guild system fought its demise in the Danish courts through the 1840s and 1850s but without ultimate success. The courts were simply unwilling to stifle the emergence of individual freedom in the arena of employment. New jobs made available by industry, merchandizing, and agriculture outmaneuvered the guilds; the freedom of occupation bill passed by the Rigsdag in 1857 did little more than confirm an already existing economic reality.

This capitalistic turn in the domestic economy as well as in Denmark's trade policies so greatly nourished the bankrupt economy that by 1840 individuals who had accumulated capital through savings were investing it in corporate enterprises. Under the leadership of Copenhagen's Industrial Society, established businesses adopted the corporate form of organization in order to expand their capital bases. New corporations were formed to undertake the construction of a national railway system, the establishment of a brewing industry, and the planning of amusement gardens. All this corporate activity in turn opened up new jobs and provided a healthy market for speculation. Because Denmark's economy continued to be heavily based in agriculture through the middle of the nineteenth century, the creation of an industrialized and corporate economy in the cities was not so rapid and dominant as to create the kinds of social and economic problems it generated in England. Only in the last quarter of the nineteenth century did the social and economic problems of industrialization appear; even then they were of an extent that could be successfully managed by government and business.

The triumph of capitalism over the guild system in 1857 represented as radical a reform in the urban economy as did the dissolution of communal agriculture in the countryside. As in the rural areas, the individual, at least in principle, was freed to pursue his own private economic interests. Individual initiative and enterprise replaced the communal and collectivist orientation of a guild-dominated labor market, and in both the city and the country the profit motive emerged as the prime incentive for labor.

The ultimate triumph of liberalism in Denmark occurred in 1848-1849 with the final ratification of the constitution by King Frederik VII. His two predecessors in the nineteenth century, Frederik VI (1808-1839) and Christian VIII (1839-1849), were both strong advocates of absolute monarchy. During their reigns, the monarchy continued to enjoy the support of Danish citizens; even the loss of Norway in 1814 and the economic collapse of the country in 1813 stirred no new political consciousness and provoked no call for a change in the character of government. As B. J. Hovde succinctly states, "between 1815 and 1830 one might almost say that there were no politics in Denmark."[3] And Hans Christian Andersen wrote in *The Fairy Tale of My Life* that "politics played no part at all in Denmark, the theatre was the 'public interest,' the most important theme

[3] Ibid., p. 511.

of conversation for the day and the evening. . . ."[4] This political passivism in the first third of the nineteenth century was largely the result of the enlightened nature of the monarchy. Frederik and Christian were not despotic in character, possessed a warm affection for their subjects, and were reasonably responsive to the agricultural and economic reforms pressed during their reigns.[5] Thus, while rapid and far-reaching changes were occurring during the first third of the nineteenth century in economic and agricultural life and in Danish foreign relations, all internal voices for political change were effectively silenced by common consent.

The second third of the nineteenth century, however, witnessed the decline of the nobility and the clergy, the two classes that had been the king's closest advisers. As the activities of banking, industry, agriculture, and commerce passed into the arena of private initiative, the nobility experienced an inexorable decline in power and influence. The nobility and the clergy were then replaced by the peasants and the bourgeoisie, and these two groups began to agitate for and ultimately brought about political reform. We have seen how agricultural reform plunged the peasants into political activity. Their politics were narrowly based on the pursuit of class interests; thus their initial goals were related almost exclusively to agricultural reform—land reform, private ownership of property, freedom of occupation, and educational reform directed primarily toward instruction in farming methods. Not until the late 1840s, when Christian VIII denied them the right of assembly and refused their request for universal conscription, did the peasants align themselves politically with the

[4] Quoted in W. Glyn Jones, *Denmark* (New York: Praeger Publishers, 1970), p. 65.

[5] Frederik tried after the war to delegate more authority to his bureaucracy of appointed officials and also attempted, though without much success, to reorganize his system of administration in the interest of greater efficiency and honesty.

bourgeoisie and come to support the latter in its demand for a constitutional form of government.

The transition to a constitutional form of government did not come about as the result of internal political pressure placed upon the king by the bourgeoisie and the peasantry. The bourgeoisie—composed of academics, the literati, and the business community—had for a decade been quietly pressing the king for a change in government. Frederik had been unresponsive, though he accidentally provided the opening needed by political liberals when in 1831 he decreed the creation of four consultative assemblies in response to pressure from Schleswig and Holstein for freedom from the Danish crown. These assemblies were created for the purpose of advising the king on how best to govern Schleswig, Holstein, Jutland, and the Danish islands. Members of each assembly were to be elected by popular vote in each province, and their role in national politics was to be purely advisory.

The intellectuals used these assemblies as their political base for articulating the principles of democratic liberalism. They stood for freedom of the individual, equality of opportunity, and political democracy, and they believed that a society based on such principles would regulate itself by the principle of intelligent self-interest. The state was to be but a policeman, making certain that no individual or group of individuals infringed upon the rights of other individuals or groups.[6] The leadership of this movement was assumed by a small group of men: the economist Christian Georg Nathan David; the theologian Henrik Nicolai Clausen, whom Hal Koch describes as "perhaps the most popular of university professors, an intrepid advocate of freedom in science and in the church, as well as in civic life";[7] the botanist Joachim Frederik Schouw; and the jurist Peter Georg Bang. Orla Lehmann represented the

[6] Hovde, *Scandinavian Countries*, II, 521.

[7] Hal Koch, *Grundtvig*, trans. Llewllyn Jones (Yellow Springs, Ohio: Antioch Press, 1952), p. 99.

9

students, Johan Christian Drewsen the industrialists, and Anton Frederik Tscherning the military; ironically, Tscherning was the most radical of all. With the establishment of the assemblies, the bourgeois liberals immediately began to press their demands for the "abolition of gild [*sic*] monopolies; free trade; improvement of the means of communication; the recognition, not of aristocratic privilege, but of 'ability' and cultural achievement . . . and finally, constitutionally established democracy."[8]

Freedom of the press became the first concrete issue behind which the liberals united in political action. In the first assembly elections in 1834, C.G.N. David's journal, *Faedrelandet* (The Fatherland), became so aggressive in its support of certain candidates and opposition to others that the king threatened to curb its role in the campaigns. This threat was strongly opposed by the liberals, and Professors Clausen and Schouw carried a petition to the king bearing 572 signatures warning him against any such repressive act. The signers of this petition also formed the Society for the Proper Use of the Freedom of the Press, which attracted thousands of members throughout Denmark and served as a mechanism for the education of the public in democratic liberalism. A compromise on this issue between the king and the liberals was reached, but it was clear that constitutional government was on the way.

Christian VIII, in an open letter dated 8 July 1846, declared himself in favor of a constitutional monarchy. He appointed Bang, a moderate, to draft a constitution, which Bang prepared to send to the king late in that year. But Christian died before he could sign a constitutional government into law. His successor, Frederik VII, called a constitutional convention into session. This convention drafted a new constitution, which Frederik signed on 5 June 1849. The constitution provided for two chambers of the Rigsdag: the Landsting, to be elected indirectly; and the Folketing, to be elected directly. Male householders thirty years of age

[8] Hovde, *Scandinavian Countries,* II, 543.

were eligible to vote.[9] The constitution guaranteed freedom of assembly, speech, and press; it also required court reform, including trial by jury. In addition, freedom of occupation, universal military service, and local self-government were placed on the agenda for future consideration by the Rigsdag. Finally, all hereditary privileges were abolished.

The tenuous alliance maintained between the peasants and the bourgeoisie during the struggle for constitutional democracy and the 1848 war with Schleswig and Holstein, from which Denmark emerged victorious, disintegrated once Frederik signed the new government into law. With these domestic and foreign matters settled, the bourgeoisie's fear of peasant leadership of the nation through their dominance of the Rigsdag resurfaced. The politics of the last third of the century centered on this struggle of the peasants for political dominance of the nation. What is important for us to notice here is that by 1850 the political consciousness of the Danish people had been thoroughly reshaped by agricultural reform, laissez-faire economics, and democratic liberalism. These broad movements had introduced changes of a quantitative nature into Danish life; more fundamentally, they brought a qualitative transformation of a people's understanding and perception of themselves. This emergence of a new self-understanding on the part of an entire people was reflected in and nurtured by Danish literature, religion, and science.

RELIGIOUS AND CULTURAL CHANGE

One of the ironies of Danish life is that the collapse of the nation through foreign and domestic difficulties early in the nineteenth century coincided with its greatest and most productive period in literature. Indeed, the period between 1802 and 1830 has been called the golden age of literature in Danish history; names like Adam Oehlen-

[9] Ibid., p. 531.

11

schläger, Nikolai Frederik Severin Grundtvig, Carsten Hauch, Bernhard Severin Ingemann, Johan Ludvig Heiberg, and Hans Christian Andersen stand out among the greatest in Danish literary history. It was an age of romanticism in reaction to the Enlightenment notion that the universe is a mechanistic unity that can be rationally expressed through the deductive systems of mathematics and metaphysics. Romantic poetry, prose, drama, historical novels, and hymns recover, praise, and proclaim the individual as the center of value and reality, as opposed to the Enlightenment emphasis upon the universal. Nature is also personified; it becomes a living being with whom each individual may share a personal and mystical union. This personal identification with nature appears as a symbol in literature for a dynamic and functional identity with God; at the same time, the nation becomes a leading symbol for identification with one's fellow men.

The thinker most responsible for the appearance of romanticism in Denmark was the young Henrik Steffens, a geologist who was born in Norway, a graduate in theology and the natural sciences of the University of Copenhagen, and an accomplished student of Friedrich Wilhelm Joseph von Schelling's philosophy of nature. Steffens returned to Copenhagen in 1802 after studying in Germany with Schelling, and during that year he gave a series of lectures at the university that was attended by Oehlenschläger and Grundtvig.

In the first nine lectures in the series, published in 1803 under the title *Introduction to Philosophical Lectures*, Steffens claimed that truth cannot be found in empirical science but must be sought through a presentment (*Ahnelse*) of the presence of the eternal in the finite.[10]

---

[10] I am indebted to Robert L. Horn's dissertation for this brief summary of Steffens's thought in these early lectures. Horn, "Positivity and Dialectic: A Study of the Theological Method of Hans Lassen Martensen" (Ph.D., diss., Union Theological Seminary, New York, 1969), pp. 7-13, 25-28.

> If we agree to this we relinquish the universal postulate of the understanding (*Forstand*) which would make our age and its way of thinking into the norm for all. . . . With this the giants awaken from their grave; gods and goddesses walk among us; every sound from the most remote ages speaks again with its own voice. . . . This presentment, whose object is always infinite, is called Poetry, since the living and creative manifests itself in an exalted mood (*Gemyth*). . . . An infinite sense seems to have concealed itself behind every visible form and beams forth mystically toward us. . . . A deep longing awakens within us.[11]

For Steffens, both the natural sciences and the study of history fall under the tutelage of speculative philosophy, for only the philosopher, in cooperation with the poet, can see through the disconnected assemblages of facts to the divine, the eternal, the infinite ground in and through which all are united.

In his seventh lecture, Steffens turned to the study of history. He claimed that the spirit of the Enlightenment offered a prosaic, rather than a poetic—that is, a mechanical rather than a religious—understanding of the universe and that it had abandoned the individual and the finite for the universal. Steffens was greatly encouraged by the spread of Protestantism, however, for in it he saw the renewal of the notion that the eternal and the divine are discovered in the individual. In Steffens's view, German idealism and romanticism were both refined expressions of the individualistic spirit of Protestantism. "The individual now becomes an expression of the Eternal, and the entire movement of nature and history can be seen as a development toward the fuller manifestation of the Eternal within more highly individualized forms."[12] Steffens was convinced that

11 Henrik Steffens, *Indeldning til Philosophiske Furlaesninger i København*, ed. B. T. Dahl (Copenhagen: Gyldendal, 1905), p. 21. Translated in Horn, "Positivity and Dialectic," pp. 8-9.

12 Quoted in Horn, "Positivity and Dialectic," p. 10.

13

philosophical idealism and the new poetry had shown that it is possible to discover a rational plan in history. "Here the Eternal Idea . . . unfolds itself, manifesting itself in an infinite evolution, not only containing in itself the possibility of everything which is to become actual, but as well the actuality of everything possible."[13] The beginning of wisdom, he argued, was to attend to *Ahnelse*, the expression of the eternal in the finite, and the clearest articulation of *Ahnelse* is poetry. The task of philosophy is to render a clearer and purer expression of the content of *Ahnelse* from its primary source in poetry.

Steffens's impact upon his audience was at first marginal. The natural philosopher Hans Christian Ørsted found nothing in the lectures that he had himself not already developed. Grundtvig dismissed them, though he subsequently admitted that his own later development depended almost entirely upon these early lectures by Steffens. Only the poet Oehlenschläger was inspired. After these lectures and long private conversations with Steffens, he suppressed two volumes of his poetry then in production and "turned his genius to the reawakening of the Norse gods, to use the historic-poetic power of the saga to create new life in his country-men."[14]

All of Oehlenschläger's works from the early nineteenth century reflect his nationalistic consciousness, and in true romantic style it is the great and glorious Danish past that he celebrated in his epic dramas, novels, and poetry. Oehlenschläger's praise in rolling verse of the greatness of the Danish past, as recorded in its ancient mythology, appealed to a people in search of an escape from the humiliating defeats and misfortunes of the present. Clausen's praise of Oehlenschläger's *Nordiske Digte* (Scandinavian Poems), which appeared in 1807, expressed the patriotic pride his works imbued in the Danish people: "The gigantic heroes of old here appeared before us in the flesh—and that in the

13 Ibid., p. 11.
14 Ibid., p. 13.

14

bitter hour of humiliation and disgrace—great in action and in resounding speech."[15]

This heroic quality of Danish antiquity was the constant theme in all of Oehlenschläger's early plays, with the exception of *Anden April* (The Second of April), which was inspired by the battle with the English fleet in the Copenhagen harbor in 1801. One of his most influential plays, *Aladdin* (1815), created a literary motif later found in the nationalistic sagas of Hauch and Ingemann. The Aladdin motif expressed the belief that certain individuals and nations were chosen by nature, God, or the gods to achieve greatness and that nothing could interfere with their success, however weak and ill-suited to the task they might appear. These twin themes of past and future national greatness had an enormous impact on a weakened and defeated Denmark. Although the grandiose predictions of future significance were satirized in the next generation by the philosopher-poet Poul Martin Møller and the dramatist J. L. Heiberg, the nationalistic consciousness awakened by Oehlenschläger did not disappear. Tempered by the criticisms of Møller and Heiberg, as well as by a realistic appraisal of the country as a small and powerless nation in the European community, Denmark's national consciousness turned inward and stimulated far-reaching reforms.

It was in relation to domestic life that the influence of Grundtvig's brand of nationalism was felt most strongly, an influence far more significant and enduring than that of Oehlenschläger. Like his former classmate Oehlenschläger, Grundtvig appealed to the past. His lifelong desire was to create in Danish life a synthesis of Nordic consciousness and Christian ethics, fusing both with the national character to form a national religion. Only by a recovery of their past, he believed, could the Danish people be true to themselves as a nation; therefore, his works on Scandinavian mythology were second in number, though greater in influence, to his writings on the Christian religion. Koch has

[15] Quoted in Hovde, *Scandinavian Countries*, II, 454.

said of Grundtvig's work that it is not the clearest in the Danish language but that it is surely "the mightiest expression of the battle of the Danish people and the Danish genius for self-consciousness." In Grundtvig's "often diffuse chatter, pointed up at intervals by a pithy saying concise as an epigraph, in his mingling of graceful lyric and rattling bombast, in his at once childishly simple and darkly enigmatic speech, coupled with a particular type of humor, he summed up widely diversified aspects of the Danish folk-mind."[16] In his scholarship, historical sagas, poetry, hymns, and sermons,[17] Grundtvig struggled to crystallize the great upheaval occurring in Danish self-consciousness during the nineteenth century. More than any other individual, he succeeded in synthesizing the many currents of change in nineteenth-century Denmark into a coherent, cohesive, and compelling nationalism.

Grundtvig's view of nationalism, Danish or otherwise, cannot be divorced from his conception of human nature. He struggled with this question throughout his life, and his most explicit answer is found in the introduction to *Northern Mythology*. He writes that "man is no ape, destined first to ape the other animals and then to ape himself until world's end, but is a matchless and marvelous creation, in whom divine powers are to reveal, unfold, and clarify themselves through a thousand generations as a divine experiment to demonstrate how spirit and matter may interpenetrate and be transfigured in a common divine consciousness."[18] Human life is a joining of spirit and clay. But spirit can never be revealed in an undifferentiated form. No particular person possesses an eternal and timeless soul —spirit, yes, but no ethereal and immaterial soul substance

16 Koch, *Grundtvig*, p. 118.

17 *N.F.S. Grundtvigs Udvalgte Skrifter*, ed. Holger Begtrup (Copenhagen: Gyldendal, 1904-09). For an edited English translation of Grundtvig's writings, see *N.F.S. Grundtvig*, trans. Johannes Knudsen, Enok Mortensen, and Ernest D. Nielsen, ed. with an intro. by Johannes Knudsen (Philadelphia: Fortress Press, 1976).

18 Koch, *Grundtvig*, p. 121.

that constitutes one's essential being. For Grundtvig, spirit always appears as clay, as earthbound, and the national is for him the clay that is shaped and formed as the expression of human spirit. Essentially, a human person is not a disembodied ego but a link in a great national chain whereby he is joined and constituted by a particular national history.

For Grundtvig, then, a nation is a people in which there exists a living and mysterious power that permeates the people from within, creating its history and fashioning its life. The human spirit is always determined as something national. Humanity is not abstract, cosmopolitan, and international in nature but is always something concrete, particular, unique, and limited by history, language, and tradition. In considering human being, it is a serious mistake to omit linguistic and nationality differences. The Enlightenment ignored all such distinctions and as a result arrived at a completely erroneous understanding of human nature. In Grundtvig's mind these differences, which had been regarded as accidental and contingent, are precisely the keys necessary to unlock the mysteries of human identity.

> Not since mankind was divided into many "peoples, races and tongues" has there been any possibility whatsoever, humanly speaking, of a mere human being, unless in the naked wilderness, for elsewhere one finds only national human beings, be they Hebrew, Greek, English, Danish. Therefore when some one people, Egyptians or Chinese, Romans or Germans, declare themselves to be the only rightful human beings, after whom all other nations must either pattern themselves or be regarded as dumb creatures, toil like domestic animals or be hunted like wild ones, mark you, it merely proves that the Egyptians or Chinese, Romans or Germans, can themselves have very little humanity in them.[19]

19 Ibid., p. 126.

17

This notion of nationality as the expression of a human identity and character distinguishes Grundtvig from earlier nationalists, whose insistence on the supremacy of all that is Danish led them to impose their will first upon Norway and later upon Schleswig and Holstein. Grundtvig's nationalism, though at times tempted by imperialistic impulses, recognized and affirmed the sanctity of national character. In the 1850s he opposed the bourgeois liberals who demanded a military solution to the Schleswig-Holstein question. He argued for the distinctiveness of the national characters of the duchies and declared that it would be wrong to impose the will of one nation upon another by force.

Grundtvig was a latecomer to the movement for constitutional monarchy. As late as 1839 he continued, like Kierkegaard, to support the idea of absolute monarchy. He viewed the constitutional struggle as a movement within the upper class, which, he thought, had a condescending attitude toward the peasants. To Grundtvig's mind, the bourgeois liberals claimed to speak not only for themselves but also for the peasants, acting as their guides, counselors, and guardians. He believed that this Whig mentality was at heart unnational in the sense that it, like the king, was fearful of radically and completely freeing the peasant class for full and equal participation in the national life. Nevertheless, Grundtvig ultimately saw in the constitutional movement the opportunity for vitalizing and stimulating the peasants to a more total involvement in the national life; only through the participation of the total populace could his concept of nationalism be achieved. He therefore sided with the bourgeois liberals in support of the constitutional monarchy; once it was established, he led the peasant opposition against bourgeois dominance of the Rigsdag.

Grundtvig's efforts to link his nationalistic ideology with Christianity was not accepted by rationalist theologians or the ecclesiastical establishment. His critics accused him of being a humanist for whom Christianity provided little more than "a higher luster to the whole."[20] They argued that he had so completely tied human identity and meaning to national consciousness that little, if any, significant room was left for an essentially religious understanding of human life. Though there is considerable justification for such a criticism. Grundtvig denied that he had ever subordinated the importance of Christianity to that of nationalism, even though it was true that he could not radically separate the one from the other. The essence of Grundtvig's position on the relation of church and state, religion and nationalism, is expressed in one of his poems:

If empty to us are the words and sound
Of "own people" and "land of our fathers,"
If we know not what more they mean
Than soil, seacoast, and population,
Then vain is every word we say
About God's kingdom's hills and dales,
God's people and congregation.

If we do not feel in our hearts,
We are spring of heaven's race,
If we cannot feel with sorrow,
That we have become debased,
Then we only make mock of the word
That God will redeem us and give
Rebirth as his own children.[21]

According to Grundtvig, a national consciousness must precede any appreciation for Christianity. By this national consciousness he meant not simply the awareness of geographic boundaries but also the participation of a whole people in a drama of struggle, conflict, and ultimate victory for the establishment of a national identity. Participation in such a drama of life against death sparks an awareness of the spiritual texture of human life. This national con-

20 Ibid., p. 151.
21 Ibid.

19

sciousness opens the world of spirit to us, where we perceive ourselves as caught in the chasm between life and death. The struggle for power, truth, and love in the national life awakens us to the highest perfection of these qualities in the life of Christ. Likewise, the threat of defeat, death, and hate in national life awakens us to the possibility of salvation promised by Christianity. Thus, a people discover in their struggle for a national consciousness a point of contact between the human and the divine. Grundtvig believed that a people must first sense the reality and value in their own lives of goodness, love, and truth on the one hand and the constant threat of failure and death on the other before Christianity, which promises the ultimate triumph of life over death, love over hate, will make any sense at all.

Northern Mythology had as its purpose the awakening of the people to an awareness of their national identity as a goal yet to be achieved. Grundtvig had hoped to arouse in them a sense of adventure, discovery, and risk and a willingness to sacrifice private interests and needs for the good of the whole. The people's spiritual deadness could only be remedied through a resuscitation of the nationl consciousness; only then would it become possible to talk with the people about Christianity. Grundtvig claimed that "if God's word is to find a prepared people, then a national word in the mother-tongue must first have turned the children's hearts to the fathers and the parents' to the children, so that they feel that death in all its forms is theirs, and mankind's, hereditary foe, and that He is the one true Savior who can and will give us eternal life."[22]

Christianity brings salvation and redemption from death, as Grundtvig acknowledges in his poem, but the salvation is social in nature in that it occurs in the restoration of the nation from the threat of death. Christian salvation is to be experienced through the triumph of Danish nationalism. No nation is self-sufficient; only Christ can restore it to

[22] Ibid., p. 163.

health. But it would be senseless and perverse, Grundtvig believed, to

> eradicate the old, primeval human life in order to give the new Christian human life room and scope, equally senseless and perverse is it to ban and as far as possible eradicate the national life in order to put the Christian life in its place. For if one says to the folk-spirit: "Depart, thou unclean spirit and make room for the Holy Spirit!" though one may thereby get rid of the folk-spirit, one will still be so far from getting the Holy Spirit in its place, as actually to be closing oneself and the people, as far as possible, to all spirits, to all spiritual influence and inspiration, all spiritual and emotional understanding and enlightenment.[23]

For Grundtvig, this meant that Christianity could only re-enter Danish life through the folk-spirit, which itself then could be redeemed, saved, and brought to full fruition in and through the Holy Spirit. It is impossible, then, to be a truly good Dane without also becoming a devout Christian. Grundtvig simply would not tolerate any sharp distinction between God and country, as is reflected in his *Nytaars-morgen* (New Year's Morning): "Now I earnestly long for a small circle of friendly co-laborers who, ignoring the witch, will depend upon the Lord and keep steadily before them the great goal He surely wishes us to attain: *the re-vival of Scandinavian heroism to Christian achievements, in line with the demands and conditions of our time.*"[24] The demands and conditions of the times included the economic, political, and social transformation of Denmark. Grundtvig in his own manner backed this transformation, indeed, was its greatest and most influential spokesman. He saw in the emerging institutions of modern Denmark the opportunity for the Danish folk-spirit to reassert itself in a modern democratic and liberal form. Hovde correctly

23 Ibid., pp. 163-64.
24 Hovde, *Scandinavian Countries*, I, 334; Grundtvig's italics.

claims that "Grundtvig had a social philosophy based upon history and religion, which championed nationalism and democracy, and was directed toward the highest ideals of middle class capitalism."[25]

Although Grundtvig tied Christianity tightly to his brand of nationalism, it is true that he did not reduce the Christian life to an attenuated civil religion. He had a strong allegiance to the Christian church, and he labored his entire life to transform the church into a living and vital community based on the sacraments of baptism and communion, which for Grundtvig constituted the essence

[25] Ibid., p. 337. Grundtvig's impact on the emergence of modern Denmark reached almost mythical dimensions, as one eulogy indicates:

For, by his worship of the people and the popular, Grundtvig has become the saint of democracy. It may with propriety be said that the Left Party movement has its roots in him. The *faith in the people* which lies back of this colossal development as its essential sustaining and propelling force,—that has been taken from Grundtvig. . . . For all sorts of enterprises, from high schools and agricultural institutes to cooperative creameries and hog abattoirs, fruitgrowers' and export societies, Grundtvig has been the patron saint. And just as surely as every enterprise begun in the genuine democratic spirit,— whether it were a bank or a newspaper—, always included in its name the word "people's" as a guarantee of its authenticity, just as certain it was that when it should name its saint it would refer to Grundtvig, among other reasons as proof that it was not committed to mere materialism, but willingly submitted to the demands of the spirit and, briefly, that "it was in compact with the higher authorities." . . . And if the object might be emancipation from ancient authority or ancient prejudice, then too it was Grundtvig to whom the appeal was made. From him was taken the great gospel of freedom, which gave to everyone the right to do somewhat as he pleased, and which especially in all personal and spiritual relationships opened the door to the fullest degree of individualism. . . . This gospel of freedom expressed self-determination, which is a basic characteristic of the age itself, which constitutes the very life nerve of democracy, which has expressed itself concretely in the steadily growing self-government of the people, as well in the political sphere as in that of church and school and in private economic enterprise. (Alfred Ipsen, "Grundtvig-dyrkelsen," *Vor fremtid*, III [1910], 341-42; quoted in Hovde, *Scandinavian Countries*, I, 338)

of Christianity. On the vital questions of faith, grace, and the priesthood of all believers, he agreed with Luther. But he believed that Lutherans had erred in making the Bible the central authority, merely substituting it for the pope as the overpowering religious authority in human life. This misplaced allegiance had generated the great enthusiasm for biblical theology and criticism and had centered Christian life on biblical interpretation. As Koch observes, "ever since Melanchthon's day there had been in the Lutheran Church a strong disposition to turn the church into a school and to make the reading and interpretation of scripture the pillar of divine service."[26] Grundtvig viewed this move as placing man's word higher than God's; interpretation of the word, not the word itself, had assumed primary importance in Christian life. Such a concept of the church made theologians and biblical scholars lords of the church and relegated the layman to the status of ignorant and passive learner.[27]

In reaction to this biblical scholasticism in Protestantism, which he labeled "exegetic popedom," Grundtvig turned his attention to the life of the congregation. What he called his "matchless discovery" was that the essence of Christianity is the congregation's life, which is centered around baptism and communion; the sacraments, not the Bible, are the foundation of the church. In the Bible, Christians find only the testimony of what happened in antiquity, but Christians cannot live by the testimony of others. Only through the living presence of God in the congregation, a presence mediated by the sacraments of baptism and communion, could Christians find renewal and salvation. Grundtvig believed that the baptism of children was theologically proper in that it symbolizes God's gift of grace to the human race, which in no way could earn or deserve it. The Lord's Supper, like baptism, is a divine event within

[26] Koch, *Grundtvig*, p. 170.

[27] J. Oskar Andersen, *Survey of the History of the Church in Denmark* (Copenhagen: O. Lohse, 1930), p. 47.

23

the life of the congregation. In communion, the individual participant encounters the saving grace of God in Christ. Both sacraments tie the individual members of the congregation to God and to one another. Through Grundtvig's influence, the sacraments recovered the place they had occupied in the Danish church prior to the Enlightenment, and they were again seen to be the means of salvation, inasmuch "as the glorified Lord here meets the individuals and speaks his word of life to them."[28]

This emphasis on tradition led Grundtvig's critics to accuse him of abandoning the spirit of the Reformation for a return to the formalism of Roman Catholicism. Grundtvig claimed that, on the contrary, he was merely extending Luther's notion of the priesthood of all believers. Yes, he was replacing Scripture with tradition, but not with a tradition presided over by the papacy and an ecclesiastical hierarchy. Rather, it was a tradition that belonged to the people and should not be controlled by the pope, the Bible, theologians, scholars, or the state. Grundtvig struggled to rescue the church from its many bondages and to reintroduce it into the lives of the people. He longed for the church to become a living community in which Christians could personally experience the redemptive power of God in their lives as they struggled individually and as a nation against the forces of death. His ultimate hope for the church was that it would implant in the people faith, courage, will, and hope sufficient to bring into existence a truly great Denmark. His great passion was for the church and the nation to be bound together in the common struggle for salvation and national identity.

While Grundtvig strove to enlist the church as the chief ally of nationalism, other currents of change surged through the religious community. These developments sometimes worked in Grundtvig's favor. In every case, he attempted to marshal change for his own purposes but resisted it when he could not use it. The three most important religious move-

[28] Ibid., p. 50.

ments in Denmark during this period were the appearance of revivalism among the peasants, the struggle to democratize the state church, and the flourishing of biblical scholarship and theology.

Religious revivalism awakened in Denmark around the turn of the century in Jutland. Initiated by two laymen, Peter Laurssen and Jens Anderssen, its immediate cause was the introduction of revised devotional books.[29] Efforts by the clergy to revise the liturgy and devotional and religious education literature were viewed by the peasants as tainted with false doctrine, and many bolted the church. The Jutlanders soon began to extend their activities through missionary journeys to different sections of the country. The movement emphasized the necessity for a dramatic and ecstatic conversion experience, the deeply sinful nature of human life, the fear of the individual for the safety of his soul, and the necessity of personal salvation.

Religious individualism spread throughout Denmark in the first third of the century. The upper class regarded the movement as "either 'pure insanity' or as 'the product of the congenital defiance of the commonality against preachers and government.' "[30] Local governments persecuted it. The revivalists, insisting on their right to determine the true content of religion, aligned themselves with the liberal democratic movement in the pursuit of religious freedom. Grundtvig, too, initially opposed the revivalists, because their movement lacked the sacramental character of his conception of Christianity. Nevertheless, despite the serious theological differences between them, Grundtvig and the revivalists eventually united.

In fact, it was the revivalists who had sought out Grundtvig. In 1825 he published a sharp polemic against the theology of Henrik Nicolai Clausen.[31] Grundtvig's opposition to Clausen found great favor among the revivalists,

---

[29] Hovde, *Scandinavian Countries*, I, 312.

[30] Ibid.

[31] The controversy between Grundtvig and Clausen is discussed below.

and the leaders of the movement recommended Grundtvig's writings to their followers. Slowly the movement began to fall under his influence, and as it did so, the revivalists began to return to the church. Grundtvig had hoped they would return, and his efforts to bring them back without requiring that they sacrifice their religious beliefs and fervor served to preserve the religious unity of the people within the state church.[32]

In analyzing this phenomenon, Hovde draws a clear connection between the breakdown of the communal structure of life in the rural areas and the individualistic nature of the revivalist movement. With the disintegration of the feudalistic social structure of rural Denmark, the character of the individual increasingly determined his possibilities for material success. Virtues like industry, thrift, ingenuity, and sobriety—all of which secure individual welfare—received increasing emphasis. Under the old social and economic structures, religion had primarily consisted of adherence to a stable institution. Individual conversion and a private relationship with God had been less important. "But now, as that society disintegrated and placed a growing emphasis upon individual self-dependence, religion necessarily became a more personal concern."[33] This individuation of religious enthusiasm and commitment not only reflected a rebellion against the aridity of religious orthodoxy but was also, and more significantly, an expression of the peasants' self-discovery in the economic and political liberalism of the day. That the revivalist movement would become

[32] Grundtvig's success in preserving national religious unity within the state church hinged on the development of his conception of religious freedom. Essentially, he believed in the right of all Christians to choose the doctrines and liturgy that were consistent with his own brand of sacramentalism, and he believed that he had no right to impose his theology upon any other person. For an excellent discussion of the development of Grundtvig's view of religious freedom and its role in preserving religious unity see Koch, *Grundtvig*, pp. 173-76.

[33] Hovde, *Scandinavian Countries*, I, 309.

the peasants' means of advancing their quest for political and economic freedom was clearly obvious by 1846.

By the 1840s the revivalistic movement had grown in complexity and had broadened its influence in the life of Denmark by forming political and ideological alliances with the liberals. Politically, the revivalists saw the liberals as allies not only in their struggle to achieve religious freedom but also in their demands for the right to free assembly and for universal military conscription. Indeed, it was this sort of practical consideration that led the peasants to support the liberals in their fight for a constitutional monarchy. Ideologically, the individualism of the revival movement and of democratic liberalism merged in the belief of each in the freedom of the individual to determine his own destiny. Thus, individualism received a religious justification for the peasantry and Grundtvig, and a philosophical one for the bourgeois liberals. In both cases, it led to an ethic conducive to economic growth and prosperity. The revivalists' demand for austerity in private life in the use of alcohol and in nonconjugal sex merged conveniently with the liberals' emphasis upon sobriety, thrift, and initiative in public life. It was no accident, then, that the revivalist movement "brought into being a sober, industrious and thrifty people, within whose ranks a very high degree of prosperity quickly arose."[34]

The movement's impact on the liberalizing of Denmark was deepened by its demand for liturgical and ecclesiastical reform within the church. The Lutheran reformation in Germany had been largely a revolt of the laity against a dominant ecclesiastical hierarchy. In the Scandinavian countries, however, Lutheranism was established from the first as the official state religion, and the clergy quickly became the sort of religious hierarchy that the Reformation had initially opposed. Throughout the eighteenth century and far into the nineteenth, pastors dominated their

[34] Ibid., p. 327.

parishes, "often in the manner of petty chieftains."[35] They in turn were dominated by the Lutheran bishops, who were identified with the government bureaucracy. The clergy resented their subordination to the monarchy and insisted that they alone should pass judgment upon matters of doctrine and practice.

In spite of the clergy's conflicts with the monarchy, the upper class, and the government bureaucracy, it quickly subordinated the conflict to the necessity of dealing with Grundtvig's free church and the revivalist movement. The march of the peasantry and the liberals toward political power in local and national government appeared to a large section of the clergy to portend dominance of the church by ignorant and lower-class people. They denounced Grundtvig and the revivalists on religious and political grounds and clearly recognized that the revivalist and liberal movements were two sides of the same coin.

Ironically, revivalism among the peasants had as its immediate cause an attempt by the clergy to initiate liturgical and theological reform within the church, especially in rural areas. Sensitive to intellectual currents in Europe and to the social and political changes occurring in Denmark, the educated clergy hoped to rescue Lutheranism from its archaic language and liturgy in order to lessen the separation between religion and life. But, as we have seen, these well-meaning clergymen helped to spark an upheaval in Danish life that went far beyond the simple internal changes in the established religious structure for which they had hoped.

The conflict between the peasants and the clergy surfaced most clearly in the quest for ecclesiastical reform. Issues concerning the pastor's authority to discipline his parishioners by withholding the sacraments, the extent to which an individual could be legally bound to the church and the pastor of the parish in which he resided, and the

35 Ibid., p. 343.

right of the laity to participate in the governance of the church were all strongly contested between 1800 and 1830. The peasants demanded the right to choose their own pastors, even if that required crossing parish lines, and they also wanted parish councils of laymen with real authority over pastors. The leadership of the clergy, with the exception of Grundtvig, the theologian Andreas Gottlob Rudelbach, and the Hebraist Jacob Christian Lindberg, resisted these demands. With the establishment of a democratically elected parliament in 1849, the debate between clergy and parishioners shifted to the Rigsdag. Slowly, the reformers gained success. A bill in 1855 dissolved the parish bond as Grundtvig had wanted, and legislation in 1868 safeguarded the right to form free congregations and the right of parishioners to call outside priests. But the free congregations were required to remain within the national church. In spite of the constitutional guarantee of complete religious freedom, the national church remained strong, primarily because of "the fear of the clergy to give the laity influence on church government . . . and the aversion of Grundtvigianism to a church constitution."[36] Although the piecemeal legislation of 1855 and 1868 went a considerable distance in protecting religious freedom, it did not dissolve the state religion. State confirmation of the pastoral office was still required, and state control of the theological content of sermons and the liturgy was not relaxed. The Grundtvigians continued up through 1870, without successes, to work for the right of ministers to follow their consciences in preaching and in the liturgy.

Whereas the political struggle within the church reflected the political and economic struggle for freedom within the larger society, the theological activity within the church reflected the influence of modern science and philosophy on the minds of the church's intellectuals. Indeed, the theological climate of the University of Copenhagen was as rich and resourceful as its European background. All the

36 Andersen, *History of the Church in Denmark*, p. 57.

major trends in late-eighteenth- and early-nineteenth-century theology on the Continent found strong expression in Danish theology. Steffens, Clausen, and Hans Lassen Martensen were the major figures during the first half of the nineteenth century. We have already seen that Steffens's 1802 lectures were the portals through which German idealism streamed into Denmark. Later Steffens published a thoroughly orthodox interpretation of the Christian religion, *On the False Theology and the True Faith* (1826).[37] Although Steffens does not mention his old friend Friedrich Schleiermacher, this book is clearly an attack on Schleiermacher's philosophy of religion as it is developed in his famous *On Religion: Speeches to Its Cultured Despisers*.[38] Steffens's book attacked Schleiermacher's attempt to make feeling *(Gefuhl)* the foundation of the relation between man and God. This "false theology," Steffens claimed, knows nothing of the love of God for man, for the only love known by man in his feelings is his own perverse self-love. Steffens maintained that it is not possible, given the sinfulness of the human race, for human beings to discover in religious feelings of dependence the love of God revealed in the New Testament. Furthermore, it is not possible for human beings to love others or God without the help of God's grace. Thus, the knowledge of God's love and the power to love are dependent upon the bringing of the New Creation through Jesus Christ. Steffens's theological position reached back deeply into Reformation theology and relied most heavily upon Luther's concept of justification by faith. "Christianity is a permanent miracle. The glory of the phenomenal world, the law of nature, the divine order of the natural man, understanding, reason, the moral law

---

[37] Henrik Steffens, *Von der falschem Theologie und dem wahren Glauben* (Breslau: Josef Max u. Komp Verlag, 1823).

[38] Friedrich Schleiermacher, *On Religion: Speeches to Its Cultured Despisers,* trans. John Oman, intro. by Rudolf Otto (New York: Harper and Row, Publishers, 1958).

—none of these can give rise to it nor can they grasp it."[39] By grounding theology in revelation and faith, Steffens signaled an all-out attack upon those who attempted to replace revelation and grace with nature and work as the starting point for religious knowledge and the religious life.

The major challenge to orthodoxy came from Clausen and Martensen. In a major work, *Constitution, Dogma, and Rite in Protestantism and Catholicism* (1825),[40] Clausen argued that the Bible must be the principle of all theology. He also maintained that the Reformation had opened the way for reason to play a decisive role in the interpretation of the Bible. Thus, if the Bible is the principle of theology, the principle of biblical interpretation is reason in the form of philosophy and philology. Theology's task, wrote Clausen, is "by philological learning and philosophical criticism to supplement its vagueness and to bring about a higher unity between the different types of doctrines and their methods of presentation."[41] The spirit of the Enlightenment, with its confidence in reason to rescue Christianity from superstition and obscurantism, shows throughout Clausen's optimistic work. His insistence upon reason as the true and best medium for understanding and grasping the Christian religion relegates faith, revelation, and experience to a secondary status in religious life. Grundtvig quickly perceived this fact and in five days wrote a stinging denunciation of Clausen's views. In *The Answer of the Church to Professor of Theology H. N. Clausen*,[42] he not only criticized Clausen but also demanded that Clausen "make the Christian Church a formal apology for his unchristian and scandalous teaching or lay down his office and

[39] Steffens, *Von der falschem Theologie*, p. 199; quoted in Horn, "Positivity and Dialectic," p. 28.

[40] H. N. Clausen, *Catholicismens og Protestantismens Kirkeforfatning, Laer og Ritus*, in Horn, "Positivity and Dialectic," p. 21. No closer citation is given by Horn.

[41] Horn, "Positivity and Dialectic," p. 21.

[42] Grundtvig, *Skrifter*, IV, 395ff.

drop his Christian name."[43] Clausen neither recanted nor resigned; instead, he sued Grundtvig for libel. He won the suit, and Denmark lost the voice of one of its ablest and most colorful spokesmen for a period of twelve years through government censorship.

Martensen claimed in his autobiography to have found much in the orthodoxy of Steffens and Grundtvig with which to agree.[44] By the time he matriculated in theology at the University of Copenhagen in 1827, he had realized that the theological debate in Denmark between the orthodoxy of Steffens and the rationalism of Clausen was at an unresolvable impasse because of the severe limitations placed on theological thought by these two categories.[45] His doctoral dissertation, *De Autonomia Conscientia Sui Humanae* (1839), was acclaimed as the work that provided an alternative between Steffens's and Clausen's interpretation of the Christian faith. Johan Alfred Bornemann, a theological colleague of Martensen's, wrote that Martensen's dissertation initiated a "new era" in Danish theology; both rationalism and supernaturalism had become "antiquated standpoints belonging to a time past."[46]

At that time the bishop of Sjaelland, the highest office in the Danish church, was Jakob Peter Mynster. After the publication of Bornemann's article, Mynster entered the debate, claiming that Martensen and Bornemann were both wrong in asserting that a philosophical theology combining rationalism and orthodoxy was possible. Mynster insisted that a religion must rest upon one of these views or the other: "insofar as one became dominant, the other would become antiquated. In any case they could not both become antiquated at once, for the very reason that they were con-

[43] Quoted in Horn, "Positivity and Dialectic," p. 22.

[44] Horn, "Positivity and Dialectic," pp. 24-25.

[45] Ibid., p. 24.

[46] J. A. Bornemann, *Tidsskrift for Litteratur og Kritik*, I (1839), 40; quoted in Horn, "Positivity and Dialectic," p. 167.

tradictories."[47] Martensen responded by arguing that the radical separation of faith and knowledge, relevation and reason, nature and the supernatural is unchristian, given the Christian notion of the incarnation. If one maintains that the contradictory predicates, God and man, cannot be united in the same subject, then all basic Christian dogma falls. According to Robert Horn, Martensen claimed that "only a position which allows that there is a fundamental and intelligible relation between the supernatural and the natural, only a position which allows the supernatural to become real for man through the natural alone, only a position which allows the supernatural to contain the natural as an element within itself is acceptable. Only such a position can avoid the inevitable destruction of the Christian faith to which the irreconcilable separation of rationalism and supernaturalism had led."[48]

The savior of the faith turned out to be Georg Wilhelm Friedrich Hegel, whose philosophy, Martensen thought, provided a compromise between orthodoxy and rationalism. Martensen claimed to have found in Hegel's *Phenomenology of Spirit*, which is a study of the dialectical relationship between historically diverse forms of self-consciousness, a method for discovering the dialectical continuity in differing theological positions. The basic insight of Hegel's phenomenology is the unity of subject and object, of thought and being. According to Martensen, this identity of subject and object, self-consciousness and revelation, is the presupposition of his speculative theology. In Martensen's new theology, our knowledge of God is God's knowledge of himself. When we truly know God, it is God who knows himself within us. The difficulty with both rationalism and orthodoxy is that they hold the subject and the object in an unmediated opposition. Orthodoxy emphasizes the object as

[47] J. P. Mynster, "Rationalisme, Supernaturalisme," *Tidsskrift for Litteratur og Kritik*, I (1839), 249ff.; quoted in Horn, "Positivity and Dialectic," p. 168.

[48] Horn, "Positivity and Dialectic," p. 172.

against reason, God as revealed and unknowable by the subject, reason. Rationalism makes the reverse mistake by emphasizing the priority of reason; in so doing, it omits the ontological reality of God, the object. For the rationalist, nothing remains over and against human subjectivity; God thereby becomes a thought purely immanent to reason. Herein lay the conflict in Danish theology, and only Martensen could see the way out by showing that both rationalism and orthodoxy are true. God is both above and in human consciousness as its motivating principle, so that we must say that in human thought God is thinking. To become attentive to this fact is to see how God reveals and discovers himself in and through human thought.

Although this speculative approach to theology was inspired by Hegel, it is clearly no carbon copy of Hegel's philosophy of religion. Martensen's Hegelianism is so highly colored by his own theological convictions that, as Horn has admirably shown, it would be a mistake to think that one could learn Hegel's philosophy by studying Martensen's theology.[49] Nonetheless, it is true to say that in Martensen's theology we find an effort to breathe fresh Hegelian life into a stalemated theological conflict. Martensen believed that both the Reformation and the Enlightenment forms of theology were destined to fail unless they were rescued by the dialectical magic of Hegelian philosophy. Ultimately, Hegel too was abandoned, but during Martensen's tenure as the dominant theological voice in Denmark (1839-1854), no theological wind would blow more strongly than Hegel's.

SCIENCE IN MODERN DENMARK

The social, economic, political, and cultural transitions in Danish life in the late eighteenth and early nineteenth centuries were preceded by the impact of the Age of Reason

[49] One of the main thrusts of Horn's dissertation is to show the distinctness and uniqueness of Danish Hegelianism.

on intellectual life in Denmark. The development of modern science in Scandinavia as a whole initially influenced only the intellectuals, though science would later be employed in the modernization of society. Not surprisingly, those who were touched by the scientific development of Europe in both the natural and the social sciences were in the vanguard of change in the economic, agricultural, and political life of Denmark.

Sweden was the first of the Scandinavian countries to make significant strides in science. For several decades after 1730 it was a prominent member of the European scientific community. The development of science in both Sweden and Denmark was tied closely to industrialization. As the slower of the two to industrialize, Denmark lagged far behind Sweden in replacing the Cartesian with a Newtonian view of the world.[50] A restrictive and conservative Lutheran orthodoxy also hampered free scientific inquiry in Denmark.

Even when Danish experimental science began to develop, it did so slowly. Newtonian physics, for example, did not reach Denmark until 1760 through the work of the Danish mathematician Jens Kraft. Experimental physics was held in such low repute that its professor at the University of Copenhagen was regarded as a charlatan and a trickster in the scientific community. Through the middle of the eighteenth century, Danish science was equally slow to develop in the fields of chemistry, biology, botany, and medicine. Indeed, it was not until Hans Christian Ørsted discovered electromagnetism in 1819 that Denmark made any scientific contribution at all to the European community. By the turn of the century, however, the Danish intellectual community had made room for all the experi-

[50] Tore Frangsmyr, "History of Swedish Science in the Eighteenth Century," *History of Science*, XII (1974), 29-42. For a full discussion of the industrialization of modern Denmark, see Ove Hornby, "Industrialization in Denmark and the Loss of the Duchies," *Scandinavian Economics History Review*, XVII (1969), 23-57.

mental sciences, and the first half of the nineteenth century saw their rapid development in Copenhagen. Moreover, science came to be accepted by most as the only medium through which knowledge about nature could be gained. The grip that Lutheran orthodoxy had held on the Danes up through the middle of the eighteenth century was gradually relaxed; by 1800 it was hardly noticeable. Those few who, like Grundtvig, still rejected the principles of modern science found little if any sympathy among the educated elite in Copenhagen. The battle between religion and science was fought in Denmark over a period of about fifty years, with science the victor there as it had been earlier in France, Germany, and England.

Not only was science accepted as a field of study within the university, but its practical value also came to be exploited by the Danes. Once economic and political liberalism were established, the utilitarian value of the sciences was seen and used in industrialization, communications, health, and transportation. We have already seen how the university played a central role in the changing economic and political life of the nation. This influence was broadened in the nineteenth century as the economy industrialized and the country was unified through its communication and transportation networks. As the state and the private sector, including business and industry, took over the planning and development of Danish life, they turned increasingly to the scientific community in the university for practical expertise.

Although the new science battled religion in Denmark as it did elsewhere, there were some Danes who saw in it a more explicit and persuasive defense for the religious notion of nature as a divine creation. While Newtonian deism flourished in Sweden early in the nineteenth century, evolutionary theories based on geological and biological evidence took on moral and religious significance in Denmark. Danish scientists and philosophers began to follow closely the work of European biologists and geologists.

Henrik Steffens, Niels Treschow, and H. C. Ørsted were thoroughly familiar with French and English work on evolutionary theory, including that of Georges Louis Leclerc de Buffon, Etienne Bonnot de Condillac, and Charles Darwin. These Danish thinkers themselves began to develop natural philosophies with an evolutionary core.

In 1807 Treschow announced a fully developed evolutionary philosophy. He argued for a nebular hypothesis of the origin of the universe; he explained chemically the formation of solids; and he knew that the more primitive fossils were to be found only in the oldest geological strata. Convinced that man had descended with other animals from some primitive animal life closely related to marine life, he pointed out the similarities of man and the ape, especially the orangutan. A complete archaeological exploration of Madagascar, he insisted, would provide much of the evidence needed to support his hypothesis. Treschow believed that in this constant appearance of novelty and variation in nature the guiding hand of a beneficient and wise God was at work. For him, the evidence supporting evolutionary theory was evidence for the wisdom, power, and goodness of God. The theory also served as the basis of an argument in defense of a philosophy of individualism. Treschow presented his position in a work entitled "Is Any Concept or Any Idea Possible Concerning Particular Things? Answered with Reference to Human Worth and Human Welfare."

> From the viewpoint to which we have come in these studies, each human being may be considered as one of the many possible forms which their common nature or idea may assume. Persons are consequently, in the first place, not inconsequential parts of the whole in his particular form. In the second place, we ought not to consider the individuals as many more or less perfect impressions of the same original, of which each would have to be worth as much less as the multitude is greater. For

37

if out of such a multitude, only a single copy should remain, there would in a certain sense be little lost by the
destruction of the rest. On the other hand, if individuals
do not compose merely a number in which all units are
equal, then their preservation, so far as their peculiar
kind is concerned, cannot be less important than that
of the species and the genera. We must, therefore, assume
that no individual ever becomes truly extinct, but that
death in actuality is progress of which it is no more permitted us to observe than what takes place in the egg before conception.[51]

Eight years later the jurist Anders Sandø Ørsted published an article in which he applied Treschow's views on
individualism to legal and moral theory.[52] Since the process
of evolution is constantly creating divergencies and varia-
tions, Ørsted argued, it follows that no classification can be
completely accurate or everlasting. This limitation has
particular implications for ethics and jurisprudence. Nature consists of individual objects related to one another
by infinitesimal graduations, and every variation has its
justification in the law of nature; therefore, it is impossible to condemn aberrations of conventional moral stand-
ards and rules. Ørsted claimed that "this constitutes no
derogation of the efforts of science to seek the ultimate unity
of all moral mandates and to bring the formulas so developed into the closest possible relation to the conditions
of individual life. It means only that the goal which the
science of ethics thus sets up for itself, as well as that which
is the object of our moral system, is an ideal, the complete

[51] Niels Treschow, "Gives der noget begreb eller nogen idee om
enslige ting?" in Harald Høffding's *Danske filosofer*, pp. 251-52; quoted
in Hovde, *Scandinavian Countries*, I, 369. Hovde gives no complete
citation.

[52] A. S. Ørsted, "Over graendserne mellem theorie og praxis i
saedelaeren," *Eunomia*, I (1815), 94-145; quoted in Hovde, *Scandinavian
Countries*, I, 370.

achievement of which is forever impossible."[53] The practical implications of this view were, from Ørsted's point of view, not license and the collapse of criminal justice but a call for humaneness and tolerance in both private and public life.

H. C. Ørsted also saw in evolutionary thought a possible defense for a belief in the spiritual unity of all things. He had heard Steffens's 1802 lectures, and he agreed with Steffens that the principle of unity of all things must be accounted for in terms of spirit. Steffens's fourth lecture was concerned with the evolutionary hypothesis, and Ørsted found in it much with which to agree. But unlike Steffens and Treschow, who defended their evolutionary philosophies in terms of geological evidence, Ørsted had a more speculative approach to the matter.

> But concerning this earth we know that it has developed through unmeasured time in a series of readjustments, and together with it the flora and fauna. The evolution began with the lowest forms, and moved toward ever more perfect ones, until finally, in the most recent of these periods, that creature was produced in which conscious knowledge revealed itself. . . . I am speaking here only of a fact which, so far as man is concerned, is undeniable, and without considering the abstrusities of the researches concerning the manner in which the corporeal and the spiritual are united. Merely to ward off every suspicion of materialism, I wish to refer to the apparent paradox— apparent because it reconciles itself—that the same nature, of which man is the undeniable product, must itself be recognized as the product of the eternally creative spirit, and to the fact that the divine origin of our spirit by no means is contradicted when the facts of nature are admitted. In other words, the concept of the universe

[53] Ørsted, "Over graendserne mellem theorie," p. 136; quoted in Hovde, *Scandinavian Countries*, I, 370-71.

is incomplete, unless it is understood as the constantly continued work of the eternally creative spirit.[54]

Here Ørsted sides with Treschow in asserting the religious implications of evolutionary theory. This theological grounding of evolutionary theory led the Danish Marxist Frederik Dreier to remark that Ørsted was a "scientist who smacked of piety."[55] In any case, it was not difficult for scientists and philosophers in Denmark to appreciate Darwin's *Origin of the Species* when it appeared in 1859.

It is also important to notice that science also helped to displace the religious conception of history in the second half of the eighteenth century. Through the work of the Danish Society for the History and the Language of the Fatherland, established in 1745, the writing of history entered a new era as rational methods slowly were adopted. The study of history had been motivated primarily by religious and dynastic interests, and the accounts of history given in the Bible and in Nordic mythology were accepted as true. Suspicion of the validity of these old religious histories mounted in the mid-eighteenth century, and the critical historical method began to be applied to old manuscripts and myths relevant to the Scandinavian past. Olaf Dalin's book on Swedish history, published in 1747, is an example of how historians were attempting to reconstruct their Scandinavian past. Dalin showed, for example, the implications of scientific discoveries regarding the falling water level in northern Europe. If the scientists were right about the diminution of the water level, then Sweden could not have been inhabited for as long as had been believed. Indeed, given the fact that Denmark was still under water at the time of Christ's birth, the claim of earlier Swedish historians that Sweden was the oldest country after the Flood

[54] H. C. Ørsted, *Aanden i naturen* (Copenhagen, 1850), I, 145-46; quoted in Hovde, *Scandinavian Countries*, I, 367.
[55] Frederik Dreier, *Aandetroen og den frie taekning* (Copenhagen, 1852), v; quoted in Hovde, *Scandinavian Countries*, I, 367.

was patently false.[56] In reconstructing Denmark's past, historians also played down the importance of dynastic history and gave the common man a more prominent place in their works. Less time was devoted to the study of military history and more to economic and institutional development in the Scandinavian past.

This shift to a critical history that included a broader spectrum of human life was accompanied by a rehabilitation of the Danish language. During the seventeenth and eighteenth centuries, Danish was spoken almost apologetically by the Danish intelligentsia. The university community wrote in Latin. Theology, the dominant cultural interest during the eighteenth century, had its roots in the writings of the Latin and German church fathers. German was the language of the military and the trading community, while the upper class, dazzled by the court of Louis XIV, spoke French. Pietism and patriotism contributed most to overcoming Danish linguistic inferiority. In its appeal to the masses, the pietistic movement was forced to use Danish if it was to be heard. Even university lectures related to the pietistic movement were given in Danish. Patriotism was also a prominent factor in the reappearance of Danish. During the third quarter of the eighteenth century, the Danish bureaucracy was dominated by Germans who had been invited into the country by the king. Their influence became so great that Danish intellectuals and politicians were ignored by their German superiors in the government. One of the results of the expulsion of the Germans and their leader, Struensee, from Denmark in 1773 was that the Danish minister Ove HoegGuldberg "taught the court to speak Danish."[57] Ludvig Holberg also startled his contemporaries by using the Danish language in his plays and novels. In his comedies he openly ridiculed the stiff and stylized language of the upper class. His young successors were more revolutionary than he. Jens Shielderup Sneedorff not

---

only regarded Danish as the best weapon against conservatism but also demonstrated in his journal, *Den Patriotiske Tilskuer*, that it could be a language of learning and culture as well. In 1761 Sneedorff published one of the first Danish dictionaries. It is obvious that the rehabilitation of the Danish language was one of the necessary conditions for the economic, social, and political reforms that followed in the late eighteenth and nineteenth centuries.

CONCLUSION

The purpose of this brief description of late-eighteenth- and nineteenth-century Denmark has been to show that one may legitimately speak of this period as the modernization of Denmark. The structural changes in the economy and politics of the country, the cultural upheaval in philosophy, literature, and religion, and the advent of experimental science laid the foundation for the building of modern Denmark. By 1850 the medieval communal economy based on agriculture had been replaced by an urban economy with a corporate, industrial, and agricultural base; the monarchical and aristocratic orientation of political life had been replaced by democracy; and new cultural forces had asserted themselves in art, literature, and philosophy to the extent that Lutheran orthodoxy was greatly weakened by an emerging secularized and scientific *Weltanschauung*. Within the church, the conflict between the old and the new orders is reflected in the battle between the conservatives and the liberals. The conservatives held to the Lutheran orthodoxy of the past, while the liberals enthusiastically sought religious and theological accommodation with European philosophy, science, and politics. We have seen how different strata within the church sided with different dimensions of the reform taking place in the society. The bourgeois liberals openly embraced German idealism, the new science, and, up to a point, the democratization of the state. Grundtvig and the peasants

sought in the church a vehicle for the complete liberation of the peasants, the achievement of political power
equal to that of the liberals, and the realization of a
nationalistic self-consciousness. In both cases, however,
the church formed a close working association with the
forces of modernization.

Modernization not only included political, economic,
and cultural change but also, and perhaps more basically,
implied a new set of values that determined both the people's self-consciousness and their behavior. Laissez-faire
capitalism and democratic liberalism were essentially
individualistic. The individual, according to democratic
liberalism, is endowed with natural rights to property, to
political self-determination, to the rewards of his own
labor, to freedom from political oppression, and to freedom of speech, assembly, and religion. The political and
economic self-determination guaranteed by nature to each
and every individual must be protected and not interfered
with by government. To be a person means to have these
rights, and the political and economic transitions occurring
in Danish government and economic life during this period
were directed toward securing and protecting this conception of the individual. Moreover, the Danes also sought cultural justification for their attempt to create a liberal state
and economy based on the value of individualism. It would
be false to say that all philosophy, religion, and art sang
the praises of the individual. Denmark, like any other
country, was too culturally diversified in the nineteenth
century for so simple a statement. Nevertheless, large seg-
ments of the religious, philosophical, and artistic com-
munities were anxious to express the spirit of liberalism
that had come to Denmark. In phenomena as diverse as
the revivalist movement, democratic liberalism, and the
evolutionary philosophies of Ørsted and Treschow we have
seen the common theme of individualism prominently at
work.

A second value to emerge in Danish life during this

43

period was that of nationalism. We have seen that the collapse of Denmark as a medium-sized power in northern Europe led the Danes to a kind of national introspection through which a renewed consciousness of their unique Nordic past was awakened. The celebration of Denmark's past in the writings of Oehlenschläger and Grundtvig and the struggle to prevent German encroachment on Danish soil in Schleswig-Holstein stimulated a new pride in all that was uniquely Scandinavian and Danish. We have seen the central role played by Grundtvig in the emergence of Danish nationalism. He accepted the principles of democratic liberalism and agreed that individuals were by nature free to pursue their own self-determination. But Grundtvig also curbed the radical individualism of liberalism by arguing that the attainment of political, economic, and religious self-determination is a social phenomenon that is defined by the history and national identity of a people. For the Danish people, this meant that the struggle for political and economic freedom was carried out on two levels. First, it implied simply the dismantling of the oppressive political and economic systems of the past and the creation of new national structures that would protect the rights and interests of each individual. Second, the fight for these basic changes in Danish life were ideologically justified by both the Danish past and the Christian religion. In both Odin and Christ, Grundtvig found moral and historical legitimation for the struggle for liberation. The new Denmark, he proclaimed, was to be a resuscitation of its old Nordic heritage, and its final achievement was both morally sanctioned and made possible by the grace of God revealed in Jesus Christ. Thus, the essentially individualistic nature of democratic liberalism in Denmark was given a significantly social and communal orientation under Grundtvig's leadership.

The third value that helped to reshape Denmark during this period was the freedom of thought and expression, which made possible the emergence of a free press and modern science in Danish life. The demise of the monarchy and the censorship that it had exerted on the press opened the way for the press to become the chief medium through which vying political and economic forces made their views known to the public. It also made possible open and free criticism of the government and other institutions, as well as public discussion of all issues related to the life of the state. Science also benefited by the freedom of thought and expression. Again, the decline of the monarchy and of Lutheran orthodoxy partially laid the foundation for the growth of experimental science. We have seen that, like the press, it slowly came to play a major role in the life of the state. Indeed, we may say that freedom of thought and expression made a substantial contribution to the shifting of the state from a monarchical and religious foundation to a democratic and scientific one.

In the preface of his important work, B. J. Hovde wrote of the enormous practical success that democracy has enjoyed in Scandinavia in confronting and resolving "the most acute problems of modern society. Enthusiastic visitors return to the United States every year with fulsome praise for the neatness and orderliness of Scandinavian institutions and for the practical sense with which these countries attack the perplexing issues of our time."[58] Hovde is not alone in praising the rational manner in which Denmark and the other Scandinavian countries have gone about establishing a democratic state and the orderly and rational manner in which they have searched out democratic solutions for the various problems perplexing their nations. It is also most important to note that a new self-consciousness was being formed by the profound political, economic, and cultural upheavals occurring in Denmark. The gradually rising degree of participation among the populace in the creation and development of democratic and economic institutions must have sown the seeds for a new consciousness distinctly political in nature and guided

[58] Ibid., p. 7.

by the sentiments of Grundtvig's nationalism and the techne of science.

The Danes met the coming of the new order with their feet firmly planted in the old. Anxious to adopt the new order grounded in politics and science, they frequently did so in religious terms. Rather than completely overthrow Lutheran orthodoxy, the Danes chose to associate it with the coming order. Indeed, it could be said that the Danes remained truthful to themselves by creating a society and a culture that represented a synthesis of their past and future. Men like Clausen, H. C. Ørsted, Mynster, Treschow, Martensen, Steffens, and the indomitable Grundtvig invited science, political and economic liberalism, and German philosophy into an alliance with Denmark's religious heritage. Philology, historical criticism, philosophical idealism, evolutionary theory, laissez-faire economics, and political liberalism—all were in one way or another accepted into the Danish household without requiring its old religion to leave. Religion became something of a grandfather to the new generation of politicians, philosophers, and scientists who frequently came to the old man asking his approval of their newfangled ideas and practices. Like a good grandfather, religion acceded to these requests, approving the new and sending it out into Danish life with great confidence and joy.

CHAPTER TWO

Christendom

KIERKEGAARD's discomfort with the modernizing influences in Denmark during his lifetime is well known. *The Present Age*[1] and *Attack upon Christendom* are by now familiar to many students of nineteenth- and twentieth-century thought, for in them one finds criticisms of modern society that later were articulated and refined by Martin Heidegger in *Being and Time* and by Karl Barth in his neo-orthodox theology. In *The Present Age*, Kierkegaard worried about the disappearance of the individual as a center of value and as a self-determining being in modern society. He successfully anticipated the depersonalization of individual life that is occurring in the twentieth century, and although this work lacks the refinement and precision of Heidegger's analysis in *Being and Time*,[2] one can see very clearly that Kierkegaard understood the general direction of Western society toward the diminution of individual autonomy.

The other dimension of Kierkegaard's social criticism with which we are familiar is his denunciation of the state church in *Attack upon Christendom*. Like Heidegger, Barth was deeply influenced by many aspects of Kierkegaard's

[1] This chapter was written a year in advance of the new translation of *En literair Anmeldelse*. Quotations in this chapter are taken from *The Present Age*, trans. Alexander Dru (New York: Harper and Row, 1962). For the recent and improved translation, see Søren Kierkegaard, *Two Ages: The Age of Revolution and The Present Age: A Literary Review*, ed. and trans. Howard V. Hong and Edna H. Hong, Vol. XIV of *Kierkegaard's Writings*, ed., Howard V. Hong (Princeton: Princeton University Press, 1978).

[2] Martin Heidegger, *Being and Time*, trans. John Macquarrie and Edward Robinson (New York: Harper and Row, 1962), pp. 149-224.

thought, including his trenchant criticisms of the symbiotic relationship that had developed between the church and the state in western European countries since the Reformation. In 1936 a group of young German pastors, including Karl Barth and Dietrich Bonhoeffer, wrote the Barmen Declaration, which denounced Hitler's effort to maneuver the state church into legitimating his government. These pastors were deeply influenced by Kierkegaard's early attack on the church's willingness to cooperate with and religiously sanction secular authority and its practices. Kierkegaard's strident attack on the Danish church in the last eighteen months of his life, like his earlier criticisms of the depersonalizing tendencies in modern society, were absorbed into a massive theological, philosophical, and social scientific literature in the twentieth century that heralded him as one of the earliest and most astute critics of these two problems in modern society. Kierkegaard has thus become in the twentieth century a defender of individualism and of separation of church and state.

Less acceptable to the sensibilities and commitments of contemporary society, however, are Kierkegaard's criticisms of democratic liberalism, academic scholarship, science, and nationalism. Although one cannot find books by Kierkegaard committed specifically to any of these subjects, he was no less sternly critical in his published works and in his journals of these aspects of modern life than he was of the two mentioned above. Many who have agreed with Kierkegaard that the individual should not be allowed to disappear in our modern bureaucratic and technological society and that the church should not be legally related to the state have also concluded that Kierkegaard was just plain wrong in his criticisms of science, nationalism, and liberalism. The maturation of science and democracy has provided the foundation of modern society and become for many the unquestionable presupposition in all discussions related to the organization of human society. That Kierkegaard would criticize the two mainstays of modern life must be merely an indication of his narrow-minded allegiance to a strictly monarchical and religious understanding of human life. If Kierkegaard was right in his defense of individual autonomy and church-state separation, he simply came down on the wrong side of the debate between the monarchists and the democrats on the one hand and the religionists and the scientists on the other.

We shall discover in this chapter that Kierkegaard viewed the loss of moral autonomy and a religious conception of human destiny as intimately linked with the emergence of the modern state based on science and self-justifying politics. This scientific and political grounding of the modern state had not only practical consequences, which Kierkegaard never objected to, but also, and more seriously, spiritual consequences in the sense that both science and democratic liberalism promoted views of human nature that worked against the way in which the human self had been understood in Christianity. What was at stake, in Kierkegaard's view, in this radical historical transition occurring throughout Europe was an equally radical alteration of the way in which human nature would be understood. Kierkegaard saw in this transition the loss of an ethical-religious view of human life—a loss he regarded as pernicious and for which the rise of modern science and politics would have to take the responsibility.

In his social criticism Kierkegaard battled for a view of human life that emphasizes both individual moral autonomy in the Kantian sense and a religious grounding of this ethical view of man. The ethical-religious state of existence so zealously defended against the speculative philosophers in the earlier pseudonymous works is in the second literature meticulously described and defended in the more practical arena of social, political, economic, and cultural change occurring in modern Denmark. What threatened Kierkegaard's ethical-religious view of the human self was not speculative idealism but the rise of science and politics as the cornerstones of the modern state. The paradigm of the aesthetic way of life was no longer the philosopher speculatively wandering in the land of possibility but the politician and scientist whose aim was to "improve human life."

REFLECTION AND PURE THOUGHT

Kierkegaard's radical opposition to his age stemmed primarily from his fear of the misuse of the power of reflection. He believed that reflection could never by itself make a significant impact upon human life, for "All my labour with respect to knowing has no effect upon my life, upon its lusts, its passions, its selfishness; it leaves me entirely unchanged—it is my action which changes my life" (*JFY*, 131). Kierkegaard clearly saw that reflection is a necessary condition for responsible and sane behavior in human life. But he also understood that reflection is not a sufficient condition for bringing about change; at best, it can only prepare a reasonable plan for and defense of actions taken. What worried Kierkegaard about his own age was its dissolving of this distinction between thinking and acting by making reflection an end in itself. "Reflection is not the evil; but a reflective condition and the deadlock which it involves, by transforming the capacity for action into a means of escape from action, is both corrupt and dangerous, and leads in the end to a retrograde movement" (*PA*, 68).[3] Indeed, one reason Kierkegaard regarded the political and cultural turmoil in nineteenth-century Denmark as a retrograde movement was that it had lost all sense of the distinction between reflection and action.

Kierkegaard expressed his criticism of reflection in a journal entry:

Self-reflection [*Selv-Reflexionen*] was a skepticism. . . . But pure thought is a still more extreme skepticism.

[3] In the same spirit, Kierkegaard wrote, "a reflective and passionless age does exactly the contrary: it *hinders* and *stifles* all action . . ." (*PA*, 51; Kierkegaard's italics).

Despite all the inwardness of self-reflection, it nevertheless could not forget its relation to actuality in the sense
of actuality, its relation to the *an sich* which pursues it.
Pure thought, however, is positive through having taken
the whole matter imaginatively into a sphere where
there is no relation to actuality at all. Pure thought does
not even dream that it is skepticism—but this itself is
the most extreme skepticism. (*JP*, III, 3702)

Kierkegaard's distinction between self-reflection and pure
thought clearly illuminates the source of his agitation
about contemporary Denmark. The life of thought in his
contemporaries had been transformed from self-reflection
to pure thought. The upheaval of the age, begun in skepticism about the old order and desire to bring about transformation, had in Kierkegaard's view culminated in a
reflective suspension of action.[4] The reflective means of
change had become ends in themselves. "Reflection for its
own sake" had become the hallmark of the age. He viewed
this suspension in reflection as a subtle imprisonment, for
Danes were convinced of "the flattering and conceited notion that the *possibility* of reflection is far superior to a
mere *decision*" (*PA*, 48; Kierkegaard's italics). Kierkegaard's
perception of this great Danish misfortune is captured in
analogy.

It is well enough known to physiologists that nothing
is more injurious to digestion than constant reflection on
digestion. And so it is also with relation to the spiritual
life the most injurious thing when reflection, as it too

[4] Clearly, action did not cease throughout Europe in the nineteenth
century; numerous reactionary monarchical governments fell and were
replaced by liberal ones. When Kierkegaard refers to the absence of
action, he does not mean political acts that topple governments but
individual actions taken by morally autonomous agents. It was this sort
of action that Kierkegaard viewed as becoming increasingly difficult
given the broad base being achieved by the reflective mentality. We
shall explore Kierkegaard's understanding of the term *action* in detail
in Chapter Four.

often does, goes amiss and instead of being used to advantage, brings the concealed labor of the hidden life out into the open and attacks the fundamental principles themselves. In case a marriage were to reflect upon the reality of marriage, it would become *eo ipso* a pretty poor marriage; for the powers that ought to be employed for the realization of the tasks of married life are employed by reflection to eat away the foundation. (*AR,* 9-10)

Here critical analysis of the presuppositions of marriage replace the act of marriage itself. It might be retorted that reflective analysis of the presuppositions of marriage in fact reveals its moral, social, and esthetic inadequacies and that such analysis saves individuals from the fatal mistake of marrying. Kierkegaard could hardly object to such a retort given his own rejection of marriage as a reasonable action for himself. Indeed, he would not disagree with anyone else who might draw the same conclusion. His only disagreement would be with those who never go beyond the point of reflection and consequently never decide for or against marriage but remain suspended in the prison of reflection.

Kierkegaard saw this suspension of action occurring on a massive scale in nineteenth-century Denmark. Rather than serving as a prelude to action, reflection was turning into pure thought and forestalling what it was initially intended to bring about. Philosophy, science, scholarship, the press, and politics were all rejected by Kierkegaard, not because he regarded them as intrinsically corrupt, but because he perceived them as having fallen victim to the fatal disease of pure thought. In all these modes of self-reflection, the religious and political immediacy of Danish life had been negated, brought under the microscopic scrutiny of critical reflection, but at the same time no private and/or public acts moved the Danes beyond this reflective mediacy. Consequently, society remained suspended in the spiritual prison of pure thought. The plight of the individual considering marriage was in Kierkegaard's view the plight of his own Denmark.

Kierkegaard viewed Hegelian philosophy as a paradigm of pure thought. As introduced into Danish intellectual life, it had a predominantly aesthetic and theological orientation. The leading literary critic, Johan Ludvig Heiberg, had developed an esthetics grounded on an interpretation of Hegel's philosophy, and Hans Lassen Martensen had done the same for theology. Without entering into an exposition of either Hegel's philosophy or its Danish interpretations in Heiberg and Martensen, we may briefly explore Kierkegaard's understanding of Hegelian philosophy as a paradigmatic expression of the reflective nature of Danish life. Kierkegaard regarded Hegelian philosophy as consistent in at least one sense with the high calling of philosophy to make human beings critically self-conscious. Like all preceding Western philosophers, Hegel engaged in, to use his own terms, a reflective mediation of immediacy. Simply stated, phenomena such as art, religion, ethics, science, and politics, which shape human consciousness, are analyzed in terms of the philosophical pursuit of knowledge (epistemology), of the good (value theory), and of the ultimately real (metaphysics). The reflective analysis of immediacy requires persons temporarily to suspend their esthetic, religious, political, scientific, and ethical presuppositions in order to examine them critically. In philosophy, the remarkable phenomenon of human consciousness turns back upon itself, making itself the object of a critical reflection that is guided by the human pursuit of truth. One easily finds in Hegelian philosophy such an analysis and on a scale unsurpassed in breadth and depth in the history of Western philosophy.

We have seen how Kierkegaard drew a distinction between self-reflection and pure thought, and it is in Hegel's failure to draw such a distinction that he found the greatest flaw in Hegelian philosophy. Self-reflection has immediacy as its beginning and ending point. Its end is not merely a critical analysis of immediacy but also, and more importantly, the transformation of immediacy. Plato's philosopher-king is a paradigm of how philosophy has believed itself capable of transforming and reshaping human life according to the philosophical pursuit of truth. Of course, Western philosophy has never been so totally influential in the shaping of human society, but religion, politics, art, and science have been positively influenced in varying degrees by philosophical reflection. When Kierkegaard states that the *an sich* pursues reflection, he is merely claiming that the ultimate end of reflection is not reflection itself but the transformation of human life through philosophical reflection.

This goal of philosophy is itself based on the presupposition that a relation exists between thought and being, between reflection and immediacy. One of the most persistent conflicts in modern philosophy has been about the nature of this relation between thought and being. Rationalists argue that being, reality, can be grasped through a priori systems of thought, while empiricists argue that thought must proceed inductively if it ever is to succeed in grasping the real. Both sides agree about the power of thought to know and to articulate in speech the nature of reality. The disagreement is over how to proceed in thought toward the attainment of knowledge of the real.

Kant, of course, brought into question this presupposition of modern philosophy concerning the unity of thought or being. As we know, Kant in his first critique argued that we can know phenomena only as they are perceived and that our perceptual experience is determined by the structure of the human mind. Our minds are so constructed that we must perceive the phenomenal world as objects in space and time and as subject to the laws of causality, but we may not conclude from this that the thing-in-itself (*ding-an-sich*) is precisely as we perceive it. This position brought radically into question the philosophical presupposition of the unity of thought and being. Furthermore, in his second critique Kant extended his theory of the limitation of thought beyond the question of knowledge of the world to the problem of self-knowledge. To philosophical thought concerning the question of God's existence, human freedom, and immortality he applied the same limitations that he did to philosophical thought about nature. Just as we are philosophically incapable of elucidating the nature of the reality that lies behind perception, so we are also incapable of demonstrating either the existence or the nonexistence of God, human freedom, and immortality lying beyond our ethical and spiritual experience. Needless to say, this radical Kantian revolution in thought cast modern philosophy into a deep skepticism about the veracity of perceptual, ethical, and religious experience. When Kierkegaard writes that the *an sich* pursues reflection, he is also claiming an allegiance to this Kantian skepticism about the capacity of human beings to realize the philosophical goal of knowing ultimate reality. But having accepted the limitations of thought, reflection must nevertheless maintain its vigil over immediacy and struggle in spite of its limitations to transform and to renew human life.

Hegel believed that the Kantian idea of the thing-in-itself, if left to stand, would undermine the very cornerstone of philosophy, which itself rested upon the presupposition of the unity of thought and being. Contrary to Kant's argument that what lies behind the phenomenal world—human freedom, immortality, and the existence of God—is inaccessible to reflection, Hegel maintained that the nature of the phenomenal world can be known in thought and that human freedom and the existence of God need not be accepted as necessary, but undemonstrable, presuppositions of morality and religion. Hegel agreed that perception, ethical striving, and religious faith constitute part of the core of human experience and that none of these modes of human consciousness is capable of knowing the true nature of reality. He also agreed with Kant that these modes of consciousness can themselves be made the object of a higher reflection in which the ordinary consciousness of common experience becomes the object of a higher reflection or consciousness. But Hegel claimed, contrary to Kant, that in this higher reflection—which he called Reason *(Vernunft)*—the absolute or the ultimate, which is only dimly and inadequately perceived in these primary modes of consciousness, is clearly grasped in human thought and rendered in philosophical speech.

We can use religion as an example of this transition from understanding *(Verstand)* to Reason *(Vernunft)*. Hegel argued that the consciousness in which human beings first gain the truth is religious consciousness. But this mode of consciousness differs from philosophical reason in that it retains what Hegel called "a form of representation [*Vorstellung*]." The truth, which is grasped in religious faith, remains tied formally with an imaginative picture or story and with the misleading suggestions that such a picture or story may imply. Moreover, this religious consciousness will be culturally influenced by the natural and social order of which it is a part. Since religious consciousness never rises above these formal and cultural limitations, it cannot be relied upon to provide truth about the absolute. Only when the absolute loses its presentation in sensuous immediacy and rises to the pure universality of conceptual thought can we be said in truth to know the absolute. It is in this manner that Hegel attempted to surpass Kant and to restore the unity of thought and being. In his analysis of Western history, Hegel sought to liberate the absolute from the prison of immediacy into the freedom of conceptual expression. Not only Western religion but also Western art, morality, politics, and philosophy are construed by Hegel to be immediate appearances of the absolute, and his philosophy is an attempt to elevate the absolute from the level of appearance to reality in human consciousness.

This high-flown philosophical disagreement between Kant and Hegel had profound existential consequences from Kierkegaard's point of view. If Hegel were correct, cultural phenomena such as religion, art, and ethics would be weakened. Hegel's intention may have been the legitimation of these phenomena by representing them as immediate expressions of truth, but the practical result is to damage their validity in human life. After all, why should anyone take a half-truth seriously? Why bother with the half-ripe fruit of religious faith, for example, when one can have its full ripeness in thought. The elevation of religious faith to the status of philosophical truth turns out, in Kierkegaard's view, to be a demotion of the significance and value of religious faith in human life. Religious faith is in fact displaced by its philosophical expression, becoming, at best, a half-truth that individuals should strive to surpass in thought.

If, on the other hand, Kant were right about the distinction between thought and being—and Kierkegaard believed that he was—then human beings are destined forever to organize experience in terms of undemonstrable presuppositions. That the world is the way we experience it, that we are morally obliged to seek the good and are free to do so, and that there is a God who ultimately guarantees a harmony of happiness and virtue—these are the undemonstrable suppositions according to which we must order our lives. For Kierkegaard, there is no surpassing the kind of life we must build on these suppositions into a higher realm of thought and reflection that transcends the limitations, the ambiguities, the uncertainties, and the risks of human life. These modes of consciousness—perception, duty, faith—constitute the immediacy of life, the *an sich*. Although reflection legitimately makes this immediacy an object of consciousness, it may not replace it as a higher form of life in the realm of pure thought, where we come to know only what we believed in the realm of immediacy. For Kierkegaard, the *an sich* tenaciously clutches at reflection, never allowing the philosopher to escape into a clean, well-lighted place where all the ambiguity, risk, and uncertainty disappear. One may build such a palace in thought, but it can

57

only be a dream, for the philosopher remains inextricably locked in the opaqueness of the *an sich*. Pure thought, however, denies the *an sich* by claiming that a philosophical dream is more real than the world in which we live and breathe. Kierkegaard accused Hegel of being comical because he constructs a palace of thought and is forced to lie in a hovel next door (*JP*, III, 3308). Surely self-reflection in the interest of improving one's life within a hovel is superior to pure thinking in the interest of building a castle in which one cannot possibly live. Though such a recognition is genuinely humbling, it seemed an obvious one to Kierkegaard. He nevertheless saw in Danish thought, especially in Martensen's theology, the reverse decision. Danish thought had embarked upon pure thought, not self-reflection, and although this commitment was most apparent in Denmark's philosophy, it also appeared in its science, scholarship, and politics—indeed, in every dimension of Danish life.

Although Kierkegaard did not describe the natural sciences and general scholarship as having fallen victim to pure thought, he clearly understood them in that way. In discussing science, Kierkegaard admitted, "All knowledge has something captivating about it, but on the other hand, it also alters the entire state in the knower's mind" (*JP*, III, 2807). It is this subtle alteration of the scientist's mind that worried Kierkegaard, for he believed that a preoccupation with science cultivates both curious and imperialistic minds. Scientific investigation elevates curiosity to the status of life style, with the consequence that the scientist forgets all but the adventure and challenge of the discovery of the secrets of nature (*JP*, III, 2813). Such an alteration of one's state of mind is in Kierkegaard's view exceedingly dangerous, for it diverts one's attention from the more important frontier of one's own subjectivity. Kierkegaard believed that to "come to oneself *in self-knowledge*" is the most significant of all epistemological tasks, and he warned that "in all other knowledge thou art away from thyself, forgetful of thyself, absent from thyself" (*JFY*, 121; Kierkegaard's italics). Like Socrates, who abandoned the Ionians' speculative quest for the basic substance of the cosmos for the search for self-knowledge through converse with persons in Athens, Kierkegaard feared that scientific curiosity diverts attention from the more fundamental and important question of self-knowledge. Kierkegaard asked, "Do I need to know the digestive process in order to eat? Do I need to know the processes of the nervous system—in order to believe in God and to love men?" (*JP*, III, 2807). Obviously not. Moreover, am I not "weakening my whole ethical passion by becoming a natural scientist? And I wonder if, with all this diverse knowledge of analogies, of abnormalities, of this and that, I do not lose more and more the impress of the ethical . . ." (*JP*, III, 2807).

Kierkegaard also worried that the power and success of the sciences in gaining knowledge of nature also engenders an imperialistic mind in that the scientist "takes it upon himself to explain all mankind" (*JP*, III, 2807). Ethics becomes the subject matter of physics and physiology. "Physiology will ultimately extend itself to the point of embracing ethics. There are already sufficient clues of a new endeavor—to treat ethics as physics, whereby all of ethics becomes illusory and ethics in the race is treated statistically by averages or is calculated as one calculates vibrations in laws of nature" (*JP*, III, 2807).[5] Science has thrust itself into an arena in which it does not belong (*JP*, III, 2807). In Kierkegaard's view, the content of the ethical and religious life is impervious to scientific inquiry. What can science possibly have to say about the reality of human freedom and the existence of God? Kierkegaard had no doubt that it can say nothing, yet he observed the growing encroachment of science upon the domain of ethical and religious subjectivity. This encroachment was in itself a

[5] Cf. *JP*, I, 927: "Finally, just as metaphysics has supplanted theology, it will end with physics supplanting ethics. The whole modern statistical approach to morality contributes to this."

great mistake, though an even greater one was the attempt to replace the ethical and religious life with a scientific invasion and explanation of it. Like the philosophers, scientists are not content merely to reflect upon phenomena distinct from themselves but insist upon absorbing these phenomena into themselves and thereby transforming the life of ethics and religion into a life of reflection upon them, that is, into a life of pure thought. Kierkegaard is unambiguously clear about this when he predicts that "What the 'race' tends toward is apparently the establishment of natural science in the place of religion [and ethics]" (*JP*, III, 2821).[6]

Kierkegaard, unlike Grundtvig, was no despiser of science. In a discussion of a book on physiology by Carl Gustav Carus, Kierkegaard accepted the significance and legitimacy of science. What he most appreciated about Carus's book was the physiologist's admission that religious and ethical issues are beyond the range of scientific investigation. In Kierkegaard's words, Carus acknowledged the distinction between the "quantitative" and the "qualitative" dimensions of life. "At all decisive points he makes unqualified room . . . for the creative power of God, for the absolute expression of worship, and says: This no one can grasp, no science, neither now nor ever" (*JP*, III, 2818). But such modesty did not generally characterize the scientific community. Kierkegaard clearly recognized that such pride is dangerous in its existential implications, but he also saw the humor in this imperialism. "If the natural sciences had been as developed in Socrates' time as they are now, all the Sophists would have become natural scientists. One would have hung a microscope outside his shop to attract customers; another would have had a sign reading: Look through our giant microscope and see how a man thinks;

6 Kierkegaard identified this tendency to make science a religion with Danish nationalism: "In the same way, no doubt, the world also wants to market a new culture-consciousness, a Christian diffusion, therefore a Christian consciousness,—and it probably will make natural science its religion" (*JP*, III, 2822).

another: See how the grass grows. Excellent motifs for an Aristophanes, especially if he has Socrates present and has him peer into a microscope" (*JP*, III, 2814). Kierkegaard found few subjects more fit for satire and ridicule than the scientific and philosophical disciples of pure thought.

Although Kierkegaard stated that "Of all scholarship, the natural sciences are the most banal" (*JP*, III, 2811), he believed that biblical scholarship ranks high in academic banality. His criticisms sound like Grundtvig's charge of "exegetical papacy": "just as the Pope secured himself by forbidding the reading of the New Testament, so Protestantism secured itself with the aid of—scholarly exegesis" (*JP*, III, 2890). Indeed, "In order to secure ourselves completely we declare that scientific scholarship exists specifically to help us understand the N[ew].T[estament]., in order that we may better hear its voice" (*JP*, III, 2872). In fact, "Christian scholarship is the human race's prodigious invention to defend itself against the N[ew].T[estament]., to ensure that one can continue to be a Christian without letting the N[ew].T[estament]. come too close" (*JP*, III, 2872). Here Kierkegaard challenged scholars who argued that a correct understanding of the New Testament is not possible without the aid of biblical scholarship. As though speaking directly to them in a journal entry, Kierkegaard asks, "can you deny, do you dare deny, that this is very easy to understand, indescribably easy, that you do not need a dictionary or commentary or a single other person in order to understand" the command in the New Testament to despise this world (*JP*, III, 2865). The scholar would no doubt respond that these words are attributed to Jesus by early Christians who believed that the return of Christ is imminent and that believers should give up their worldly cares and concerns in order to prepare for the Second Coming. In short, the passage reflects the eschatological character of the early Christian community; its meaning and truth are largely determined by its *Sitz im Leben*.

Kierkegaard believed that this approach to the New

61

Testament transforms the understanding of it. Instead of being recognized as God's word, which literally determines human values, a sense of guilt and forgiveness, and a hope for a final reconciliation of heaven and earth, it is merely appreciated "as an exceedingly notable document of olden time upon which one expends an astonishing amount of diligence and acumen, etc. . . ." (*FSE*, 58). Kierkegaard claimed, "While the pastors dispute about who can write most beautifully, while journals and periodicals with deep seriousness criticize the artistic aspects of the language, the construction, etc., we completely forget that we are to act according to this, that God has not really given his word as material for a literary exercise to see who is able to present it most elegantly" (*JP*, III, 2911). However, he never asserted that the findings of biblical scholarship are false or that this scholarly activity is in some sense intrinsically evil. What concerned him was that in the scholarly investigation of the Bible one forgets that it is essentially an existential form of life that challenges the values and priorities that normally or conventionally govern our lives. Scholarship shrouds this existential form of life in the garb of academic respectability. The New Testament is understood in one of two ways: as an antiquarian document that is worthy of textual and literary analysis, or as the receptacle of universal truths wrapped in the mythology of an antiquated world view. In either case, biblical scholarship serves the truth of the New Testament by revealing its literary and artistic or doctrinal value (*JP*, III, 1906).[7] In both cases, the notion that it is an existential possibility for

[7] A similar sentiment appears in *For Self-Examination*, where Kierkegaard writes that "I do not put myself into any personal (subjective) relation to God's Word, but on the contrary, with the seriousness for which people so highly commend me, I transform the Word into an impersonal entity (the objective, the objective doctrine, etc.), to which I, a man not only serious but cultured, relate myself objectively, so that I am not so uncultivated and vain as to bring my personality into play, and to suppose it was I who was addressed, I and constantly I who was being spoken about" (*FSE*, 60-61).

each of us is forgotten. And where we continue to think of it as a possibility for our lives, scholarship omits and confuses "the existentially strenuous passages in the New Testament. We hush them up—and then we arrange things on easier and cheaper terms" (*JP*, III, 2881), which we then offer to children (*JP*, III, 2895).

This criticism of biblical scholarship is the same one that Kierkegaard leveled against science and philosophy. All three disciplines make the scholarly understanding of morality and religion superior to the activities themselves. Reflection does not lead the individual back into the ethical and religious life but abrogates it. The existential texturing of subjectivity by ethics and religion is suspended by the marvelous discovery of pure thought, the matchless deception that maintains that infinite thought about the nature of marriage is superior to marriage itself.

REFLECTION AND LEVELING

The reflective negation of ethics and religion leads not only to pure thought but also to politics. The political and social philosophers made religion an object of reflection as well in the nineteenth century, and they, no less than the speculative philosophers and scientists of the day, repudiated the understanding of human nature in their common ethical and religious traditions. Although their rejection takes the form not of flight into pure thought but of political action, it, like pure thought, culminates in the displacement of God and king as the authorities of history and history's social and political institutions. Ludwig Feuerbach and Karl Marx had tried to empty the entire cosmos, nature and history, of all vestiges of the divine. Democratic liberalism had been more genteel in its quiet removal of God to the fringe of the cosmos; once having set nature in motion, he left its maintenance to human reason and freedom. The subtle distinctions between atheism and deism have little influence on the practical struggle for political autonomy, however. Certainly there are serious ethical and ontological distinctions to be made between liberalism and socialism, but the two movements are alike in their rejection of divine authority in the social and political affairs of men. This release of human life from the bondage of monarchy and religion politicized human life on the most basic level in that politics emerged as a way of being in the world. No longer the priority and responsibility of kings and nobles, governance became the overriding concern of the common man. In his new-found freedom the common man discovered not simply the possibilities for a better life but, more fundamentally, a new understanding of himself as a human being. We have seen how this politicizing of human life came to Denmark in the form of liberalism, with its overriding emphasis on the individual. We have also noted how Danish literature, religion, and philosophy both celebrated and sanctified the individualism of democratic liberalism.

In turning to an analysis of Kierkegaard's conception of the role politics occupied in nineteenth-century Danish life, one first notices that his critique does not go to the theoretical sources of either liberal or socialist thought. Kierkegaard had read both Feuerbach and Locke, but he had never heard the names John Stuart Mill and Karl Marx.[8] In any case, Kierkegaard's analysis is more empirical in the sense that it is related to what he observed going on around him rather than to theoretical sources. This empirical orientation, however, does not lead to a simple-minded cataloguing of events but to two central criticisms of democratic liberalism. First, he argued that it defines the individual in terms of an abstract egalitarian ideal that

[8] For a study of Kierkegaard's understanding of communism and a comparison of the political thought of Kierkegaard and Marx, see Gregor Malantschuk, *The Controversial Kierkegaard*, trans. Howard V. Hong and Edna H. Hong (Ontario: Wilfrid Laurier University Press, 1979).

levels him. Second, this individualism entails an egotism that degrades human life.

In the work of reflection Kierkegaard saw the emergence of an abstraction that levels human life (*PA*, 55). The leveling process being carried out by reflection in the service of an abstraction is so powerful, he predicted, that it is "bound to continue, like a tradewind, and consume everything" (*PA*, 55-56). This abstraction will be all-consuming, because all thought and practice will be so pervaded by its influence that even its opposition will emerge as a mere reflection of it. "[N]o society or association can arrest that abstract power, simply because an association is itself in the service of the levelling process" (*PA*, 55). Kierkegaard envisioned a future in which this abstraction would have gained such a hold upon human consciousness that all thought, practice, and speech would be totally absorbed by its power.

The abstraction that Kierkegaard feared and that "not even the individuality of different nationalities can arrest" (*PA*, 55) is the ideal of human equality. The "dialectic of the present age tends toward equality, and its most logical—though mistaken—fulfillment is levelling . . ." (*PA*, 52). In this abstraction of equality, the "*representation* of *humanity pure and unalloyed*" (*PA*, 55) transforms one into "a man and nothing else, in the complete equalitarian sense" (*PA*, 57). Kierkegaard believed that democratic liberalism in both thought and practice brings forward simultaneously liberation from enslaving traditions and institutions and a new definition of human nature. The French Revolution, which was "built on an untruth" (*JP*, IV, 4136) and carried out in the interests of human rights, freedom, and equality, which individuals have by nature, brought into being a citizen of the world. In Kierkegaard's view, the democratic revolutions sweeping across Europe destroyed the concrete and historical community, replacing it with the abstract and ahistorical public. The individual is defined no longer by contingent factors like nationality, race, community, and occupation but by his membership in the human race, which is defined in the universal ideals of democratic liberalism. Once an individual is captured by these ideals, he becomes a member of the public, "which is everything and nothing, the most dangerous of all powers and the most insignificant. . . . The qualification 'public' is produced by the deceptive juggling of an age of reflection, which makes it appear flattering to the individual who in this way can arrogate to himself this monster, in comparison with which concrete realities seem poor. The public is the fairy story of an age of understanding, which in imagination makes the individual into something even greater than a king above his people . . ." (PA, 63). Kierkegaard here sounds like Grundtvig, who castigated the Enlightenment notion of the individual as a universal category that defies the crucial and identity-forming limitations of nationality, culture, and race. There is indeed significant agreement between the two on this point. Kierkegaard conceived of the public as a "phantom . . . spirit, a monstrous abstraction" (PA, 59), a denial of all accidental and concrete contingencies of fate and history in the determining of the being of human life. The denial of contingency and concreteness as ontologically definitive of human nature levels all persons to a universal abstraction. Kierkegaard objected to this leveling because it recognizes as ontologically definitive in any single individual *only* what it recognizes in all.

Kierkegaard calls this ideal of equality a "negative unity" and a "negative reciprocity of all individuals" (PA, 52). That is to say, the philosophical question of human nature turns on the political notion of human equality and rights and excludes a priori any consideration of social, historical, political, and physical contingencies. Kierkegaard construed this denial as itself a rejection of individuality. Once the individual is leveled by reflection, he "no longer belongs to God, to himself, to his beloved, to his art or to his science, he is conscious of belonging in all things to an abstraction to which he is subjected in reflection . . ." (*PA*, 53). Thus, the individual belongs to "a public [which] is neither a nation, nor a generation, nor a community, nor a society, nor these particular men, for all these are only what they are through the concrete . . ." (*PA*, 62).[9] This leveling process is, then, "the victory of abstraction over the individual" (*PA*, 52);[10] indeed, it is the "destruction of the individual" (*PA*, 54). To the extent that the individual exists at all, "he only exists in an external sense . . . as a

[9] A passage from Unamuno reflects the sense of Kierkegaard's concept of the public:

Homo sum; nihil humani a me alienum puto, said the Latin playwright. For my part I would rather say: *Nullum hominem a me alienum puto*: I am a man; no other man do I deem a stranger. For in my eyes the adjective *humanus* is no less suspect than its abstract substantive *humanitas*, humanity. I would choose neither "the human" nor "humanity," neither the simple adjective nor the substantivized adjective, but the concrete substantive: man, the man of flesh and blood, the man who is born, suffers, and dies—above all, who dies; the man who eats and drinks and plays and sleeps and thinks and loves; the man who is seen and heard; one's brother, the real brother.

For there is something else called man, the subject of many lucubrations, more or less scientific, and he is the legendary featherless biped, the ζῷον πολιτικόν of Aristotle, the social contractor of Rousseau, the *homo economicus* of the Manchester school, the *homo sapiens* of Linnaeus, or, if you like, the vertical mammal. Such a man is a man from nowhere, from neither here nor there, neither of this age nor of another, who has neither sex nor country, who is, in short, a mere idea. That is to say, a no-man.

Our man is the other one, the man of flesh and blood: you and I, that man yonder, all of us who walk firmly on the earth. ("The Man of Flesh and Blood," in Miguel de Unamuno, *The Tragic Sense of Life in Men and Nations*, trans. and ed. Anthony Kerrigan, Bollingen Series LXXXV, no. 4 [Princeton: Princeton University Press, 1972], pp. 3-4)

[10] Kierkegaard viewed his contemporaries as "false reprints," since all are alike. They fail to understand that "every man as he comes from God's hand is an original edition . . ." (*CD*, 66). We shall see in Chapters Four and Five that Kierkegaard, as this passage suggests, provides a religious justification for his emphasis on the ontological and moral significance of individuality.

numeral within the crowd, a fraction within the earthly conglomeration" (*PH*, 184). Clearly, this abstraction is for Kierkegaard a trivialization of the notion of individuality. Without those contingencies that distinguish one individual from another, the only distinguishing mechanism that remains is the quantitative one. The irony in the loss of individuality within the movement of liberalism was not lost upon Kierkegaard, for he saw clearly how contradictory it is for liberalism to culminate, as he thought it would, in the disappearance of the very individual who is exalted in its theory and practice.[11]

There is a second sense in which Kierkegaard employs the term *leveling* in order to describe the events occurring around him. Persons belonging to the public not only deny their individuality by selling their birthright for an abstract conception of the human self, but they also are unable to make a real commitment. In fact, to be a member of the

[11] Kierkegaard's analysis of the rise of the modern depersonalized society does not rely solely on his view of liberalism as internally contradictory. Although his analysis lacks the sophistication of modern sociology, he saw clearly that the depersonalization of modern life was the product of all the factors creating the modern state—science, industrialization, communications, transportation, etc. Though he could not see how this was happening in any technically accurate way, *The Present Age* is clearly prophetic in its anticipation of the central fact of modern life. Two passages from his journals illuminate his understanding of the complexity of the process he described in *The Present Age.*

The advance of civilization, the rise of the large cities, centralization, and what corresponded to all this and essentially produced it— the press as a means of communication—have given all life a completely wrong direction. (*JP*, IV, 4166)

The railroad craze is altogether an attempt à la Babel. It also fits together with the end of a cultural period; it is the last lap. Unfortunately, almost simultaneously the new era began, 1848. The railroads are related to the idea of centralization as a potentiation. (*JP*, IV, 4179)

For a discussion of the processes of abstraction at work in contemporary society, see Peter Berger, *Facing up to Modernity* (New York: Basic Books, 1977).

public is to become part of something that *"hinders and stifles* all action" (*PA*, 51; Kierkegard's italics) and transforms "the capacity for action into a means of escape from action . . ." (*PA*, 68), so that one comes to ignore his "eternal responsibility" for himself and the other (*PA*, 53). Just as we discover the individual in his concrete historical and cultural situation, so we also discover the individual in his capacity to act within this situation, which makes him what he is. Indeed, the two are closely related, for it is possible for a person to act as an individual only if he conceives of himself as such. His facticity not only constitutes his being but is also the condition for an awareness of himself as a personal agent who is responsible both for himself and the other. The leveling process neutralizes the notion of the person as a unique individual with distinct responsibilities toward himself and the other. Moreover, this process is intimately related to reflection: reflection's attack on religion is one of the conditions that makes possible the leveling process.

In Kierkegaard's view, it is the West's religious tradition, more than any other phenomenon, that emphasizes the ontological uniqueness of each individual and his moral obligation to all other selves. Paradoxically, however, the reflective mediation of this tradition laid the necessary foundation for the disappearance of the individual. The "abstract levelling process, that self-combustion of the human race, [is] produced by the friction which arises when the individual ceases to exist as singled out by religion . . ." (*PA*, 55-56). The work of reflection is to dissolve the individuating force in human life and to replace it with an abstract conception of the individual as one who is distinguished by neither his facticity nor his private responsibility for the other.

This triumph of reflection as pure thought and as leveling agent in the modern age entails the eradication of the ethical-religious form of life as Kierkegaard understood it. The modern state emerged from that activity which shifts the foundation of human life from ethics and religion to science and politics. The union of democratic liberalism and scientific rationalism with laissez-faire capitalism created the modern state and freed the individual from the tutelage of God and king on the one hand and from the restraints and obligations of his facticity on the other. Defined no longer in terms of his moral obligations and religious destiny but in terms of natural rights, he set a worldly course toward personal economic and political aggrandizement. Kierkegaard is unequivocally clear about the emergence of the economic man within the modern state. "In the end . . . money will be the one thing people will desire," even though it is only "an abstraction" (*PA*, 40). The leveling of all facticity that defines and obligates us leads ultimately to the creation of an abstraction that itself becomes the agent that shapes and directs human striving. Kierkegaard's suspicions of the modern state in which such a thing could happen are not difficult to imagine. He thought that once the individual is liberated from the discipline of the ethical-religious form of life, what remains is an unchecked egotism that is sanctioned and cultivated by the modern state.

> The state is human egotism in great dimensions, very expediently and cunningly composed so that the egotisms of individuals intersect each other correctively. . . . Just as we speak of a calculus of infinitesimals, so also the state is a calculus of egotisms, but always in such a way that it egotistically appears to be the most prudent thing to enter into and to be in this higher egotism. But this, after all, is anything but the moral abandoning of egotism. The state cannot go beyond this; so to be improved by living in the state is just as doubtful as being improved in a prison. Perhaps one becomes much shrewder about his egotism, his enlightened egotism, that is, his egotism in relation to other egotisms, but less egotistic he does not become, and what is worse, one is spoiled by regarding

this official, civic, authorized egotism as virtue—this, in fact, is how demoralizing civic life is, because it reassures one in being a shrewd egotist. (*JP*, IV, 4238)[12]

The modern state, then, is based on an acknowledgment of the acquisitive character of human nature and the tacit admission that it cannot be ethically transformed or negated and hence must be controlled. Thus, the state sets as its twin tasks the control of acquisitiveness through its political institutions and the rational planning of the means for satisfying the ever-expanding demands of the acquisitive instinct. What remains, Kierkegaard thought, is the necessity of making this collective egotism into a virtue. Kierkegaard may have had Hegel in mind when he wrote this passage,[13] but it is more likely that he was thinking of the Grundtvigian populists and the bourgeois liberals. Both groups in their own way attempted to justify religiously the self-justifying politics of liberalism. Thus the absorption of religion into pure thought and its displacement by the leveling process do not entail the complete rejection of religion but only its separation from ethics and its subsequent realignment with science and politics in order to sanctify the new order.

Religion and the Modern State

Kierkegaard praised Feuerbach and David Friedrich Strauss for their public repudiation of Christianity. He believed that "resolutely and definitely to have no religion at all is something passionate" (*AC*, 185) and that these two freethinkers were to be praised for their forthright atheism. Passionate antireligion is in Kierkegaard's view superior to "a religion which is watered down and garbled into mere

---

12 Cf. *JP*, II, 2037.

13 Kierkegaard recognized that Hegel locates evil in "isolated subjectivity," and he agreed that "isolated subjectivity as the age understands it is evil, but restoration to health by means of 'objectivity' is not a hair better" (*JP*, IV, 4555).

twaddle, so that one can hold this religion in a perfectly passionateless way" (*AC*, 185). Through his pseudonyms, Kierkegaard had earlier criticized those who attempted to find a theological accommodation of Christianity and Hegelian philosophy, but in his second literature it is Mynster and Grundtvig who are found guilty of the sin of acculturating Christianity by wedding it to the modernization of Denmark. That both men were regarded, "in different ways, as representatives of true Christianity" (*AC*, 183) infuriated Kierkegaard. He saw in their political and ecclesiastical commitments the attenuation of religious earnestness. "But inasmuch as Christianity came to be served in homogeneity with all finite objectives (something achieved especially in Protestantism, especially in Denmark), Christianity essentially dropped out, eternity dropped out; that which was supposed to represent the eternal became exactly like all other finite things, a living for finite objectives" (*JP*, IV, 4242).[14] Christianity has been identified exclusively with "finite objectives" in the sense that it places "a divine blessing upon all the trivialities and putterings of finitude and the temporal enjoyment of life" (*JP*, IV, 4998).[15] The modernization of Denmark may appear to us to be considerably more than trivial putterings, but Kierkegaard did not think so. Indeed, given the scorn he pours upon modernization in other texts, this is a modest criticism. His criticisms are, however, less important here than his claim that Christianity had become a "blessing" on the modernization of Denmark.

Grundtvig, as we have seen, sought to align Christianity

[14] The terms *finite* and *eternal* are easily misleading, for they imply a supernatural or otherworldly understanding of Christianity. Kierkegaard agreed that Christianity is a rejection of the finite and the temporal for the infinite and the eternal, but these terms have an ethical rather than a metaphysical meaning in Kierkegaard's understanding of Christianity. We shall explore the meaning of these terms in Chapter Four in discussing Kierkegaard's concept of the self.

[15] Cf. *JP*, II, 1860.

with modernization in his religious nationalism and in his support of the state church, which he regarded as a "civil institution." He worked for its reform in order that it might "provide good living conditions for the true church,"[16] which he identified with the Apostles' Creed and the sacraments of baptism and communion. Grundtvig's strongest commitment, of course, was not to this civil institution but to his religious nationalism. We should make a distinction between Grundtvig's support of the state church on the one hand and his religious nationalism on the other. Kierkegaard, however, seems not to have made this distinction; he perceived Grundtvig's support of both as equally representing the marriage of religious faith and nationalistic self-consciousness. The clearest of Kierkegaard's criticisms of Grundtvig's religious nationalism is found in a journal entry from 1850:

> It is obvious that one of the factors in Christ's death was that he repudiated nationalism, wanted to have nothing to do with it. Nowadays the orthodox are—the true nationalists; they produce theories about Christian states and Christian peoples. . . .
>
> Grundtvig, who has always hated discipline and rigorousness, has also produced a theory that the true Christian takes part in everything—he has presumably forgotten the metaphor about those who run in the race and are abstemious in everything. It is unbelievable what nonsense they have made out of the story of the wedding in Cana. The Grundtvigians, to be consistent, must be upset by the fact that Christ was not married, let alone many times. (*JP*, IV, 4171)[17]

Moreover, this "Grundtvigian nonsense about nationality

16 Hal Koch, *Grundtvig*, trans. Llewellyn Jones (Yellow Springs, Ohio: Antioch Press, 1952), p. 124.

17 Cf. *JP*, VI, 6724: "In his younger days he [Grundtvig] represented the old, the old-fashioned, the hoary past, primitive, primeval Christianity; now in his old age he has spruced up to be the latest thing out, a regular fashion-setter."

is also a retrogression to paganism. It is unbelievable what foolishness delirious Grundtvigian candidates are able to serve up. Th. Fenger says, for example, that no one can be a true Christian except through nationality" (*JP*, IV, 4121).

The Grundtvigians, according to Kierkegaard, had taken Christianity into a Babylonian captivity in which its assimilation with the conquering forces of nationalism would be so complete that the captive would totally disappear. Indeed, the acculturation of Christianity would be so thorough that being a Christian would become "synonymous with being a human being . . ." (*JP*, IV, 4175). This passage from the journals echoes one of the main criticisms of Danish Christianity in *Attack upon Christendom*, where Kierkegaard scorns the practice of making citizenship and church membership Danish birthrights. Less obviously, yet more significantly, this passage reflects Kierkegaard's criticism of Grundtvig's identification of nationalism with Christian faith. We have seen that Grundtvig's nationalism was an attempt to anchor liberalism in a folk tradition. That is, Grundtvig tried to correct what he regarded as the excessively abstract individualism of liberalism by identifying the individual's struggle to secure and protect his natural rights with a concrete cultural tradition. Furthermore, this acculturation of liberalism was religiously sanctioned by Christianity. Grundtvig was fond of saying "man first, then Christian . . . ,"[18] meaning that human beings achieve their full humanity in a nationalistic self-consciousness that is then made possible and sanctioned by the grace of God. Odin and Christ symbolically represent the Danish struggle for political, economic, and cultural freedom in and through which the Danes are perfected as human.

To Kierkegaard, liberalism disguised as nationalism was no better than liberalism naked and unadorned. In both cases, the individual is defined ontologically by his natural

18 *N.F.S. Grundtvig*, trans. Johannes Knudsen, Enok Mortensen, and Ernest D. Nielsen, ed. with an intro. by Johannes Knudsen (Philadelphia: Fortress Press, 1961), p. 141.

rights and by the political activity by which he secures and protects those rights. Indeed, to paint human being in the colors of nationalism merely conceals the leveling impact of liberalism on human life and the egotism that it unleashes. Kierkegaard thought that this concealing of the true nature of liberalism in a religiously inspired nationalism culminates in a religious sanctification of these two related components of democratic liberalism. "We center all our attention," Kierkegaard complained, "upon the race, community, Church, in short, upon a collective— whereupon the category 'the single individual' disappears" in the ideal of equality and in the political struggle to organize human society in terms of that ideal (*JP*, II, 1906). This political struggle is itself interpreted by Grundtvig both as the historical realization of Danish destiny and as God's will. Thus, in the hands of the Grundtvigians, Christianity becomes a priest rather than a prophet in relation to the new order. In Kierkegaard's words, "The result of the Christianity of 'Christendom' is that everything, absolutely everything, has remained as it was, only everything has assumed the name of 'Christian' . . ." (*AC*, 164). This statement is in one sense completely false. One cannot say that everything has remained the same in Denmark; the absolute rule of the king was replaced by a constitutional monarchy. Yet, from a religious point of view, things have not changed; God continues to be a patron, though now of the "people" rather than of the king.

Bishop Mynster was not at all sympathetic with the people's movement. He and Grundtvig had been on different sides of political, theological, and ecclesiastical issues all their professional lives. The aristocratic Mynster supported the Danish bloodless revolution, though he was no radical in the Grundtvigian sense. What he had hoped for was the transfer of power from the king to the bourgeois liberals. He had no taste whatsoever for the rise of the proletariat to political and ecclesiastical power. He saw correctly that the revivalist movement and later the struggle for ecclesiastical reform—essentially lower class movements—were the religious side of the people's struggle for power, and he staunchly opposed both.[19]

Kierkegaard's antagonism toward the religious fervor of his day was directed against not only Grundtvig's religious nationalism but also Mynster's conservative orthodoxy.[20] His attacks on Mynster are a perplexing mixture of *ad hominem* arguments, personal vindictiveness, and theological disagreement. Yet in all these attacks Kierkegaard consistently focused on Mynster's priestly role to the middle and upper classes in Copenhagen.

One may well imagine that these classes, caught up in the economic and psychological tensions of laissez-faire capitalism, found great solace in Mynster's sermonizing assurances that the decisive event in the Christian life is the reception of God's grace, by which each individual is justified before God. The theological slant is clearly Lutheran: individuals are saved by grace, not by works. As did the revivalists, Mynster emphasized the need for a personal conversion experience,[21] though no doubt without the ecstatic and emotional trappings that characterized the lower classes' religious experience. Mynster's stress on grace and justification rather than on works must surely have soothed aching consciences, bolstered weakened egos, and assured the successful that their well-being was a divine blessing. Mynster's religion was just what the Copenhagen

[19] J. Oskar Andersen, *Survey of the History of the Church in Denmark* (Copenhagen: O. Lohse, 1930), p. 46.

[20] One of the few times that Kierkegaard supported Mynster was in 1839, when Mynster attacked Martensen for claiming that some middle way between rationalism and supernaturalism had to be developed theologically. Mynster claimed that both oppositions could not be right and that one had to settle for one or the other. Kierkegaard agreed with Mynster's position and publicly stated his support.

[21] Andersen, *History of the Church in Denmark*, p. 46. See *JP*, II, 1913, for an example of Kierkegaard's attack on the conservative Lutheran orthodoxy of his day. His criticisms of this mode of Christianity will be discussed in Chapter Six.

middle class required in the new liberal order. In two journal entries that are remarkably Marxist in tone, Kierkegaard complained that "it is actually the favored ones who have taken possession of Christianity, the rich and the powerful who in addition to all their enjoyment of life also want all their power and might and wealth interpreted as proof of God's grace and a sign of their piety . . ." (*JP*, IV, 4682). Furthermore, "The state thought it prudent to accommodate this teaching of eternity and instruction about another world in order to tranquilize people and thus be better able to control them" (*JP*, IV, 4242). As Kierkegaard saw it, Mynster's Christianity ideologically secured the new middle class. Set free to make a good living, each individual finds in Lutheranism a companion who could be trusted and relied upon to conduct him safely and with a clear conscience through the rigorous compromises of free enterprise competition.

In characterizing Mynster as "worldly shrewd," "weak," and "self-indulgent" (*AC*, 9), a man who "enjoyed in the greatest measure all possible worldly goods and enjoyments" (*AC*, 11),[22] Kierkegaard must surely have had the bishop's parishioners in mind as well. They, like Mynster, conceived of religious earnestness in this way: "in a humanly allowable and honest way, or indeed in a humanly honorable way also, to get through this life happily and well" (*AC*, 183). That religion might entail contending "in mortal combat with this world" (*AC*, 184) seems never to have occurred to Mynster and his flock, for "the Mynsterish lifeview . . . is Epicureanism, enjoyment of life and the lust for life, belonging to this world . . ." (*AC*, 183).

We have seen that the theological and ecclesiastical conflict between Grundtvig and Mynster, in whose hands Lutheranism proved to be so remarkably malleable, was in Kierkegaard's view a religious reflection of a more funda-

[22] Kierkegaard claimed that Mynster was prone "to idolize the establishment" (*JP*, V, 5961) and had "adhered to the secular mentality as much as anyone . . ." (*JP*, VI, 6412).

mental social and political conflict occurring within the emerging modern state. *And this intimate connection between class conflict and religious belief and practice is the main target of Kierkegaard's criticism of Christendom.* Both Grundtvig and Mynster saw the promise of liberalism from the perspective of class. For Mynster, liberalism offered the preservation of privilege, power, and wealth; for Grundtvig, it promised the attainment of the same. Religion became the ally of both. The "lust for power and human ambition . . . turned its attention to Christianity to see if it could cunningly take possession of it and then with respect to other men play our Lord, who rules with the help of eternity as background. The really great attempt in this direction is the pope. . . . The other effort in this direction is that of the state" (*JP*, IV, 4504). This passage refers equally to Mynster and Grundtvig. Each represented a class within the state that was seeking to gain power "with the help of eternity as background." In both cases, Christianity was being "adroitly shifted into human egotism" (*JP*, III, 3779).[23] The modern state turns out to be an egotistical struggle for power masquerading as a virtue in a religious disguise. This is what Kierkegaard meant by his famous term *Christendom*. Christendom is not simply the state church; more fundamentally, it is the modern liberal state, which is legitimated and sanctioned by religion in the form of the Danish church. Christendom is the fall of life from the high plane of ethics to the aesthetic view of life, where pleasure is conceived of as the highest good. Christendom is the legitimation of the political pursuit of one's private interests devoid of ethical obligation to the other.

Kierkegaard's criticisms of Danish pastors, which are so shrill and prominent in *Attack upon Christendom*, are a starting point for his more fundamental criticism of religion in society. The role that they occupy in the state church, according to Kierkegaard, is only a manifestation of the alli-

23 In another journal entry Kierkegaard accused his age of "abolishing God and making the age into God . . ." (*JP*, II, 1375).

ance between egotism and religious faith. In this pastoral religion, "what man likes becomes religion. . . . The rest of the
community, when one examines the case more closely, are
seen to be egotistically interested in upholding the estimation in which the priests are held—for otherwise the
falsification cannot succeed" (*AC*, 221). There are two sides
to the deception perpetrated by this priestly religion. On
the one hand, the priests stand to gain financially by maintaining the deception; they shrewdly and correctly "saw that
profit and numbers go together" (*JP*, III, 2996).[24] Kierkegaard never tired of identifying the Danish pastors with the
Sophists in Plato's dialogues who profit through deception
(*JP*, IV, 4309, 4313). On the other hand, the priests represent the nobility, dignity, and propriety of the way of life
pursued by the parishioners. The pastors "decorate life;
'they assuage the sorrows and ennoble the joys' " of human
life (*JP*, I, 386).[25] From their pastors the Danes receive no
jeremiads, only soothing assurances that things are as they
should be.

It is worth noting that Kierkegaard could discuss this alliance between religion and the state in strictly theological
terms, as a journal entry indicates: "Throughout Christendom the dialectical element has been abolished. The doctrine of 'grace' is moved a whole stage too high. Christianity has demanded the genuine renunciation of the worldly,
has demanded the voluntary, and then, on top of this, one
is to acknowledge that he is nothing, that all is grace. Christendom removes the former entirely—and then lets grace
move up; it grafts 'grace,' if you will, directly onto the
secular mind" (*JP*, I, 763).[26] In his pseudonymous writings,

[24] Cf. *AC*, 87: pastors "love the customary order of things, which
they are very loath to let go."

[25] Cf. *JP*, VI, 6256, 6257.

[26] Cf. *TC*, 206: "Wherever there seems to be . . . an established
Christendom, there is an attempt to construct a triumphant Church,
even if this word is not used; for the Church militant is in process of
becoming, *established* Christendom simply *is*, does not become" (Kierkegaard's italics).

Kierkegaard had been explicit about the theological impropriety of speaking about God's grace independently of ethics.[27] One may legitimately refer to God's grace only as that which makes possible the fulfillment of ethical obligation. Any other use of the term *grace* is unacceptable. The preceding passage expresses the same conviction. The word *voluntary* refers to the ethical. Only when one acknowledges that he is bound by the ethical task yet incapable of completing it is grace a possibility in human life. In Christendom, however, ethical obligation, the voluntary, has been discarded, with the result that God's grace is cheaply and falsely acquired without any expenditure of ethical passion. The theologian and the pastor alike have completely forgotten the ethical in their willingness to graft God's grace onto the secular order. Conversely, the state sees in Christianity such a possibility, and, once it has been worn down by the assault of pure thought, what remains is an attenuated and enfeebled Christianity that is "spavined and decrepit and on its last legs, spoiled and muddle-headed, then the state said: See, now I can bid on it; and smart as I am I can see very well that I can use it and profit from it enough so that I can properly see my way to spending a little to polish it up" (*JP*, IV, 4232). Polish it up, indeed. Kierkegaard understood perfectly the subtle and devious interaction between theological thought and religious life on the one hand and social and political class conflict on the other. He perceived clearly that religion, once detached from the obligation of the ethical, becomes the shadow of the material struggle for power within the modern state.

A Confusion of Categories

At its deepest level the alliance between religion and class conflict results in category confusion on both the theoretical and practical levels of life. As early as 1846, Kierkegaard attacked this problem in his unpublished *On Authority and*

[27] *CUP*, 133, 135, 144, 284, 348. *JP*, I, 981; II, 1372, 1373, 1414.

Revelation, which deals with the claims of the Danish pastor Adolph Peter Adler to have experienced a direct revelation from God. After being relieved of his pastorate, Adler wrote a number of books in which he attempted to interpret this revelation with the help of Hegelian philosophy. Adler repudiated speculative idealism after his experience but returned to it in order to make sense of his alleged revelation. Kierkegaard condemned Adler's use of idealistic terminology to account for his religious experience and to express its truth. By relying upon the alien terms and categories of speculative idealism, Kierkegaard argued, Adler enervated Christian terms like *revelation* and *authority* to the point of destroying their meaning. The result is a vast confusion of theoretical categories, which makes it impossible for Christians to know what their own speech means.[28]

Kiergegaard believed that Adler's confusions about the nature of religion were symptomatic of the confusions throughout Denmark. Grundtvig and Mynster were no different from Adler in Kierkegaard's view, for they also suffered from and perpetuated a fundamental confusion about the nature of religion. Adler sought, at times unwittingly, an alliance between religion and idealism, while Grundtvig and Mynster sought an identical alliance between religion and nationalistic and class consciousness. The confusion in Grundtvig's and Mynster's cases lies in the identification of nationalism and liberalism with virtue and in the religious sanctification of this view of virtue. Terms such as *freedom, equality, justice, truth,* and *happiness* became the coinage of Danish liberalism, thereby bestowing upon it the notion of virtue that these terms had encompassed in ethical and religious discourse. Though Grundtvig was no Hegelian, he certainly favored Hegel's view that participation in the state is the individual's ulti-

---

[28] For an excellent discussion of Kierkegaard's *On Authority and Revelation,* see Joe Jones, "Some Remarks on Authority and Revelation in Kierkegaard," *The Journal of Religion,* LVII (1977), 232-51.

mate ethical achievement. No doubt Grundtvig would have quarreled with Hegel about the ethical and ontological status of the individual within the state and about the role that nationalistic historical consciousness plays in the state, but he would have been in agreement with Hegel about the centrality of the state in the perfecting of human life.

For Kierkegaard, this ethical emphasis on the state and on historical self-consciousness was at the root of the category confusion plaguing Denmark. He was unequivocal about this confusion. "That the state in a Christian sense is supposed to be what Hegel taught—namely, that it has moral significance, that true virtue can appear only in the state (something I also childishly babbled after him in my dissertation), that the goal of the state is to improve men— is obviously nonsense" (*JP*, IV, 4238). In an obvious reference to Grundtvig, he charged that the Danes had made "a wrong turn which has established the historical in place of the primitive. . . . As I have often pointed out, we shudder at the strenuousness of having to be primitive *I*—and so we become third person and become tranquilized in the historical and trace the historical" (*JP*, II, 2077). "[E]thically dissipated," he claimed, the Danes want to "establish the generation, one abstraction or another, fantastical social definitions, and the like . . ." (*JP*, II, 2021). In opposition to these emphases on the state and historical self-consciousness as means to human perfection and self-actualization, Kierkegaard placed "what is fundamental for all morality, constructive life, religion—the single individual," who is also the "passage way through which 'Christendom' must go . . ." (*JP*, II, 2021). The perception of oneself as historically destined to participate in the creation of the modern liberal state in and through which one morally perfects oneself is the basic confusion of the age, according to Kierkegaard. Yet that is precisely the understanding that emerges in the Grundtvigian synthesis of Danish nationalism, democratic liberalism, and the Christian religion.[29]

[29] The consequences of this category confusion are severe, as Kierke-

Nowhere is this confusion of categories more apparent for Kierkegaard than in his perception of the Danes' understanding of the vote. In numerous journal entries, Kierkegaard criticized the Danes' confusion about the nature of the vote. "Truth and everything connected with it cannot be decided by ballot" (*JP*, IV, 4875). "Is not this (voting with regard to 'truth') the old idolatry, a worship of the human race or of statistics, based on the idea that 'truth' has no higher origin, no higher authority" (*JP*, IV, 4874). "Through incessant voting ethical concepts will ultimately vanish from the race. The power of ethical concepts is the context of conscience; but voting externalizes everything" (*JP*, I, 986). This last passage captures the sense of those preceding it. Voting symbolized the awakening of a political self-consciousness within the Danish people, which expressed itself in terms traditionally belonging to ethics. Words like *freedom, equality*, and *truth* became the property of the new politics, with the consequent loss of the ethical concepts associated with them. As Kierkegaard saw it, "The idea of genuine equality, essential equality, has been given up; equality has now become a political question

---

gaard indicated in a journal entry:

And since Christianity has been abolished . . . the whole realm of the temporal has also come to be muddled. . . .

. . . when a man or when a generation must live in and for merely finite ends, life becomes a whirlpool, meaninglessness, and either a despairing arrogance or a despairing disconsolateness.

There must be weight—just as the clock or the clock's works need a heavy weight in order to run properly, and the ship needs ballast.

Christianity would furnish this weight, this regulating weight, by making it every individual's lifemeaning that whether he becomes eternally saved is decided for him in this life. Consequently Christianity puts eternity at stake. Into the middle of all these finite goals, which merely confuse when they are supposed to be everything, Christianity introduced weight, and this weight was intended to regulate temporal life, both its good days and its bad days, etc.

And because the weight has vanished—the clock cannot run, the ship steers wildly—and for this reason human life is a whirlpool. (*JP*, I, 1003)

discussed throughout Europe" (*JP*, IV, 4131).[30] Again, "What has confused everything and above all the whole of Christendom and the whole of Christianity is that the contemporaries, the generation, etc. are regarded as the authority in matters of truth" (*JP*, II, 2015). Without investigating Kierkegaard's own definitions of equality and truth, we can see in these journal entries his fear of the absorption of ethical terms by what he regarded as nonethical dimensions of life. These two passages reflect as clearly as any Kierkegaard's awareness that in Denmark issues traditionally belonging to ethics and religion had shifted into the domain of politics and science. The questions of equality and truth had become political and scientific problems and no longer ethical and religious ones. This shifting of the basis of culture from religion and ethics to science and politics was for Kierkegaard the root cause of the confusion of categories, and he viewed this confusion as a great disaster. "Here again we see . . . that the whole modern trend is a disastrous caricature of religiousness—it is politics. . . . But politics is egotism dressed up as love, is the most frightful egotism; is Satan himself in the form of an angel of light" (*JP*, IV, 4206).[31] Kierkegaard sounds like a man ahead of his time in his concern over satanism. He is not concerned about individual possession, however. Rather, he feared a collective possession in which our worst impulses are disguised so that they cease to be recognized for what they are. Political goals and priorities become ethical problems to the extent that the distinction between the two dissolves. Kierkegaard did not deny that politics raises ethical problems, but he argued that politics and social and political philosophy cannot alone become normative for ethical judgments and behavior.

[30] Equality is determined, according to Kierkegaard, not by natural rights but by the moral law. See *WL*, 53.

[31] Kierkegaard complained that Christianity had become "secularism" and that "the medium for being Christian has been shifted from existence and the ethical to the intellectual, the metaphysical, the imaginary . . ." (*ANOL*, 35).

CONCLUSION

We shall see in the following chapter that Kierkegaard saw serious psychological and social consequences in this dissipation of ethics. The demise of the individual as an ethically autonomous agent, in Kierkegaard's view, gives birth to the psychological maladies of envy and anxiety and to an unjust society that allows for the economic and political survival only of those who manage to gain power. We have already seen that Kierkegaard repeatedly referred to the modern state as Christendom because of its success in maneuvering Christianity into the position of legitimating it. And we have also seen that Kierkegaard insisted that the solution through which Christendom must go is the reappearance of what Kierkegaard called "the single individual." It is to this most important of all Kierkegaard's categories that we now turn.

CHAPTER THREE

The Natural Self

ONE FINDS in Kierkegaard's second literature a continuation of his earlier emphasis in the pseudonymous writings on ethics as the search for self-knowledge. This Socratic principle is clearly a present and unifying theme in the pseudonymous literature, and Kierkegaard did not lose sight of this philosophical commitment in his later works. He continued to stress the search for self-knowledge as a subjective passion that receives its most exemplary expression in the ethical-religious form of life. More importantly, the second literature significantly deepens Kierkegaard's preoccupation with self-knowledge by disclosing self-love as its essential motivation and the social-political context in which all self-love and self-knowledge take form.

Before looking more closely at the way in which the second literature expands the view of ethics developed in the pseudonymous works, it would be useful to recall Kierkegaard's three stages of human existence. The pseudonymous works develop a conception of human existence as composed of aesthetic, ethical, and religious stages of life. The aesthetic stage is characterized by the desire for pleasure, the ethical by the obligation to become morally good, and the religious by the faith that one can with God's help fulfill one's ethical obligation. The pseudonyms, who themselves are developed personalities, admirably portray the formal relations of pleasure, duty, and faith. They also succeed in presenting these relations existentially in a series of characters who are seized by dread and despair in their struggles to come to terms with the subjective dimensions of the human self. Few philosophers in the history of Western thought have so thoroughly penetrated and exposed the complex terrain of human inwardness. Moreover, through his pseudonyms, Kierkegaard illuminated not only the texture of human inwardness but also its irreducibility. That is to say, the desire for pleasure, the demands of duty, and the promise of faith are ontologically constitutive of persons, and the reconciling of these desires, obligations, and hopes is a private task that each individual must accomplish: this self and the existential task that it poses are inescapably mine and mine alone. It is in this sense that Kierkegaard called attention to the irreducibility of the human *qua* individual, and the virtue of this achievement is its recognition of the character of human selfhood.

The conception of the human self developed by the early pseudonyms is deficient in at least two respects, however. First, the role of the other is included neither in Kierkegaard's ontological analysis of the nature of the self nor in his analysis of the way in which individuals come to a knowledge of who and what they are. The pseudonymous writings leave one with the impression that the human other is not a necessary condition for either the existence of the self or for self-knowledge. This omission lends an abstract quality to Kierkegaard's conception of the self and leads to the charge that he has an atomistic view of the human self like that of the liberals. The second deficiency in the early pseudonymous literature is its lack of emphasis on the material conditions constituting the human self. Kierkegaard noted in *Either/Or* that the self is constituted by social, historical, economic, and cultural factors, as well as by biological and psychological ones, but he did not develop this insight in early writings. Moreover, the earlier works pay little attention to the social and political developments of Denmark in the nineteenth century. This neglect of the material conditions constituting the human self and the social and political events occurring in his lifetime, along with his failure to include the other in his ontology of the human self, has led some critics of the pseudonyms to conclude that Kierkegaard was an eccentric and isolated genius who was content to write for an equally isolated and, indeed, abstract individual exclusively concerned with his private destiny. If left with only these early materials, the critic might well argue that Kierkegaard's irreducible inwardness is merely the psychological side of the alienated consciousness produced by the liberalism of modern social and political thought.

Kierkegaard anticipated this sort of criticism. Commenting in a journal entry on the publication of his *Edifying Discourses*, which accompanied the publication of his pseudonymous books, Kierkegaard noted that his critics "will presumably bawl out that I do not know what comes next, that I know nothing about sociality. The fools! Yet on the other hand, I owe it to myself to confess before God that in a certain sense there is some truth in it, only not as men understand it, namely that always when I have first presented one aspect sharply and clearly, then I affirm the validity of the other even more strongly. Now I have the theme of the next book. It will be called *Works of Love*" (*SKP*, VIII¹, A 4). Here Kierkegaard is up to his dialectical mischief again. The concern with the individual leads dialectically to an equally strong concern for the social. The transition may not be as dialectically neat as Kierkegaard hints that it will be, but it is a clear and unmistakable move nonetheless. Not only *Works of Love* but also all of the second literature is concerned with precisely these deficiencies plaguing the pseudonymous literature. In his later literature, Kierkegaard's ontology of the human self takes on a social dimension, as does his epistemology. The self cannot exist or know itself without the other. Thus, Kierkegaard's struggle to come to terms with the nature of the human self continues in this later literature, though the development of his thought is significantly informed by both the social and historical dimensions of human life.

If Kierkegaard broadened his conception of the human

self and the quest for self-knowledge by placing both in a social-political context, he also broadened it by introducing self-love as the essential motivation of self-knowledge. Self-love and self-knowledge are related in the sense that the former is a necessary condition of the latter. Self-love is the desire to become a concrete, identifiable, and worthy self, and the satisfaction of this desire requires a social and historical context. In other words, self-love is the desire for self-respect. One cannot become a self independently of the other and of history. Indeed, human relations on both a private and a public scale and historical movements are most clearly understood, Kierkegaard argued, when they are construed in terms of the human self and its development toward concretion, identifiability, and a sense of worth. This desire, as we shall see, is similar to the desire for pleasure that is so thoroughly analyzed in the pseudonymous works as the heart of the aesthetic mode of existence. The ethical and religious task of life is portrayed not as transcending this desire but as mediating it by disclosing the necessary ethical and religious character of the desire's satisfaction. We shall see that the ethical-religious task is the same in the later literature. How is self-love, or the desire for self-respect, to be ethically and religiously mediated? In confronting this question, Kierkegaard began with the notion that self-love is unsurpassable: one cannot not love oneself. He also recognized the impossibility of loving oneself without directly implicating others. What Kierkegaard seems to have discovered in these later works is a social dimension of human being based on the phenomenon of love. All human beings love themselves, and it is this self-love that casts us into relations with others. For without the other it is not possible to love oneself.

The inescapability of self-love and the other as its necessary condition are the grounds for both selfish and unselfish self-love. Self-love is like pleasure. The pseudonymous writers are anxious to persuade their readers that pursuit of pleasure that is unmediated by the ethical-religious mode of consciousness contradicts itself by culminating in despair. In the later works, Kierkegaard tried to persuade his reader that self-love that is not mediated by an ethical-religious mode of consciousness will culminate in selfishness. Selfish self-love *(Elskov)* is a contradiction in the sense that one who selfishly loves himself can never actually become the concrete, identifiable, and worthy self that he desires to become. Moreover, selfish self-love is self-defeating, because it legislates the existence of a world characterized by conflict, manipulation, and envy. To exist in such a world is to exist in a manner that contradicts the natural end *(telos)* of self-love. Kierkegaard argued that only when one wills all selves as ends is it possible for one to become the self one desires to become. Proper self-love *(Kjærlighed)* is love for all as one loves oneself.

The transformation of selfish self-love by the recognition of one's ethical obligations and religious hopes is the only way in which the natural *telos* of self-love can ever be actualized. Kierkegaard's transition to the social and the historical in his second literature, then, places aesthetic desire, ethical obligation, and religious faith in a living and concrete situation. Yes, it is true to say that these are the irreducible dimensions of the human self. But one must also say that the self always desires something particular, is always obligated to will specific and concrete ends, and also hopes for the realization of those same ends. Thus, Kierkegaard placed his conception of the dialectical development of selfhood in a concrete social and historical situation that makes concrete and specific human desire, obligation, and hope.

In this chapter, we shall examine Kierkegaard's conception of selfish self-love. This analysis will lead us to a consideration of both its private and public forms, as well as to an exploration of the psychology generated by selfish self-love. This chapter also includes a discussion of how Kierkegaard perceived contemporary political, social, economic, and cultural movements as functions of selfish self-love.

Finally, we shall see that Kierkegaard's opposition to the religious movements represented by Grundtvig and Mynster proceeded from his perception of these religious movements as justifying and sanctioning the selfish self-love that permeated public and private life in Denmark. In the fourth chapter, we shall investigate Kierkegaard's conception of unselfish self-love.

THE NATURAL SELF

In Kierkegaard's discussion of the human situation in his second literature and in his journal writings, one of the terms most frequently used to describe human beings is *natural man*.[1] One finds in most of these references to the natural man the notion of human beings as selfish. Kierkegaard believed that "natural qualifications," such as human "drive and inclination," are always selfish (*JP*, IV, 4447). Indeed, "naturally, there is nothing a man clings to so tight as to his selfishness—which he clings to with his whole self!" (*FSE*, 97).[2] This passage correctly reflects Kierkegaard's suspicion that there is little, if anything, undertaken by the natural man that is not tainted by the perversity of selfishness. Kierkegaard, like Aristotle, whom he followed closely on this point, related the problem of selfishness to the issue of self-love.[3] The natural man is one "who loves himself selfishly" (*TC*, 119), and Kierkegaard would agree with Aristotle that such persons "assign to themselves the greater

[1] *AC*, 122, 128, 150, 158; *CD*, 179-80; *ED*, IV, 29ff.; *JFY*, 154, 205; *FSE*, 68, 96; *TC*, 113-15, 119, 121; *JP*, I, 330, 507, II, 1823, 1943, III, 2902, 2908, 2919, 2970, 3031, 3224, 3317, 3681, 3779, IV, 4349, 4360, 4690, 4711, 4798, 4885, 5031.

[2] Cf. *FSE*, 19.

[3] Kierkegaard approvingly referred to Aristotle's *Nicomachean Ethics*, IX, 7, and IX, 9, in his discussion of selfishness. Though he did not mention IX, 8, it is obvious that he depended upon this chapter as well in his analysis of selfish self-love in *JP*, III, 2441. Aristotle, *Ethica Nicomachea*, trans. W. D. Ross, in *The Basic Works of Aristotle*, ed. with an intro. by Richard McKeon (New York: Random House, 1941).

share of wealth, honours, and bodily pleasures . . . [and] gratify their appetites and in general their feelings and the irrational element of the soul. . . ."[4] But for Kierkegaard, an equally serious form of selfish self-love is rooted not in greed but in power. The more perverse form of selfish self-love is the love that masquerades as love for another but is in reality the overpowering of the other for one's own ends. Kierkegaard asserted that "what we men extol under the name of love is selfishness . . ." (*FSE*, 102).[5] Natural qualifications like human "drive and inclination" are directed not only at the possession of such physical and social objects as food, shelter, money, and fame but also, and more fundamentally when disguised as genuine love, at the possession of other persons.

Kierkegaard claimed an allegiance to Aristotle in his observation that most expressions of love are in fact expressions of selfish self-love (*JP*, III, 2441), and he relied heavily on Aristotle in explaining how such a phenomenon is possible. In the *Nicomachean Ethics*, Aristotle argued that craftsmen and poets love their handiwork and poems more than those objects would love their creators if they were to come alive.[6] This is true also of benefactors who love those whom they have helped more than the benefited love their benefactors. "The cause of this," explained Aristotle, "is that existence is to all men a thing to be chosen and loved, and that we exist by virtue of activity (i.e. by living and acting), and that the handiwork *is* in a sense, the producer in activity; he loves his handiwork, therefore, because he loves existence. And this is rooted in the nature of things; for what he is in potentiality, his handiwork manifest in activity."[7] The actualization of oneself in the object of one's activity is pleasant.[8] Furthermore, Aristotle claimed that

[4] *Nicomachean Ethics*, IX, 8.

[5] Cf. *FSE*, 97: "For love precisely is one of the strongest and deepest expressions of selfishness."

[6] *Nicomachean Ethics*, IX, 7.

[7] Ibid.; Aristotle's italics.   [8] Ibid.

"love is like an activity";[9] thus, an object of love is loved because it represents the lover as actualized. It is therefore improper to draw a sharp ontological distinction between the actor and the acted upon, the producer and the product, the lover and the beloved.[10]

Kierkegaard saw in Aristotle's observations about some forms of love a principle governing the behavior of the natural man. Love within nature is a mode of self-production through which each individual attempts to pass from a state of potentiality to one of actuality by creating himself in and through the other: "To be specific, he who has produced something loves it more than the production loves him. Why is this? Because there is more 'being,' more egotism, in the first relationship than in the second, because author-love is the highest egotism. . . . This whole chapter by Aristotle is valuable" (*JP*, III, 2441). Kierkegaard also drew from this chapter an inference that Aristotle perhaps would not have drawn. Aristotle says that "activity" is pleasurable, but Kierkegaard claimed that this activity is also selfishness, because "what is sought after is not the other's good, or not that alone" (*FSE*, 103), but essentially one's own transition from possibility to actuality through action upon another.[11] Kierkegaard agreed with Aristotle that the self's handiwork is the "producer in activity," but he felt that it is mistaken to distinguish ontologically the subject and the object acted upon by the subject. Kierkegaard extended this principle into the domain of human relationships in order to show that such relationships, when grounded in nature, are expressions of selfish self-love (egotism). The self is a being that is in the process of becoming, and in the realm of nature one finds that this becoming self exploits other selves in its quest to be. This struggle to become a self within nature—the natural man's egotism—

9 Ibid.
10 Ibid.
11 Aristotle discusses selfish self-love in ibid., IX, 8, and there relates it to greed.

occurs in both the private and the public spheres of human life.[12]

THE NATURAL SELF IN PRIVATE RELATIONS

Kierkegaard's discussion of egotism in the private sphere of life is most thoroughly developed in *Works of Love*. There and elsewhere, Kierkegaard identifies a number of concrete relations between individuals as expressions of egotism. The list of examples include: maternal love (*JP*, III, 2412-2425); relations based on admiration (*JP*, I, 974) and on ownership of property (*WL*, 248ff.); marriage; sacrificial love; paternal love (*JP*, III, 2412); the religious relation between God and the individual (*AC*, 150, 191, 221-22); sexual relations (eros); and friendship (*WL*, passim). Only eros and friendship receive extended analysis in *Works of Love*, although it is clear that the arguments against eros and friendship as modes of egotism apply equally to the other types of relationships. Indeed, for Kierkegaard, all natural relations between individuals, whatever their forms, are subject to the contagion of egotism.

It should be pointed out that in his later works and in the journals Kierkegaard did not seriously examine the classical analyses of friendship and eros in Aristotle and Plato. Only in his earliest published work, *Either/Or*, where he discusses Aristotle's view of friendship (*E/O*, II, 321-27), is it possible to find any attention given to the classical position on these two forms of love. *Works of Love* cannot be regarded as a full treatment of eros in Plato's thought. One distinction between the Kierkegaardian conception of love in this book and his understanding of the Aristotelean

[12] The distinction between private and public is here loosely drawn to designate relations between individuals as opposed to relations between groups of individuals. It is recognized that public as well as private relations may be political, since both involve power, but in this chapter and the one following, the use of the term *political* will be confined to discussions of relations among groups of individuals.

and Platonic notions is clear, however. This distinction rests in Kierkegaard's belief that from a Christian point of view one must regard love as an obligation that has a religious grounding. Kierkegaard was correct in assuming that the Greeks thought it contradictory to consider oneself obligated to love another person. Admittedly, friendship and eros for Plato and Aristotle entail duties, but these obligations are dimensions of the love relation, not its ground. Kierkegaard correctly observed that love in classical philosophy is viewed as a spontaneous and immediate (pre-reflective) phenomenon. And it is precisely in the immediate and unreflective character of eros and friendship that Kierkegaard discovered difficulties that require that both be grounded in a new way.

In discussing these forms of love in *Works of Love*, Kierkegaard resorted to a conceptual framework that he had used in earlier works to illuminate the nature of self-consciousness, freedom, anxiety, and despair. According to Kierkegaard, "in erotic love the I is qualified as body-psyche-spirit, the beloved qualified as body-psyche-spirit. In friendship the I is qualified as psyche-spirit and the friend is qualified as psyche-spirit. Only in love to one's neighbour is the self, which loves, spiritually qualified simply as spirit and his neighbour as purely spiritual" (*WL*, 69). Without entering into a long discussion about the meaning of these terms in Kierkegaard's writings,[13] it is sufficient to say that human relations that are not essentially spiritual in nature but are instead sensuous or psychical are grounded in what Kierkegaard called "natural determinants (tendencies, inclinations)" (*WL*, 68).

Eros and friendship are by definition naturally determined, and when the individual does not exist as spirit, they are only modes of immediacy. As such, both are

[13] Those familiar with Kierkegaard's earlier works will recognize these three terms as the ones he uses in the development of his concept of the self.

[14] Cf. *WL*, 65.

spontaneous, preferential, and accidental in nature. Their spontaneous character results from their existing prior to that mode of reflection that leads to self-consciousness. That is to say, individuals whose responses of love to others are spontaneous are motivated in part by impulses of which they are not conscious; they are unaware and uncritical of the impulses that motivate much of their behavior. Neither eros nor friendship requires reflection as a necessary condition for existing; they are accidental in the sense that they are in part "determined by the object" (*WL*, 77),[15] that is, by certain features and qualities of the other. It may also be the case that the lover and friend prefer[16] certain features and qualities to others, so that the beloved and the befriended are preferred to the exclusion of others. Thus, the very nature of these modes of loving includes spontaneity, exclusivity (*WL*, 62ff.), and preferentiality. It is in this sense that both are by nature modes of immediacy. The immediate individual is one who is not self-reflective and, as such, exists in social relations that are by definition spontaneous, exclusive, and preferential.

Kierkegaard observed throughout *Works of Love* that these immediate social relations have been praised by poets and philosophers as the epitome of goodness and fulfillment in human relations. He does not in the least share their enthusiasm. In his view, eros and friendship as immediate phonemena are nothing more than disguised forms of selfish self-love: "self-love, egocentricity, is sensuality" (*WL*, 65). "In [erotic] love and friendship one's neighbour is not loved but one's other-self, or the first I once again, but more intensely" (*WL*, 69). In eros and friendship, self-love "selfishly . . . unite[s] the two in a new selfish self" (*WL*, 69).[17]

15 Cf. *JP*, III, 2449.

16 Kierkegaard noted that "*erotic love and friendship are preferential and the passion of preference*" (*WL*, 65; Kierkegaard's italics).

17 "But falling in love is self-love; erotic love is self-love. In erotic love I keep my own idea of what is lovable and find that the object completely suits my head and my heart; this is why I love the beloved so ardently—that is, I ardently love myself" (*JP*, II, 1411).

One might dismiss these remarks as examples of Kierkegaard's polemical extravagance; they have a polemical value but are not seriously intended as propositions about the nature of eros and friendship. Or one might dismiss them as the pronouncements of a resentful social cripple who himself failed to enter into meaningful erotic relationships and friendships. They are, one might conclude, polemical or spiteful and resentful remarks that are without substance. But Kierkegaard does not leave these claims undefended.

He maintained that erotic love and friendship are conventionally understood to include reciprocal devotion, respect, and admiration. In both relationships, two persons meet and come to recognize each other as equals. Such relationships are also characterized by a degree of selflessness in at least two senses. First, one's selflessness is recognized in the need for the other. The other contributes to and makes possible one's happiness and fulfillment, which would be impossible without the other. Selflessness is also included in the sense that each is expected to sacrifice certain immediate and long-range interests and needs in the interest of the other. The relationship's history is viewed ideally as a continuing struggle to achieve a proper and congenial equilibrium between receiving and giving. This struggle for harmony and balance is nurtured by positive responses felt for and evoked by the other.

Kierkegaard claimed that this understanding of eros and friendship requires the dimension of selflessness. In his view, it is precisely the necessary dimension of selflessness that is lacking in relations of eros and friendship.[18] Consequently, the description of these social relations by poets and philosophers is at best romantically naive. Eros, friendship, and all other social relations not qualified by spirit are selfish, not selfless, in the sense that they are functions of the individ-

---

[18] "The basis for erotic love is a drive, the basis of friendship is inclination, but drive and inclination are natural qualifications, and natural qualifications are always selfish . . . therefore there is still a hidden self-love in erotic love and friendship" (*JP*, IV, 4447).

ual's struggle to achieve self-respect. The other is not an equal but a means to the end of self-constitution.

This selfish self-love is not simple greed or a crude narcissistic infatuation with one's own body and feelings but is dialectically conceived as the narcissistic infatuation with the other in whom one sees oneself. Thus, "the one whom self-love in the strictest sense loves is also basically the other-I, for the other-I is oneself, and this is indeed self-love" (*WL*, 69).[19] For Kierkegaard, eros and friendship are trapped in this pessimistic scenario of self-seeking. Even the commitment of "devotion" and the feeling of "boundless abandonment" toward the other are self-deceptions, since they too are disguised modes of self-constitution in and through the other (*WL*, 67).

Kierkegaard's analysis of the ways in which love can be a mode of self-constitution is not as developed as one would like. His reflections at this point are ambiguous and suggest at least two ways in which an individual may relate to the other as a means to the end of becoming a self. First, the relation between the loved and the beloved is compared, as we have noted, with the relation between creator and created. The beloved is something that the lover forms, shapes, fashions, brings into being; he is an expression of the lover. As the product of the lover, the beloved becomes the lover in the Aristotelian sense of the self's becoming.[20] Kierkegaard, as we have already seen, agreed with Aristotle's claim that when the lover is related to the beloved as creator to product, the lover loves the beloved more than the beloved loves the lover. This is so, Kierkegaard asserted, because "there is more 'being' . . . in the first relationship than in the second . . ." (*JP*, III, 2441). The lover loves him-

---

[19] Cf., *WL*, 66: The beloved is "called, remarkably and significantly enough, the *other-self*. . . . But wherein lies self-love? It lies in the I, in the self. Would not self-love, then, still remain in loving the other-self, the other-I?" (Kierkegaard's italics).

[20] *Nicomachean Ethics*, IX, 7.

self only when he *is* something to love. In objects that he creates he becomes a real, tangible, identifiable thing. In love the lover ceases to be merely a possibility, an imaginative reality, a mere image in his own mind. The individual becomes a concrete, identifiable, and worthy self in the transition from possibility to actuality in and through the beloved.

In a departure from his discussion of eros and friendship, Kierkegaard described the person who seeks to create himself through the domination of others as one who is utterly incapable of genuine love. Such persons who use eros and friendship as disguised modes of self-assertion do not love the other at all, for

> only true love loves every man according to his own individuality. *The strong, the domineering* person lacks flexibility, and he lacks a sense of awareness of others; he demands his own with everyone; he wills that everyone shall be recreated in his image, be trimmed according to his pattern for human beings. . . . If the strong and domineering individual cannot create, he wants at least to remodel; he seeks his own so that wherever he points he can say: see, this is my image, this is my idea, this is my will. Whether the strong and domineering individual is allotted a great sphere of activity or a small one, whether he is a tyrant in an empire or a house-tyrant in a little attic room, the essence is the same: domineeringly unwilling to go out of oneself, domineeringly wanting to crush the other person's individuality or make life miserable for him. (*WL,* 252-53)

For those persons lacking the internal resilience to assert themselves over others, there is the possibility of identifying with a larger group of people through which one collectively accomplishes the same goal of self-constitution. Kierkegaard identified the weak as those who band together in groups to attain for themselves what they cannot acquire individually.[21]

Other passages in *Works of Love* (*WL*, 69) suggests a second mode of self-constitution through a relation of love that is very close to Jean-Paul Sartre's analysis of love in *Being and Nothingness*, where he argues that to love is to want to be loved.[22] This definition of love does not mean that the lover, in addition to loving the beloved, also wants to be loved. On the contrary, Sartre means that loving is nothing more than wanting to be loved. In this case, the lover becomes a concrete and identifiable self not through acting on the beloved but by being acted upon by the beloved. The characters Garcin and Estelle in Sartre's *No Exit* are illustrations of this analysis of love in *Being and Nothingness*.[23] Garcin understands that his role in the French Resistance and his attempted flight to Mexico in order to start a Resistance newspaper cannot be an act of heroism unless it is so construed by someone else. Garcin cannot decide whether his effort to leave France, resulting in his arrest for desertion, is an act of cowardice or courage. He acts as if the only way in which the ambiguity can be resolved is for someone to regard him as a hero. He seeks this respect first in Estelle, whom he subsequently abandons because he suspects her motives for cooperating with him. Later Garcin decides that it is the lesbian Inez whom he will approach, since her acknowledgment of him as heroic would not be sexually motivated. The case is the same with Estelle, who understands that she cannot *be* desirable unless she *is* desired; she therefore seeks the cooperation of Garcin in becoming a self that is sexually attractive and appealing. Garcin and Estelle each require another person in order to

[21] This mode of self-constitution will be discussed in the following section of this chapter, "The Natural Self in Public Relations."

[22] Jean-Paul Sartre, *Being and Nothingness*, trans. Hazel Barnes (New York: Washington Square Press, 1968), pp. 474-84.

[23] Jean-Paul Sartre, *No Exit*, trans. Stuart Gilbert (New York: Alfred A. Knopf, Inc., 1946).

become a concrete and identifiable self. Sartre's version of the social constitution of human selfhood is the basis of his own version of the war of all against all.

In this type of selfish self-love, the lover is not an active agent, as in the first case, but a passive object desiring only to be acted upon by the beloved. The lover wants to become a concrete and identifiable self through the agency of the beloved (WL, 69). Kierkegaard quite correctly saw that this mode of self-love leads in the direction of self-deification: the lover desires ultimately nothing less than to become the center of the beloved's life (WL, 69)—in Sartre's terms, the beloved's "project." Put another way, the lover wants to become the beloved's absolute. All actions and values are then decided upon with reference to this center of one's world, in which case the lover becomes a god in the eyes of the beloved.

This desire to become a self in and through the other naturally insinuates itself into every form of human love. Eros and friendship are the examples most frequently cited in Kierkegaard's later writings, but they are not the only victims of the natural egotism that flaws all immediate human relations. In both cases, "selfishness would be wounded very deeply indeed by being deprived of the object . . ." (FSE, 98).[24] In stating the conflict between persons in this way, Kierkegaard gives an entirely different character to the nature of our most basic social relations and institutions. He claimed that society at this level, including not only eros and friendship but also all social relations and institutions, is a function of the individual's pursuit of self-identity through the domination of other selves. In these social relations we discover the impulse to use the other as a means to the end of self-actualization. In eros and friendship we

[24] Kierkegaard understood his reluctance to break with Regine and Abraham's reluctance to sacrifice Isaac in this manner. Both loved persons are, in Kierkegaard's view, the actualization of other selves; for this reason, they are difficult to release, since their loss entails the lover's loss of himself as well. See FSE, 98ff.

101

discover not a battle growing out of the impulse to survive but, more fundamentally, a struggle for self-respect. In the use of the other one comes to an awareness of oneself as somebody, as an identity standing out from all other things, as ontologically distinct, unique, and worthy. One sees in eros and friendship the "natural tendency" to reach out, dominate, and order all things in the basic interests of one's own self-constitution. To make this point, Kierkegaard selected the seemingly most benign and gracious of all social relations, eros and friendship, to expose the basic egocentricity of all human selves.[25]

This discussion of Kierkegaard's conception of the natural self has highlighted three constituent elements of all immediate relations between individuals. First, the individual in an immediate social relation is not self-conscious. That is, the individual is lacking in a full awareness of the nature of his own self and mistakenly views himself exclusively in and through the other. Both eros and friendship are devoid of what Kierkegaard called spirit and are therefore incomplete expressions of oneself. Second, we have seen how in the state of immediacy all relations of love are attempts at self-constitution. The other is required for the emergence of the individual as a human self. In this state of nature we discover the social nature of human selfhood. Third, we have seen that immediacy, though social in nature, is also a state of conflict. The social fabric of im-

---

[25] It is important to state explicitly that Kierkegaard made a distinction between egotism and all forms of love, including eros and friendship. The different forms of love are not essentially evil; they are merely the victims of the natural man's inclination to attempt to become a self through the possession of another person. The possession frequently takes the misleading form of love, which led Kierkegaard to conclude that in most instances love is a deception in the sense that lovers, friends, and parents, for example, deceive themselves in failing to see that their own interests and needs dominate these relations. In Kierkegaard's view, eros and friendship are life's greatest fortune (*WL*, 249). The issue is how to preserve them from the contamination of egotism.

mediacy is one of struggling for power over the other in the pursuit of one's self-identity and self-respect. Immediacy is painfully paradoxical: we cannot *be* without the other, yet the other is the greatest possible threat to achieving success in one's struggle *to be*. Selfish self-love generates conflict in that each individual who loves himself selfishly relates to the other as a means to the end of becoming a concrete and identifiable self.

THE NATURAL SELF IN PUBLIC RELATIONS

Kierkegaard observed the egotism of the natural man in property and class relations as well as in private relations. Whereas the egotism of private relations often masquerades as love, the egotism in public relations is often disguised as political activity ostensibly committed to the eradication of human poverty and oppression. The struggle for property and political power is also, in Kierkegaard's view, a struggle for self-identity. In his discussion of the anxiety that accompanies one's social, economic, and political status (*CD*, 5-94), we see clearly Kierkegaard's perception of the spiritual character of human conflict in the public dimensions of human life.

Human beings in their natural state, unlike other species, require the other in order to be. We have already seen how this is the case in private relations, and we find that Kierkegaard appealed to this same principle in his analysis of class relations. Describing man in his natural state, Kierkegaard claimed that "in order to be himself, a man must first be expertly informed about what the others are, and thereby learn to know what he himself is—in order then to be that" (*CD*, 42). Given the impossibility of being human without the other, "it seems as though he must constantly wait for the others in order to learn to know what he is now, at this moment" (*CD*, 43). Existing, for the natural man, "lies in existing only before others, in not knowing anything else but the relationship to others" (*CD*, 44). Therefore, "he

103

is what the others make of him, and what he makes of himself by only being for others" (*CD*, 47).

This self-determination based on one's reference to others is no less a reality in public than in private human relationships. The complicated network of collective and public relations established in the economic, political, social, and cultural arenas of life may also become the medium through which individuals seek to establish themselves as concrete, identifiable, and worthy selves. In these cases, the human qualities that become desirable as the source of identity and worth may include a variety of phenomena. It may be, for example, that money, race, cultural heritage, or sexuality becomes the identifying and valuing distinction. In any case, conflict among groups is based on the struggle to maintain either the valuable phenomenon—for example, money —or the phenomenon as valuable—for example, sexuality of race—in order to maintain one's view of oneself as a being concrete and worthy. Coercion is an essential ingredient of human relationships within nature, for it becomes necessary at times to resist forcibly those who would deprive one of that which identifies one as a concrete and worthy being.

In *Christian Discourses*, Kierkegaard analyzed this conflict between groups as class conflict based on the struggle for economic and political power. However, his analysis of class conflict does not settle on the economic and political dimensions of such conflict but on the spiritual nature of the tension. Class conflict is an essential feature of all natural human relations because it rises out of the struggle for identity. To be sure, economic and political issues are genuinely at stake in class conflict. But underlying these tangible struggles Kierkegaard saw a more fundamental struggle for human self-identity. Since one's identity is dialectically constituted in relation to the other, the conflict between classes is nothing less than a conflict generated by the struggle to be a concrete, identifiable, and valuable self. In fact, from Kierkegaard's perspective, it is a mistake to distinguish the struggle for political and economic power from the spiritual struggle to become a self. All natural human relations are egotistical; therefore, political and economic power becomes the means whereby members of the ruling class establish their identity through the domination of the lower class. Moreover, "the lowly man . . . sinks under the prodigious weight of comparison which he lays upon himself" (CD, 48). He is "tortured by the thought of being nothing, tortured by the fruitlessness of his effort to be something (CD, 48). His "anxiety is *to become something* in the world. . . . To be [simply] a man . . . is not to be anything—that is in fact to be nothing, for in this there is no distinction from nor advantage over all men. . . . But to be Councillor of Justice—that would be something . . ." (CD, 47; Kierkegaard's italics).

To have power is to be something; to be powerless is to be nothing. Since one cannot be powerful unless there is powerlessness, one must have a powerless other in order to be. To maintain these class distinctions between the powerful and the powerless, the wealthy and the poor, is essential for the natural man if he is to have any possibility of gaining identity, being, in the world. Thus, it is not ironic that members of the lower class cling to the system that suppresses them, for without it there would be no chance of ever becoming a concrete, identifiable, and valuable self. The lowly man "desires to belong to the temporal . . . he will not let it go, he clings tighter to being nothing, tighter and tighter as he seeks in vain to be something . . ." (CD, 48). Likewise, the high man clings to the same system, for it is the source of his identity and self-respect as well. The low man's anxiety is that he is nothing, the high man's that he will become nothing. The anxiety of highness is the fear that one will lose one's identity through the loss of class position (CD, 60).

It is clear, then, that this dialectical constitution of selfhood is not only conceptually grasped by the thinker but also directly experienced by all human beings as fear of the other and as anxiety about one's identity or being. The high

105

man, for example, "secures himself in every way, since he descries danger everywhere, plots everywhere, envy everywhere . . ." (*CD*, 60). His fear of the other is anxiety over himself; the loss of class identity is self-dissolution. Since class identity and being are essentially related, one requires the other in order to be, and yet the other is the greatest possible threat to one's becoming a concrete self within the realm of immediacy.

While this struggle for identity may be carried out publicly in the struggle for economic and political power, it may also be present in social and cultural conflict. In *Works of Love*, Kierkegaard described as "small-minded" those persons who band together and prejudically exclude all who do not share in some common trait or characteristic that they regard as peculiarly distinguishing. "Small-mindedness has fastened itself tightly to a very particular shape and form which it calls its own; only this does it seek, and only this can it love. If small-mindedness finds this, then it loves. Thereby small-mindedness sticks together with small-mindedness; they grow together like an ingrown nail, and spiritually speaking it is just as bad. This association of small-mindedness is then praised as the highest love, as true friendship, as true, steadfast, sincere harmony" (*WL*, 254). Such prejudicial and cowardly small-mindedness feels "a damp unpleasant anxiety upon observing another person's individuality and nothing is more important than to get rid of it" (*WL*, 254). Those not possessing the valued trait or characteristic are excluded yet feared, for their individuality stands as a constant threat to the identifying and valuing trait of such a closed society.

This tension is forcefully illustrated in Flannery O'Connor's excellent short story "Everything That Rises Must Converge."[26] The story takes place on a bus in a small town in the Deep South. Its main characters are a middle-aged, middle-class white woman, who is fiercely proud of her

[26] In Flannery O'Connor, *Everything That Rises Must Converge* (New York: Farrar, Straus and Giroux, 1965).

Southern aristocratic heritage, and her son, Julian, who has just graduated from a small Southern college and is presently selling typewriters until he can launch a writing career. The main portion of the story occurs as the two are riding to the downtown YWCA, where Julian's mother plans to attend her weekly weight-reducing class. At a stop the bus is boarded by a black woman and her four-year-old son, who immediately attracts Julian's mother's attention. Throughout the remainder of the bus ride, the white woman treats the child with gratuitous and condescending gestures of the sort that one makes to an inferior. As the four persons get off the bus, Julian's mother gives the young boy a "shiny new penny." The black mother's rage, which has been slowly building throughout the ride, finally erupts with a slap across the white woman's face. She then grabs her son's hand and storms down the sidewalk, leaving Julian's mother dazed and sprawled on the ground.

Julian accepts this violent reproach as a lesson justly deserved. "He saw no reason to let the lesson she had had go without backing it up with an explanation of its meaning. She might as well be made to understand what had happened to her. 'Don't think that was just an uppity Negro woman,' he said. 'That was the whole colored race which will no longer take your condescending pennies. . . . What all this means,' he said, 'is that the old world is gone.' "[27] His remonstrance at the end of the story, "you aren't who you think you are,"[28] is a direct attack on her earlier assurances that she knows who she is. It is clear that her identity is linked with her white heritage, which requires the continuing servitude of the blacks. That the blacks will no longer allow Julian's mother this identity is symbolized by the black woman's attack on her at the bus stop. The story ends with O'Connor's description of the woman's face as "fiercely distorted." Julian "was looking into a face he had never seen before."[29] The black woman's violence left

27 Ibid., p. 21.   28 Ibid., p. 22.
29 Ibid.

107

Julian's mother without a recognizable identity. Self-consciousness and class consciousness were indistinguishable in the sense that her entire being was predicated on the subjugation of the black. The black woman's denial of this social arrangement constitutes nothing less than the denial of white identity. Moreover, O'Connor portrays this social arrangement as one of "innocence," as "natural" as breathing. Only Julian, who has been away to college and has gained a critical reflective distance on his own heritage, is able to understand and criticize the black-white relation as it had developed in the history of the South.

O'Connor's story forcefully conveys Kierkegaard's notion of the spiritual ground of cultural and class conflict in its portrayal of Julian's mother as one who "naturally" and "innocently" builds an identity in and through the subjugation of the black. It is important to note, however, that this example is not intended to imply that egotism is present only in extreme and dramatic situations involving prejudice and exploitation. According to Kierkegaard, all group relations within immediacy are essentially governed by this self-seeking principle. So subtle are these relations at times that it is not always possible to see the egotism that is so clearly apparent in O'Connor's short story. In Kierkegaard's view, all group conflict within immediacy has egotism as its chief motivating principle, even though such conflict may be expressed in political, economic, and cultural terms. This is not to suggest that the conflict as it appears is an unreal one; rather, one does not get to the root of such conflict until it has been construed in terms of egotism.

THE PSYCHOLOGY OF THE NATURAL SELF

In considering the social nature of the self, Kierkegaard did not abandon his concern for human inwardness. Perhaps more than any other nineteenth-century philosopher or theologian, he was preoccupied with the complex and unchartered terrain of human subjectivity. So central is this concept in his analysis of the human situation that one might well characterize him as an apostle of inwardness. His phenomenology of despair in *The Sickness unto Death* and *Either/Or,* along with his introduction of the concept of anxiety in *The Concept of Dread,* rank him as a pioneer in the psychology of human inwardness, which has become so commonplace in contemporary psychological investigation.[30] We should also mention that the specifically religious and moral psychology developed in *Concluding Unscientific Postscript* is comparable to Augustine's psychological investigations into the religious personality.

Kierkegaard's second literature continues this preoccupation with the character of human inwardness, although his approach takes on the features of what we now call social psychology. Though his work here is not nearly as well developed as are his earlier psychological treatises, Kierkegaard was nevertheless deeply concerned with the nature of human inwardness, which is influenced by social environment. In the earlier pseudonymous works, despair and anxiety, for example, are conditioned by the individual's internal struggle to discover himself and to actualize his ethical-religious destiny. In the later works, it is social conflict that generates the psychology of human inwardness. Envy becomes the dominant feature of human inwardness. Jealousy, hatred, and anxiety are also discovered as prevailing psychological realities in a society dominated by the kind of social conflict that Kierkegaard found in both the private and the public dimensions of human life.

According to Kierkegaard, one is envious of another per-

[30] The term *psychology* here does not carry its twentieth-century connotations. Unlike contemporary psychologists, Kierkegaard was not empirically and statistically oriented. His psychology is, on the contrary, a priori in nature in that it is conceptually dependent on a theory of human nature. Moreover, Kierkegaard is in the Platonic and Augustinian tradition in that his psychological investigations have a moral and religious content and occur within a much broader range of philosophical, religious, and ethical concerns.

son when one regards that person as a threat to one's identity.[31] This person is not a physical threat but is rather a threat in the sense that he is perceived as possessing a something that bestows identity and worth upon him, a something that the perceiver himself lacks. One may react to such a person either by coming to admire him or by feeling envy (CD, 136).[32] To admire another person is to acknowledge and affirm distinguishing, even ennobling, qualities in him that one does not oneself necessarily possess. Kierkegaard describes the admirer as one who "loses himself in admiration of the one who is so far greater" (CD, 136). The refusal to admit that one has lost oneself in admiration is envy that "tortures itself because it will not be, what at bottom it is, admiration" (CD, 136). It tortures itself because the other is perceived as a sign of one's nonbeing. Envy is different from greed as a motivation of opposition to another person. One is greedy for things, whereas one is envious of persons. To say that conflict is based on envy is to assert that the opposition is conditioned by a quest for identity and not merely for material gain. If one is envious of another person because of his possessions or his social status, it is not simply the possessions and status that are desired but the identity and worth that they bestow upon their owner.

The egotism that prevails within immediacy either dom-

---

[31] The Danish term *Misundelse* has been mistranslated by Dru as *ressentiment* in *The Present Age*. The term must be translated as envy. Dru was obviously attempting to link Kierkegaard's social criticism in *The Present Age* with Nietzsche's criticisms of Christianity. There appears to be little similarity between the two. Nietzsche's *ressentiment* is the essential quality of Christian morality, whereas the term *Misundelse* in *The Present Age*, *The Sickness unto Death*, and *Works of Love* is defined by Kierkegaard as the opposite of admiration. Whether there is any significant agreement between the two can be determined only by a serious comparative study of the two concepts. Happily, Howard and Edna Hong have properly translated *Misundelse* as envy in their translation of *Two Ages*.

[32] Cf. *SUD*, 217-18.

inates the other or is envious of him. The other *qua* individual stands as a contradiction to one's own claim to worthiness, and when it is not possible to triumph over the other, one stands related to him in envy. It is in this sense that Kierkegaard spoke of envy as the "negative unifying principle" (*PA*, 47) of his age. Envy unifies in the sense that it actively expresses the social character of human nature and the dominant psychological characteristic of his society. It is negative in the sense that within immediacy this social nature of selfhood necessarily expresses itself as opposition and conflict. Kierkegaard writes that "the envy which surrounds . . . [the individual] and in which he participates by envying others, is envious in a negative and critical sense" (*PA*, 48). Individuals who perceive others as contradictions of their desire for identity and worth are tortured internally by a persistent envy and therefore take up a negative and critical relation toward those who stand as a contradiction of their own desire to become a self.[33]

Envy in both public and private relations is described by Kierkegaard as having two possible objects. The object of envy may be a quality that is acquired by virtue of one's possession of something desirable, such as wealth, fame, social status. In this case, some of those objects are more readily attainable than others by the envious person. Or the object of envy may be a quality that is a function of character or moral excellence and is not easily attainable by those who are envious. As an example, Kierkegaard cited the fate of Aristides in Aristophanes' play *The Knights.* Aristides was voted into exile by his peers in the Athenian senate, and Kierkegaard regarded this ostracism as "a negative mark of distinction" (*PA*, 50). "The man who told Aristides that he voted for his exile 'because he could not endure hearing Aristides called the only just man' did not deny Aristides' eminence, but admitted something about

[33] Kierkegaard described envy as being "twofold in its action: it is selfish within the individual and it thus results in the selfishness of society around him, which thus works against him" (*PA*, 47-48).

himself. He admitted that his relation to distinction was the unhappy love of envy, instead of the happy love of admiration . . ." (*PA*, 50).

Kierkegaard also seems to have thought of himself as an object of the "unhappy love of envy." His journals are filled with references to the abuses he received from the Copenhagen populace as expressions of an envy that could not tolerate excellence and eminence in one of its members (*JP*, V, 5192).[34] The envy of moral eminence and courage is directed toward an object that people admire but at the same time lack the tenacity and courage to emulate. Rather than be judged by their own indolence, they seek to demean and to destroy the credibility of such eminence. Kierkegaard, for example, believed that Meïr Goldschmidt's public derision of him through articles and cartoons in his journal, *The Corsair*, was intended to destroy his credibility by making him the laughingstock of Copenhagen. Kierkegaard referred to Goldschmidt as "the characterless instrument of envy and demoralization" (*JP*, IV, 4149). The harsh and unfair satire of Kierkegaard's legs and dress and of his unusual relation with Regine Olsen served to reduce him to a level beneath the readers of the journal so that he became a figure of contempt rather than a figure of honor—a perfect example of envious persons seeking to discredit the qualities of character that others possess and that they themselves lack.

Kierkegaard's rather aristocratic view of envy is complemented by a more pedestrian view of its role in Danish society. He found that individuals envy not only the eminent but also one another. Anyone who is "favored by some advantage" (*WL*, 89) will become in time an object of envy. By "some advantage" Kierkegaard no doubt meant the attainment of money, power, and social standing. Though far from advocating social structures that allow, indeed encourage, the attainment of earthly advantages by

[34] Cf. *JP*, V, 6031, 6852.

some but not all, he recognized that in the new liberal order earthly advantages will not be apportioned equally. Even so, those who are not favored must not fall victim to that envy which is a tacit admission of the desirability of those advantages (*WL*, 90). Werner Stark has nicely described the possibility for egotism and envy unleashed by the new liberal order. In the new order, he writes, "society continues mainly as an economic entity, for the sake of the material advantages which it has to offer to its members; but these members will—not unnaturally—be supremely watchful that they should each reap as high a share of these advantages as they possibly can. Thus there will arise a state of mutual ill-will, or envy as Kierkegaard terms it, a struggle of all against all, such as we see it unfolding in the thousand-and-one processes of competition which have clearly characterized classical capitalism."[35]

This envious ill-will is both collective and individual, public and private, and Kierkegaard did not hesitate to portray the division of Danish society into political and economic factions as an expression of envy. Within nineteenth-century Denmark, "envy ascended and came to the top. Now everything was changed. Through the power that lies in numbers they wanted first and foremost to get rid of all eminence, and through numbers (by being a group, a crowd, a party, etc.) they wanted to upgrade themselves" (*JP*, IV, 4227).[36] For Kierkegaard, of course, the very idea of wanting to upgrade or to improve oneself through political acts is mistaken. Politics is for Kierkegaard a quantitative discipline (*JP*, IV, 4200).[37] It cannot in any way resolve the problems associated with the basic passion to become a self. Nor can it in any way purify the impulse of egotism and envy that characterizes that passion in its immediate and natural state. This passion is for Kierkegaard the most

[35] Werner Stark, *Social Theory and Christian Thought* (London: Routledge and Kegan Paul Ltd., 1958), p. 87.
[36] Cf. *GS*, 133.
[37] Cf. *AC*, 127.

113

essential and inescapable fact of human life, and the great catastrophe of his Denmark was that such a passion found collective expression in the new liberal politics of his day. Such a passion requires discipline, purification, and a moral direction that politics cannot provide. Within the political realm, this passion in its egotistical and envious forms is merely collectivized, so that the worst impulses motivating individuals are expressed as the will of the people.

Kierkegaard concentrated less in his second literature on the inwardness that is generated by egotism within what we have called private relations. One finds in *Works of Love*, however, a discussion of jealousy, hatred, and boredom as constituents of egotistical relations (*WL*, 47-54). Here Kierkegaard shows how this unhappy consciousness will inevitably take its toll within human relations that are simply immediate in nature. Like the inwardness of envy generated on both a private and a public scale, jealously will emerge eventually as a primary constituent of immediate relations. The psychology of social immediacy is as negative and painful as are the relations that ground them. In his psychological analysis of egotism, Kierkegaard rigorously holds to the notion that the inside and the outside are mirror reflections. One cannot escape psychologically from the struggle to triumph over others egotistically within the realm of immediacy. This triumph can never be complete; thus, envy and jealousy are ever present psychological features of the inwardness generated by such an orientation. Even if one appears to triumph, there is always present the anxiety that tomorrow one may lose the identity and respect one has gained today.

Egotism and Politics

Judging from Kierkegaard's discussion of Danish public life in the nineteenth century, he obviously believed that it had fallen victim to the twin demons of envy and egotism. Kierkegaard had no illusions about the nature of political activity in such a situation. He was suspicious of men like Grundtvig who sought to masquerade their politics as a selfless activity devoted to the common good, one that expressed its high and virtuous ideals in the rhetoric of religion. Referring to Grundtvig's political coalition, Kierkegaard wrote, "it is really presumptious that a group will call itself 'the people of love': it is vain and selfish" (*SKP, VIII*[1], A 309). In Kierkegaard's view, Danish politics was essentially ideological; stripped of its blandishments, it was nothing more than the expression of the collective egotism of a particular class. Kierkegaard understood that Danish modernization hinged on the awakening of a political consciousness of an entire people and their subsequent organization into political parties for the purpose of achieving common interests. He insisted that "Egotism has understood this and has abated to the extent that egotism has become somewhat social, blocks and parties. . . . But the fact that egotism became social certainly does not mean it ceased to be egotism" (*JP*, II, 2037).[38] More strongly, "politics is egotism dressed up as love, is the most frightful egotism, is Satan himself in the form of an angel of light" (*JP*, IV, 4206). Kierkegaard's extension of egotism into the political realm is an indication of his refusal to draw a sharp distinction between the private and public spheres of life. Indeed, there could not be an essential but only a formal difference between the two. Thus, the dynamics governing natural relations between parent and child or between spouses are no different from those governing public relations in the political, economic, and cultural realms of human life. For the natural man, class consciousness is no less his self-consciousness in his public relations than is role consciousness in his private relations.

Given this dissolving of all essential distinctions between human nature and public life, Kierkegaard could view the political life of the natural man in modern Denmark—in

[38] Cf. *JP*, IV, 4238.

spite of the material gains it made possible for those who most needed them—as a civilized expression of the untamed and darkened side of human nature. Politics is the public side of the individual's struggle to be in and through the subjugation of the other. The spiritual struggle to be is, according to Kierkegaard, the principle by which we make clear the nature of politics within the natural man. To claim that egotism has become social and political in nature in the modern liberal state is to claim that democratic liberalism does not alter this fundamental flaw in human life but only provides it a new form of expression. Given the egotistical character of the natural man, liberalism leaves open the door for a collective form of egotism in which, as we have seen, class consciousness and self-consciousness become one. In Kierkegaard's view one of the primary flaws of Grundtvigian nationalism, as with all forms of liberalism, was its failure to recognize this fact and to be anything more than just another expression of the natural man's spiritual quest to become a concrete, identifiable, and worthy self. Grundtvigian nationalism was all the more abhorrent to Kierkegaard because it garbed itself in the ethical and religious discourse of Christianity, which, ideally, demands an essential transformation rather than a cultural justification of the natural man's politics.

Kierkegaard's opposition to the natural man's political activity must be understood in terms of envy and egotism. People like Grundtvig saw in political life the promise of the good life; participation in the life of the state was for them the highest virtue. From Kierkegaard's perspective, however, the politics of Danish modernization became simultaneously an expression and a concealment of the human dilemma of egotism. Those engaging egotistically in political life, then, are as ignorant of the nature of the human self as are those who selfishly love themselves in private personal relationships. We see here a similarity between the public and private aspects of the life of the natural man, a similarity that lies in his ignorance of his real self. This igno-

116

rance leads to activities—eros, friendship, and politics—that themselves become further expressions of ignorance rather than cures for it. No less significant is the fact that in both the public and the private spheres of life human action is directed toward the establishment or constitution of one's identity or selfhood. In both dimensions of life, the other becomes an instrument in the quest for self-realization. To be sure, a formal distinction exists between the two in the sense that in political activity the goal is attained not individually but collectively through identification with others with whom one aligns oneself in the pursuit of power, wealth, and social position. Nevertheless, exploitation of the other—as a class or as an individual—in the interest of becoming a self is no less the result of egotism in political relations than it is of egotism in private relations. The necessity of the other in order to be a self is an inescapable fact of human nature that characterizes all natural private and public relations. This law of our nature is the basis of conflict within the private and public spheres of human life. Conflict within all natural relations is inescapable, since all human beings strive to become concrete, identifiable, and worthy selves in and through the other.

From Kierkegaard's perspective, the only significant formal difference between the private and the public is the scale of the conflict. Given that the public dimension of life, like the private one, is qualified by each individual's ignorance of what a self is, it is not surprising that Kierkegaard insisted that, in spite of all the political turmoil in Denmark and western Europe, nothing revolutionary had really occurred (*PA*, 33-35). We can begin to see in what sense he meant that nothing had changed, no action had been taken, no revolution had been completed. The political, economic, social, and cultural upheaval that brought about the new liberal order was powerless to make essential changes because it rested on a fundamental ignorance of the nature of the human self. Socrates, not the political revolutionary, is in Kierkegaard's view the arbiter of real and

117

genuine change (*JP*, IV, 4118), and Kierkegaard regarded his own task as essentially Socratic. The real problem lies within each person's lack of self-knowledge and in his capacity for self-deception, and not within the social and political arena.

Kierkegaard believed that the true revolutionary is one who seeks to expose the possibilities for egotism released by the new liberal order. It was necessary to rescue ethics and religion, as he understood them, from the bondage of the new liberal order. Only then would it be possible to challenge in a Socratic sense the ignorance and self-deception on which the new order was based. Finally, and most difficult of all, it was necessary to find a way in which to accomplish these goals. Kierkegaard recognized that he could not stand on a street corner and preach to the masses about their envy and egotism any more than he could tell them that they were not Christians. An indirect approach was required. He would have to approach his fellow citizens from behind and surprise them with the truth by making them discover it for themselves—a Socratic approach. The individual must be educated as to his own nature and the nature of the new liberal order. Only then could one ask what kind of social order honest men should pursue. Like Socrates in the *Gorgias*, Kierkegaard believed that social and political injustice is rooted in human inwardness and lack of character. The creation of a just social order hinges on the reorientation of the other in the individual's self-consciousness. Any genuine change bringing about a really new social order requires the transformation of human self-consciousness, and in Kierkegaard's view such a transformation can occur only through the power of ethics and religion.

CONCLUSION

It should be evident by now that it would be mistaken to believe that Kierkegaard's term *natural man* refers to

118

some ahistorical or asocial state of nature in which human beings exist independently of history and social structures. As is apparent, the natural man may exist in varying sorts of social structures but is necessarily a social animal. To exist in a natural state or in a state of nature implies for Kierkegaard a social mode of existing. Indeed, the existence of what Kierkegaard called the natural man *requires the existence of the other. So closely aligned are the natural man and social existence that one cannot exist without the other.* Thus, the state of nature is necessarily social in character. The theological notion that egotism and selfishness are natural dispositions owing to our fallen nature may have been working in the back of Kierkegaard's mind, but he never made much of it. More prominent in his thought is the relation between this natural man and the new political and economic order of nineteenth-century Denmark. When Kierkegaard describes and criticizes the natural man, he does not seem to have in mind so much the fallen man as he does the nineteenth-century Dane who is happily, eagerly, and uncritically participating in the new liberal order. Thus, Kierkegaard used the term *natural man* not as an abstract theological principle but as a descriptive term.

Although Kierkegaard does not use economic and sociological jargon, he nevertheless seems to be describing and criticizing what we would call a market economy. In the nineteenth century, Denmark experienced the demise of its feudal economy and the emergence of a new capitalistic system. When Kierkegaard criticizes the natural man, he more often than not seems to be criticizing the sort of individualism that was fostered by Denmark's simple and developing market economy. The principles of a simple market economy were already in place in Kierkegaard's lifetime: (1) No central authority allocates work; individuals freely expend their talents and energies as they will. (2) The state does not authoritatively provide rewards for work; individuals are not guaranteed compensation or rewards appropriate to their social function. (3) All individuals seek

119

to maximize the return on the expenditure of their talents and energies. And (4) all individuals are free to use whatever material resources they possess to make a living. It is just this sort of economic arrangement that, in Kierkegaard's view, nurtures the capacity for egotism in human relations by economically and politically institutionalizing it.

Kierkegaard complained that the natural man "admires everything that has power, cunning, selfishness etc.—successfully—that is, so that it wins money, honor, esteem" (*JP*, IV, 5020). Moreover, "the merely human view" of life encourages individuals to attain an "accurate knowledge of and shrewd calculation upon one's own powers, talents, qualifications, possibilities, and in the same measure [become] familiar with what human and worldly shrewdness teaches the initiated . . ." (*JFY*, 121). This sort of knowledge offers the "probability of attaining power" but "does not in a deeper sense lead a man to himself, but farther and farther away from his deeper self; it is only in the sense of selfishness that it brings him nearer and nearer to himself . . ." (*JFY*, 121). The emphasis of the contemporary order on the cultivation of one's natural talents and abilities in the interest of power, money, honor, and esteem encourages that sort of human selfishness that Kierkegaard observed in all natural relations that are grounded only in themselves.

Clearly, Kierkegaard never fully developed his view of how society ought to be structured. We have only some general, though interesting, statements about what society will become once the age of individualism has been surpassed: "when the dialectical period (the romantic) in history is over (a period which I certainly very aptly call the period of individualism) social life will begin to play its part in the highest sense, and ideas such as 'state' (e.g. as it existed among the Greeks; 'church' in the older Catholic sense) must necessarily return richer and fuller than before, that is to say enriched by all the values which the surviving differences of individualism can give to the idea, *so that the individual means nothing as such, but every thing as a link in a chain"* (*SKJ*, 1836). We should not be too quick to dismiss this early journal entry as an example of the Hegelian influence on the young Kierkegaard. The chain analogy, for example, would be an apt one in describing human selfhood within the state of nature as Kierkegaard understood it: human beings require each other in order to be human. Even the non-egotistical person must necessarily exist with and through others.[39] Although Kierkegaard developed this point along ethical lines of thought rather than in terms of a positive social theory, we can see nevertheless the aptness of the chain analogy in discussing the egotistical and the ethical spheres of human life.

Kierkegaard did not develop a social theory along the lines suggested by the early journal entry. Once he moves beyond critical analysis to offer positive alternatives, his discourse becomes ethical in nature. As we shall see, he regarded the overcoming of egotism in human relations as a necessary condition for the establishment of a nonexploitive and just society. But the surpassing of egotism must be essentially an ethical and religious, not a political, achievement. This claim does not imply that Kierkegaard's ethical solution to egotism excludes political activity: Kierkegaard claimed only that individual ethical resolve is a necessary condition for overcoming the state of nature. If, then, the social is opposed to anything, it is not the natural. The natural is distinct not from the social but, as we shall see in the next chapter, from the ethical. Of course, it does

[39] Kierkegaard was adamant about the human need for community, as is evident in this much later passage in *Works of Love*: "No, the cure is precisely to learn all over again the most important thing, to understand oneself in one's longing for community. So deeply is this need grounded in the nature of man that since the creation of the first man there has been no change, no new discovery made . . . this need [is] grounded in the nature of man and . . . *essentially* . . . belong[s] to being a human being . . ." (*WL*, 153-54; Kierkegaard's italics).

121

not follow that all modes of social existence are natural and that the ethical is somehow opposed to or independent of the social. In the following chapter we shall see under what conditions social exsitence ceases to be natural and becomes ethical.

CHAPTER FOUR

The Ethical Self

THE CONCEPT of neighbor is so central to Kierkegaard's second literature that it is impossible to understand other key concepts in this literature without constant reference to it. The concepts of freedom, law, duty, love, willing the good (purity of heart), not willing the good (double-mindedness), self-deception, repetition, equality, God, action, conscience, suffering, ethics, and religion are all allied with the notion of neighbor in the second literature. Indeed, another way of expressing Kierkegaard's negative reaction to his own age is to say that he perceived it as having lost the notion of the other as neighbor. His writings in this second period are devoted to a rediscovery of the other as neighbor in and through the discovery of one's own self. The two are for him inseparable. Just as the other is a necessary constituent of oneself in all natural relations, so the neighbor is a necessary condition of one's self-consciousness and self-becoming. Kierkegaard cannot be more explicit about this than when he writes that "the concept of *neighbour* really means a duplicating of one's own self" (*WL*, 37; Kierkegaard's italics). In ethical terms, the question continues to be: How should I love myself? And the answer continues to settle on the other as a necessary condition for the existence of self-love. Just as one cannot selfishly love oneself without the other, so one cannot properly love oneself without the other. Thus, "to love oneself in the right way and to love one's neighbour correspond perfectly to one another; fundamentally they are one and the same thing" (*WL*, 39). In this chapter we shall investigate the many alliances Kierkegaard established between the concept of neighbor and the other key concepts in the second literature and the way in which

123

these alliances form Kierkegaard's ethical understanding of human selfhood.

Kierkegaard set the tone for his analysis of love for one's neighbor by distinguishing this mode of love from all forms of love in natural relations like friendship and eros. "As the poet understands them, love and friendship contain no ethical task. Love and friendship are good fortune . . . but ethically understood this is simply a way of saying that there is no task at all. On the other hand, when one has the *obligation* to love his neighbour, then there is the task, the ethical task, which is the origin of all tasks" (*WL*, 64; Kierkegaard's italics). The passage states that to be a neighbor is an obligation required by the moral law, that the neighbor is the one whom I am obliged to love. Indeed, "*if it were not a duty to love, then there would be no concept of neighbour at all*" (*WL*, 58; Kierkegaard's italics). Or, "he towards whom I have a duty is my neighbour . . ." (*WL*, 38). Again, "choosing a lover, finding a friend, yes, that is a long, hard job, but one's neighbour is easy to recognise, easy to find—if one himself will only recognise his duty" (*WL*, 39).[1] These passages suggest that when the other is chosen not aesthetically but ethically, one's relation to the other is grounded not in one's needs and tastes but in the moral law. Thus, to choose to live ethically entails recognizing the other as one's neighbor.

Without the moral law it would be as absurd to speak about one's neighbor as it would be to speak without passion about one's lover. Kierkegaard admitted that anyone who exists essentially in natural relations will find this talk about the neighbor to be absurd and senseless, an offense to one's understanding (*WL*, 41). "Anyone who clings to earthly life [that is, exists in natural relations] does not love his neighbor—that is, for him the neighbor does not exist"

[1] Cf. *WL*, 38: "This means that by recognising your duty you easily discover who your neighbour is." And, "If it were not a duty to love, then there could not be any question of loving the neighbor; for the concept 'neighbor' corresponds to loving as a duty" (*JP*, I, 943).

124

(*JP*, IV, 4603). For one who exists before the moral law, however, the neighbor not only exists but is also every man. In natural relations, one makes distinctions on the basis of one's tastes and needs and the desirability of the other. The moral law allows for no such distinctions within oneself or the other. Thus, the "neighbor is every man, and this is so far from being a natural qualification, an impulse of drive or of inclination to love the neighbor, that on the contrary one *shall* love him" (*JP*, IV, 4447; my italics). The *shall* universalizes the object of love. To exist before the law is to exist for all persons in a certain way that categorically excludes the way in which one exists toward other persons in all natural relations. We must, of course, distinguish between existing for all in principle and in fact. Obviously, an individual cannot exist for all in fact. But that one exists for all in principle means that one cannot and ought not exist in fact for anyone except as neighbor.

Before turning to a detailed analysis of this conception of the neighbor as the other whom one discovers when one exists before the law, it is important to make two preliminary points. First, it is true that in *Works of Love* Kierkegaard does not distinguish sharply between ethics and religion. The law governing ethical relations between all men does not "rise up in any human heart" (*WL*, 41); rather, it is disclosed to man, revealed in the words of the prophets and Jesus Christ. Christianity makes "every human relation between man and man a relationship of conscience" (*WL*, 137).[2] We should not overlook this point, for Kierkegaard's ethics is not intelligible without a serious consideration of its religious form. But in this chapter it is important to analyze the ethical content of the moral law, as Kierkegaard conceived it, without considering its religious form. Ulti-

---

2 Cf. *WL*, 36: "on the other hand, the Christian teaching is to love one's neighbour, to love all mankind, all men, even enemies, and not to make exceptions, neither in favouritism nor in aversion." "Just as the blood throbs in every nerve, so will Christianity in the relationship of conscience penetrate everything" (*WL*, 137).

125

mately, of course, the content of the law and its form (as divine command) should not be separated, but we shall better be able to discuss the ethical content of the law if we delay discussion of its form until the following chapter. There we shall see why Kierkegaard believed that the law must come in the form of a divine command and what impact, if any, this form has upon the content.

Second, we have already seen in a preliminary manner that the concepts of neighbor and moral law are interrelated in the sense that one discovers the other as neighbor in the discovery of one's duty. By means of the law, one comes to exist for the other as neighbor. Other key terms in Kierkegaard's ethics are similarly derived—for example, "love . . . fulfills the law and more" (*JP*, III, 2403). Love is existing for the neighbor, or, as Kierkegaard liked to put it, love is practicing the law (*WL*, 37). The concept of freedom is similarly allied with the concepts of law and neighbor. " 'Only law can give freedom.' Alas, we often think that freedom exists and that it is law which binds freedom. Yet it is just the opposite; without law freedom does not exist at all, and it is law which gives freedom" (*WL*, 53). Freedom, like love and neighbor, is a derivative concept. Without prior conception of the moral law that ethically binds each to the other, there can be no conception of human freedom. I am free to choose either to do X or not to do X only when I exist before the law. Otherwise, all activity is simply behavior that is determined by nature.

Finally, Kierkegaard claimed that "it is in fact the law which makes everyone equal . . ." (*WL*, 53).[3] Human equality is to be found most properly in relation to our common humanity before the law. In our common obligation and duty toward one another, rather than in natural rights, we discover genuine human equality.

[3] Cf. *WL*, 315: "The thought of God's presence makes a person shy in relationship to the other person, for God's presence makes the two essentially equal."

It is not difficult to see the essentially ethical content of these terms in Kierkegaard's mind as they are derived from the concept of the moral law. What Kierkegaard saw happening in nineteenth-century Denmark was the linking of these terms, especially freedom and equality, with the concept of natural right and the consequent politicizing of these terms in the rhetoric of liberalism. Grundtvig, as we have seen, even tried to construe his brand of liberalism as a politics of love, wresting this term as well from its moorings in an ethical philosophy of obligation. More than anything else, to Kierkegaard's mind, the politicizing of these terms by the activists of nineteenth-century Denmark and the emergence of the liberal notion that self-realization occurs through collectivized political power rather than through Socratic introspection threatened the loss of the human self in the modern state.

CHOOSING ONESELF AND SELFISHNESS

In Kierkegaard's attempt at a moral resolution of the problem of egotism, self-love is as much at the center of the solution as it is the center of the problem. The twin facts of human self-love and of the other as a necessary condition of all human self-love are inescapable. And, in Kierkegaard's view, it is to Christianity's everlasting credit that it has not failed to notice and to accept these facts as presuppositions in its ethical philosophy. Referring to the Hegelians' claim to begin philosophy without presuppositions, Kierkegaard countered that Christianity "by no means begins, as do certain high-flying thinkers, without presuppositions—nor with a flattering presupposition, either!" (*WL*, 34). For "Christianity presupposes that men love themselves and adds to this only the phrase about neighbours *as yourself*. And yet there is the difference of the eternal between the first and the last" (*WL*, 35; Kierkegaard's italics).[4] This "difference of the eternal" between

[4] The reference is to Matthew 22:39: "And a second is like it, You shall love your neighbor as yourself."

127

selfish self-love and love for one's neighbor is established by the law and, more specifically, by the particular form of the law that requires that one love the other *as one loves one-self*. For the law simply to state that one shall love one's neighbor leaves room for equivocation and deception. But when the phrase *as yourself* is added, all grounds for equivocation, ambiguity, and deception are removed. Self-love, as we have seen, is desiring to become a concrete, identifiable, and worthy self; the law requires one to love the other in the same manner.

In expressing the radically reorienting power of this phrase, Kierkegaard affirmed that "the whole thing is as quick as a turn of the hand; every thing is decided . . . 'in a moment, in the twinkling of an eye.' (I Corinthians 15:52)" (*WL*, 35). This is so because "selfishness absolutely cannot endure . . . duplication, and the words of the command *as yourself* are simply duplication" (*WL*, 38; Kierkegaard's italics). What is duplicated is oneself in the sense that what one wills for oneself, one wills for the other; therefore, "the concept of *neighbour* really means a duplicating of one's own self" (*WL*, 37; Kierkegaard's italics). The consequence of this sort of duplication is, as Kierkegaard says, the abrogation of selfish self-love. "As Jacob limped after having struggled with God, so shall [selfish] self-love be broken if it has struggled with this phrase, which never-theless does not seek to teach a man not to love himself but in fact rather seeks to teach him proper self-love" (*WL*, 35). Here Kierkegaard insisted that self-love is not abrogated in love for the other as neighbor but that such love brings "proper" self-love into being. Without getting into the is-sues of what kind of self-love is generated in and through love for one's neighbor and why this new form of self-love, whatever it might be, is "proper" self-love, we can readily see that loving the other as one loves oneself requires a dif-ferent form of self-love. Within nature, self-love takes the form of relating to the other as a means to an end. Ethically,

128

one can no longer love oneself in this way, because the other ceases to be the means of one's own self-seeking.

Thus, the moral law, as it is here stated, transforms one's relation to the other, and in so doing it transforms one's love for oneself. The law does not command that one cease loving onself when one loves one's neighbor. No, "the command of love to one's neighbour therefore speaks in one and the same phrase, *as yourself*, about this neighbour-love and about love to oneself" (*WL*, 40; Kierkegaard's italics). Or, "when the law's *as yourself* has wrested from you the self-love which Christianity sadly enough must presuppose to be in every man, then and then only have you learned how to love yourself. The law is, therefore: you shall love yourself in the same way as you love your neighbour when you love him as yourself" (*WL*, 39; Kierkegaard's italics).[5] Here is Kierkegaard at his dialectical and murkiest best; yet the sense of this passage is clear enough. The law requires the individual to love the neighbor as he loves himself and to continue to love himself when he loves his neighbor as himself. Indeed, the two in some manner require each other. "To love oneself in the right way and to love one's neighbor correspond perfectly to one another; fundamentally they are one and the same thing" (*WL*, 39). The passage is a perplexing one. Clearly, we can understand in what sense the law requires one to love the other as one loves oneself. But in what sense can one continue to love oneself when one's self-love takes the form of willing the other as a means to one's own end? The law no longer allows this sort of self-love. Indeed, and more correctly, the law does not even allow the existence of such a self. In what sense, then, is one a self that one can love when one relates to the other as neighbor? This is the key question.

5 Cf. *WL*, 39: "The command reads thus, 'You shall love your neighbour as yourself,' but if the command is properly understood, it also says the opposite: '*You shall love yourself in the right way*.' If anyone, therefore, refuses to learn from Christianity how to love himself in the right way, he cannot love his neighbour either" (Kierkegaard's italics).

In what sense is one a self when one exists before the law that obliges one to love? We have seen that the self in nature is in a state of incompletion and requires the other in order to be. The other becomes the means whereby the self's becoming materializes as a concrete, identifiable, and worthy project. Thus, *to pursue oneself in and through the other is what it means to love oneself.* The form that this striving takes in the state of nature is no longer allowable, yet something similar appears to be required by the law. One must love oneself, and one must love the other. Moreover, the two are in some way mutually dependent. Just as the other is a necessary condition for becoming a self in nature, so the other continues to be a necessary condition for becoming a self in the ethical sphere of life.

A long passage in *Works of Love* illuminates the vagaries and complexities of this central Kierkegaardian claim that love for the other is the proper form of self-love.

> As soon as love, in its relation to its object, does not in that relationship relate just as much to itself, although it still is entirely dependent, then it is dependent in a false sense, then the law of its existence is outside itself, and therefore it is in a contemptible sense, in an earthly, in a temporal sense, dependent. But the love which has undergone the transformation of the eternal by becoming duty and which loves because it *shall* love—this love is independent; it has the law of its existence in the relationship of love itself to the eternal. This love can never become dependent in a false sense, for the only thing it is dependent upon is duty, and duty alone makes for genuine freedom. Spontaneous love makes a man free and in the next moment dependent. It is as with a man's existence. By coming into existence, by becoming a *self*, he becomes free, but in the next moment he is dependent on this self. Duty, however, makes a man dependent and at the same moment eternally independent. "Only law can give freedom." (*WL*, 52-53; Kierkegaard's italics)

This passage is as remarkable as it is complex, for in it Kierkegaard manages to synthesize the main point of his earlier pseudonymous writings with his later emphasis on love in the nonpseudonymous literature.[6] The central issue in the earlier literature is how an individual becomes a self. Indeed, this question is the guiding preoccupation of all the pseudonyms' philosophical, religious, esthetic, and psychological explorations of human existence. With the completion of *The Sickness unto Death* in 1849, Kierkegaard appears to have been satisfied that he had resolved the question; he never again took it up in any sustained and systematic manner. The achievement of the pseudonyms is the settling of this question, and their answer appears as the ground for the resolution of yet another question: How shall I love my neighbor? Put differently, Kierkegaard seems prepared to say that the questions concerning the nature of human selfhood and love for one's neighbor are two sides of the same issue and that an explanation of one side requires an intimate familiarity with the other. The references in the above passage to duty, freedom, "becoming a *self*," and love's "relating just as much to itself" as to its

---

[6] The relation of Kierkegaard's pseudonymous and second literatures is a complex problem that cannot be approached systematically in this book. In the Chapter Seven and the Conclusion some comparisons between these two literatures are made with respect to Kierkegaard's literary style in both. These comparisons are not intended to exhaust all the issues clustering around the relation of the pseudonymous and nonpseudonymous literatures. It is important, however, to point out here that in the transition to the second literature Kierkegaard abandoned both the styles and many of the philosophical positions taken by the pseudonyms. Nevertheless, a point of coherence remains in the concept of the self. This unity of thought is evident from a comparison of the two literatures and a reading of the journals. One can see in the journals the concept of the self at work in both the earlier and later literatures. In the present study, the concept of the self in the pseudonymous works, which is summarized in the following pages, will appear in references cited from the second literature throughout the rest of this book. For references to recent studies of the concept of the self in the pseudonymous works, see n. 10 below.

object evidence Kierkegaard's appeal to the pseudonymous literature in solving the questions raised in the second literature.

It is impossible here to investigate extensively the notion of the self that is developed in the earlier pseudonymous literature. Kierkegaard there spoke about the self in various modes: in very complicated, almost algebraic formulas, such as the famous one in *The Sickness unto Death* (*SUD*, 146); in religious terms, where he referred to it as spirit;[7] in Hegelian terms, when he spoke of the self as a synthesis of opposites;[8] or in psychological terms, when he referred to the self as characterized by anxiety and despair.[9] This complex terminology is deeply rooted in nineteenth-century German philosophy and is drawn especially from theories of the self in the thought of Kant, Fichte, and Hegel. These different approaches form a single and coherent theory of the self. The task of reconstructing systematically and completely Kierkegaard's concept of the self in these terms has already been completed by a number of scholars and need not be repeated in detail here. Nevertheless, it is necessary to summarize this concept of the self before we can proceed with our analysis of love in *Works of Love*.[10]

The first point to notice is that Kierkegaard had a clear sense of a determinate dimension of human selfhood. He

[7] *CDR*, 37ff., 44ff., 83ff.; *CUP*, 128, 169-70, 309; *SUD*, 146.

[8] *DODE*, 149, 153ff.; *SUD*, 140-41, 149, 162-75; *CD*, 39, 44, 47, 76, 79; *CUP*, 176, 268.

[9] *CDR*, 37ff., 55, 64-65, 82; *SUD*, 148-49.

[10] For extensive discussions of the concept of the self in Kierkegaard's pseudonymous literature, see: John W. Elrod, *Being and Existence in Kierkegaard's Pseudonymous Works* (Princeton: Princeton University Press, 1975); Helmut Fahrenbach, *Kierkegaards existenzdialektische Ethik* (Frankfurt: V. Klostermann, 1968); Gregor Malantschuk, *Kierkegaard's Way to Truth*, trans. Mary Michelsen (Minneapolis: Augsburg Publishing House, 1963); George Price, *The Narrow Pass* (New York: McGraw-Hill, 1963); Adi Shmueli, *Kierkegaard and Consciousness*, trans. Naomi Handelman (Princeton: Princeton University Press, 1971); Mark Taylor, *Kierkegaard's Pseudonymous Authorship* (Princeton: Princeton University Press, 1975).

recognized that any answer to the question about the nature of selfhood must begin with an appreciation for firm, unalterable, and empirically determinable qualities. Thus, one aspect of the self is constituted by its particular organic, social, and cultural environment and by a specific history (*E/O*, II, 179, 220). The self is further determined by physiological qualities—race, sex, physical structure—as well as by psychological temperament and natural talents, interests, and intelligence (*E/O*, II, 220).[11] Kierkegaard used a variety of terms to describe this dimension of human selfhood. The self is, for example, *finite* (*SUD*, 162-68) in the sense that it is not all things that a self can possibly be; the self is always a particular and concrete self. It is, for example, black and feminine rather than white and male. To be finite means to be limited by those multiple qualities that make the self what it is. This aspect of human selfhood is also referred to as the self's *reality* (*DODE*, 147-48).[12] Just as Descartes spoke of the self's reality as a thinking thing, so Kierkegaard spoke of the self's reality as a historically determined thing. The term *necessity* (*SUD*, 168-75) is also used to describe this aspect of the self, and it conveys the notion that this aspect or dimension of life is inescapable. One cannot escape being the self that one is made to be by the determining factors that constitute it. This finite self, which is one's necessity, is also qualified by the dimension of time (*CDR*, 75-81). The self is not a static and rigidly fixed substance but a continually expanding and changing phenomenon by virtue of its immersion in history and the political, social, cultural, and physiological changes impinging upon it.

11 Cf. *E/O*, II, 227, 267, 337.

12 In a note in *DODE*, Kierkegaard identifies *reality* and *actuality* (*DODE* 148), but this identification is peculiar to this posthumously published work. In his major pseudonymous works, the term *actuality* refers not to the concrete and historically constituted dimension of the self but to the individual's choice of himself as a synthesis of the finite and the infinite.

Although the self is limited by its finitude, it is not reducible to it, for human selfhood includes the dimension of consciousness. In the analysis of human consciousness in *De Omnibus Dubitantum Est*, Kierkegaard specified two modes of consciousness. We may refer to the first as finite consciousness (*DODE*, 148-52). By this Kierkegaard meant that all human beings who engage objects external to themselves are finitely conscious. This mode of consciousness takes a multiplicity of forms, including perceiving, thinking, believing, judging, playing, loving, and worshiping. Kierkegaard would have had little difficulty agreeing with the phenomenologists' claim that human activity is to be defined in terms of the category of consciousness and that consciousness is always consciousness of something. Finite consciousness always has a specific and determinate thing as its object—a material phenomenon, an abstract idea, a promise to be kept, a goal to be achieved, a god to be worshiped, a person to be loved, a tradition to be defended, a proposition to be believed. Moreover, through consciousness of and interaction with these material, historical, and cultural objects, a finite and temporal self comes into being. It is through the self's conscious assimilation of the objective world into which it is thrown that it becomes the finite, necessary, and temporal reality that it is.

In the second mode of consciousness, which we may refer to as self-consciousness (*DODE*, 152-55), finite consciousness itself becomes the object of consciousness. The Danish term *Bevisthed*, which Kierkegaard used frequently in his analysis of human consciousness, is defined in Christian Molbech's *Dansk Ordbog* as "the characteristic of being aware of one's own existence, to have knowledge of it and of oneself."[13] *Bevisthed*, generally expresses self-consciousness, and it has two aspects. First, self-consciousness is consciousness of one's finitude. That is to say, through self-consciousness one comes to know what in fact one is as this particular

[13] Christian Molbech, *Dansk Ordbog* (Copenhagen: Gyldendal, 1833).

finite self. Second, self-consciousness includes the awareness that one's finite self is one's necessity, that one's self is constituted by the material, historical, and cultural objects that one encounters and that one cannot finitely, at any given moment, be anything but that particular self. Self-consciousness is, then, a kind of "transparency" (*SUD*, 147) in which one becomes completely aware of the substance (reality) and nature (necessity) of one's being.

Kierkegaard frequently described the transition from consciousness to self-consciousness as a mediation of immediacy (*DODE*, 148, 152). The self that is only finitely conscious is an immediate self in the sense that it *is* a set of relations that themselves are not examined, ordered, harmonized, judged, or transformed in any sense *by the subject whom they constitute*. To mediate this confusion is to negate it in the sense that one gives it a new form. This mediated self is what Kierkegaard called the ideal self (*DODE*, 148), which is to the real self what a map is to unexplored terrain. Mediation is not in any sense an abrogation or transcending of the real self; it is merely an idealization of it. To emphasize that self-consciousness is always consciousness of one's real self, Kierkegaard characterized the process of becoming self-conscious as a repetition. At the conclusion of *De Omnibus Dubitantum Est*, he explained that "when we speak of Repetition we get collision, for Repetition is only conceivable of what existed before (*DODE*, 153). Again, "There is an opposition here, because that which was existing, exists again in another manner" (*DODE*, 154). The real self "exists again" as an ideal self, so that self-consciousness is always consciousness of one's real self, which "existed before."

Kierkegaard, therefore, continually criticized those who argued that the real is taken up into the ideal as thought, such that one can say that thought possesses reality.[14] Such a claim presupposes the identity of thought and being, which in Hegel's philosophy takes the form of negating

[14] See my *Being and Existence in Kierkegaard's Pseudonymous Works*, pp. 46ff.

in thought whatever is immediate—that is, prior to thought —in order to discover there what is real. The view of speculative idealism—at least as Kierkegaard understood it —is that the immediate, concrete, and sensible phenomenon is always in fact an appearance that contains hidden within itself a reality that can be made universal, which in coming to expression destroys the view that the phenomenon, as it immediately presents itself, is unsurpassable. Kierkegaard believed that one should not view the immediate as containing within itself possibilities for higher forms of historical development. Each individual, each culture, each historical epoch is what it is precisely by virtue of its facticity, its concrete reality. It is mistaken to view the concrete as a husk of some higher and universal mode of existing that can be grasped in human thought as the ideal self. Such a view impels the philosopher to look beyond the immediate to the mediate, beyond the concrete to the abstract—indeed, in Kierkegaard's view, beyond the real to an illusion.

For Kierkegaard, it is the concrete in all its contingent, accidental, and multifaceted dimensions that is the real. It is not a mere appearance, a state in the development of some higher social life form. Each historical moment in both public and private life must be taken seriously on its own terms as the fact that is ultimately and materially real and final for the individuals existing in that moment. Historical necessity makes each of us what we are and can become by presenting us with a limited range of possibilities from which we must choose. All possible modes of existing for any given individual are embedded in his historical necessity, and one should not look elsewhere for possibilities in the making of one's existence. In Kierkegaard's view, the Hegelian notion of negation (*aufheben*), with its presupposition of the identity of thought and being and its commitment to discover the universal ideal self concealed in the particular, the real in the appearance, leads individuals toward an abstract self-conception that denies the ultimacy of the concrete as grievously as does religious mysticism.[15]

Mysticism is as mistaken as speculative idealism, for it also views the concrete, temporal, and finite dimension of life as ultimately the dimension of mere appearance. Kierkegaard unequivocally rejected mysticism and its conception of the self in *Either/Or*, where he claimed that mysticism teaches that the finite is "vanity, illusion, sin" (*E/O*, II, 253) and that the historical is "unprofitable labor" (*E/O*, II, 254). This view of finitude and history is metaphysically mistaken because it also divests the individual of his concretion (*E/O*, II, 266) and brings about a loss of contact with reality (*E/O*, II, 255). Mysticism "always ends with 'nothing' " (*JP*, III, 2797). This confusion over the nature of reality is particularly troubling because of its ethical consequences. Mysticism's most serious failing, in fact, is that it does not trouble itself to determine "ethically my relation to existence" (*E/O*, II, 253). The mystics, of course, cannot be expected to be ethically concerned about what for them is ultimately unreal, and for this reason Kierkegaard was mistaken in his failure to be more philosophically critical and less polemical in his discussion of mysticism. In any case, Kierkegaard perceived in religious mysticism an attempt to deny that for human beings history and temporal-

15 A distinction between the normative and material modes of development should be made here. When Kierkegaard speaks of the concrete as ontologically unsurpassable, he means to suggest that the concrete, with its social, political, and cultural traditions, is unsurpassable. Whatever any given individual or epoch is or can become is limited by the material conditions that constitute it. It cannot and ought not attempt to become what materially is not possible for it. It is, of course, possible to make normative judgments about the behavior of an individual or the traditions, customs, and conventions of a historical epoch in the life of a people. Such normative judgments, however, involve the obligation to seek not to transcend one's material conditions but to develop ethically within them. This distinction will be developed below in our discussion of Kierkegaard's conception of a community of ends as the goal that is ethically binding on all human selves.

ity are the surest paths to human freedom and salvation. He eloquently urged upon his reader the awareness that the temporal "exists for man's sake and is the greatest of all the gifts of grace. For man's eternal dignity consists in the fact that he can have a history, the divine element in him consists in the fact that he himself, if he will, can impart to this history continuity, for this it acquires only when it is not the sum of all that has happened to me or befallen me but is my own work, in such a way that even what has befallen me is by me transformed and translated from necessity to freedom" (*E/O*, II, 254-55).

Kierkegaard's rejection of Hegelian and mystical conceptions of the ideal self hinges on his view that the finite dimension of the self is ontologically inescapable. Kierkegaard's use of the term *repetition* is extremely significant, for the term expresses, as he himself stated, the notion that the ideal self is neither a mediation nor a repudiation of the finite, temporal, and concrete self but a repetition of it. Kierkegaard viewed the self as a synthesis precisely in this sense. The ideal self is neither more nor less than a reconstruction within the human imagination of the real self as ideal. The self's ideality consists in its being, first, for consciousness and, second, for freedom and hence an ethical obligation. This difference between Kierkegaard's ontology and that of the idealists and the mystics leads unavoidably to the ethical question. For the question of how human beings ought to behave is always predicated on the prior metaphysical or ontological question concerning the nature of the real. We are now in a position to turn more directly to the way in which Kierkegaard's ontology lays a foundation for his ethics.

The emergence of self-consciousness as the repetition of reality as ideality brings into focus the third dimension of the self. The self as a synthesis of reality and ideality "is a relationship which, though it is derived, relates itself to itself, which means freedom" (*SUD*, 162). We have seen that self-consciousness is the repetition of reality as ideality.

This is what Kierkegaard means when he speaks enigmatically about the self's relating itself to itself. This repetition, which is self-consciousness, gives rise to human freedom. The task is now "to transform repetition into something inward, into the proper task of freedom, into freedom's highest interest, as to whether, while everything changes, it can actually realize repetition (*CDR*, 17n). This realization of repetition "consists in appropriating what is already given. Consequently, the individual is, through freedom, absolutely dependent upon that which is given" (*SKP*, III, A ii). In fact, in freely becoming oneself, one "cannot relinquish anything in this whole, not the most painful, not the hardest to bear . . ." (*E/O*, II, 220). Kierkegaard thus aligns self-consciousness and freedom in the sense that the former is a necessary condition for the existence of the latter (*E/O*, II, 264). Those who are only finitely conscious, knowing themselves only as they are determined and defined by their facticity, cannot be free, since self-knowledge is a condition of freedom.

This conception of freedom does not imply the possibility of abandoning one's real self in thought or mystical intuition or by appropriating a reality radically new and different from the reality that one is. Kierkegaard spoke of freedom as "appropriating what is already given" and as not "relinquish[ing] anything in this whole" so as to emphasize the ontological necessity of one's reality. To be free in Kierkegaard's sense of the term means, at least minimally, becoming and accepting one's necessity. Self-acceptance is, of course, not the totality of freedom; there is the further task of choosing from the range of possibilities that authentically constitute the accepted self. Nevertheless, self-acceptance is a necessary condition for making concrete and particular choices.

Kierkegaard nowhere better captured this notion of self-acceptance than in his concept of choosing oneself, which he developed most completely in the second volume of *Either/*

Or. Two key passages will orient our discussion of this concept.

> But what is it I choose? Is it this thing or that? No, for I choose absolutely, and the absoluteness of my choice is expressed precisely by the fact that I have not chosen to choose this or that. I choose the absolute. And what is the absolute? It is I myself in my eternal validity. (*E/O*, II, 218)

> But what, then, is this self of mine? If I were required to define this, my first answer would be: It is the most abstract of all things, and yet at the same time it is the most concrete—it is freedom. (*E/O*, II, 218)

When Kierkegaard claimed that the self is an absolute, he meant that it is "its own end and purpose" (*E/O*, II, 269). The self is "the absolute which has its teleology in itself" (*E/O*, II, 267). That is to say, whatever the self is to become is legislated by the nature of the self and not by anything external to it. We have already seen that the self is a unity of particularity and of its capacity to make this particularity the object of consciousness and freedom. Kierkegaard's way of making this point in the passage above is to say that the self is both the most concrete and the most abstract of all things. More clearly, he claimed that the self is "the unity of the universal and the particular" (*E/O*, II, 269). The particular self is, as we have seen, the self that is constituted by its facticity. The universal dimension of one's self is its capacity for making one's particularity an object of reflection, so that one becomes self-conscious and thereby capable of choosing the self that one is. Freedom means, in this sense, the choosing of one's necessity.[16] It is also clear that the relation between the particular and the universal dimensions of the self is a dialectical one in the sense that one cannot exist freely unless one chooses one's

---

[16] See *The Sickness unto Death* for Kierkegaard's discussion of necessity.

particularity, and one cannot so choose unless one is free. To exist freely means that one has chosen oneself as a unity of the particular and the universal.

According to Kierkegaard, any conception of freedom that does not remain wedded to particularity is bound to lead the individual not only toward an abstract self-understanding but also toward an abstract life. "If one does not hold fast to the fact that the individual has the ideal self in himself, his *Dichten und Trachten* [thought, aspirations, endeavors, studies] remain abstract" (*E/O*, II, 264). Any individual who wants "to cast reality from him . . . is nothing at all, an abstraction. Only as the particular is he the absolute . . ." (*E/O*, II, 270). Kierkegaard warned, "If one does not adopt this doctrine [of the self], personality becomes abstract, its relation to duty abstract, its immortality abstract" (*E/O*, II, 269).[17] The references to duty and immortality in this last passage indicate Kierkegaard's fear that both the ethical and the religious life become abstract when the concrete particularity of the human self is ignored in the individual's striving to become himself. Thus, the self that one chooses must not be "an abstract self which fits everywhere and hence nowhere, but a concrete self which stands in reciprocal relations with these surroundings, these conditions of life, this natural order. This self which is the aim is not merely a personal self but a social, a civic self" (*E/O*, II, 267).[18]

[17] In this connection, it would be useful to consult Kresten Nordentoff, *Kierkegaard's Psychology*, trans. Bruce H. Kirmmse (Pittsburgh: Duquesne University Press, 1978).

[18] Kierkegaard also stated in this connection that each individual has a history in which "he stands in relation to other individuals of the race and to the race as a whole . . . and . . . he is the man he is only in consequence of this history" (*E/O*, II, 220). We have seen in the preceding chapter the sense in which the individual's concreteness includes a social dimension. The self that each individual chooses is a social self, that is, a self that is constituted by its relations to other human beings. Kierkegaard seems to have recognized this point as early as the writing of *Either/Or*, even though he does not begin to develop it until after the completion of most of the pseudonymous writings.

One other point needs to be made about Kierkegaard's conception of human freedom. The term *freedom* is conventionally related to the idea of novelty in the sense that when an individual freely chooses something, he is changed by the act of choosing. The thing chosen modifies the subject such that he is in some sense different after the choice is made. Kierkegaard did not want to deny this notion of novelty, although his definition of freedom as the choice of necessity appears to resist the claim that free choices introduce novelty into the lives of human subjects. Kierkegaard insisted that even though the choice is the choice of necessity, the subject is transformed by the choice itself. When an individual "becomes himself, quite the same self he was before, down to the least significant peculiarity, . . . he becomes another, for the choice permeates everything and transforms it" (*E/O*, II, 227). In other words, when the individual chooses himself, "he chooses himself as product . . . [but] when he chooses himself as product he can just as well be said to produce himself" (*E/O*, II, 255-56).[19] By this transformation, then, the subject produces himself for consciousness and freedom. The self that in the state of immediacy has the capacity (κατὰ δύναμιν) for self-consciousness and freedom in fact becomes self-conscious and free. This transformation occurs when the real self as idealized is made an object of consciousness and freedom. Thus, the self is transformed by virtue of its knowledge and acceptance of itself. In Kierkegaard's words, the self "comes into existence" (*PF*, 89-110) with the choice.[20] Prior to the choice, the self does not exist, since it neither is conscious of nor has chosen itself. It is at this point of coming into existence that the individual is transformed and confronted with the possibility of living his life ethically and religiously. For Kierkegaard interpreted both ethical obligation and religious

[19] Cf. *E/O*, II, 219: "This self did not exist previously, for it came into existence by means of the choice, and yet it did exist, for it was in fact 'himself.' " Cf. also *E/O*, II, 263.

[20] Cf. *CUP*, 176, 277-81, 311.

faith in terms of the individual's striving to become himself. It would be beside the point to launch into an analysis of the relation between becoming a self and the ethical and religious stages of existence developed by Kierkegaard in the pseudonymous literature. Here it is important for us to realize that when Kierkegaard speaks about becoming a self in *Works of Love*, he is referring to what has been described above as choosing oneself.

Choosing Oneself and Loving the Other

In what sense does the notion of choosing oneself help to resolve the problems generated in our analysis of love in Kierkegaard's *Works of Love*? The first point we must notice is that the entire second literature considerably deepens the conception of the social dimension of the self's necessity that Kierkegaard began to develop as early as *Either/Or* (*E/O*, 220, 267). In the second literature, particularly in *Works of Love, Christian Discourses*, and *Purity of Heart*, Kierkegaard disclosed the social form of human finitude. The individual, as finitely conscious, is not a passive observer of a social and organic environment that is ontologically separate from him. Nor does this finitely conscious individual dispassionately assimilate his organic, social, and cultural environment. On the contrary, he is supremely interested in becoming an identifiable and worthy self and seeks to accomplish this goal through the internal assimilation of his social environment. Sexuality, race, cultural heritage and traditions, political affiliation, and class identification constitute the self's finitude, and the individual's appropriation of that finitude is motivated by the supreme interest, need, to become a self. In the language of *Works of Love*, the passionate assimilation of finitude within the realm of finite consciousness is motivated by a self-love that is selfish in nature. The selfish use of the other as a means to the end of self-actualization is what Kierkegaard referred to in *Works of Love* as false dependence

143

(*WL*, 52-53), which, as we have seen, is present in both private and public relations.

Once the social form of necessity is made clear, the whole notion of choosing oneself, as it is developed in *Either/Or*, becomes problematic. We have described this choice as a self-acceptance that is made possible by infinite or self-consciousness. In choosing his self, the individual acknowledges what he is by necessity and refuses to be deceived into accepting a self other than the one he discovers in self-consciousness. In this choice is his freedom, and the strength of this notion of freedom can be assessed both historically and ethically. As we have seen, one may legitimately read the second volume of *Either/Or* as a polemical statement against the idealistic and mystical notions of the self that were dominant in the nineteenth century. Kierkegaard's notion of freedom may be positively evaluated along ethical lines as well. The existentialist movement that built on Kierkegaard's pseudonymous literature has as its central axiom the notion of choosing, in Kierkegaard's sense, as a good. Kierkegaard himself was unambiguously clear about the value of choosing when he wrote that "The good is the *an-und-für-sich-Seiende* posited by the *an-und-für-sich-Seiende* [being-in-and-for-itself], and this is freedom" (*E/O*, II, 228). Although the form of this sentence is a blatant parody of the tortured syntax of speculative philosophy, Kierkegaard was serious in claiming that freedom, in the sense of choosing oneself, is a good. In Kierkegaard's view, self-choosing is a good because it is the actualization of the self as a synthesis of reality and ideality and necessity and possibility. In choosing, the self as a potential unity is realized as an actual one. Such an achievement involves the individual's assimilation of his necessity by simultaneously making it his own and himself a part of it. To choose one's necessity requires both self-knowledge, which precedes and makes the choice possible, and active acceptance of the self disclosed in self-consciousness.

This notion of freedom as a good, however, is not without

144

a serious difficulty, which stems from the way in which the possibility of choosing is derived. We have observed that in *Either/Or* self-consciousness generates the possibility of free choice. Moreover, we have seen that self-consciousness is a negation of necessity and can contain only what is discovered in such a negation. Consciousness, as such, is empty. It can contribute nothing of itself since it is merely a reflecting pool in which the individual sees clearly his own necessity and its social form. In Kierkegaard's scenario for becoming a self, this social self, which is the individual's reality, must be reflected as an ideal self and chosen. Such a reflection would allow only for the choice of oneself as one is, and that self, as we have seen, is an egotistical one. The choice would simply entrench the already egotistical character of one's relations with others. Self-consciousness enables one to see that one becomes a self in and through the other, and the choice of that self would involve one's internal assimilation of it, with a consequent hardening of the conflict and inequity that characterize that self. Simply to assert that choosing oneself is the good is to say that one ought to continue behaving in the manner one has always behaved but with a clear knowledge and acceptance of oneself in that behavior. Since consciousness is the negation of nature and can contain only what it discovers there, it can provide no ethical principle that might guide the individual's assimilation of necessity. And if nature is egotism, then one cannot expect to find in infinite consciousness any ethical rule or law according to which one might ethically judge one's behavior.

Kierkegaard understood the limitation of this conception of freedom as a good even in *Either/Or*. There he describes the choice as including the dimension of repentance. In choosing, the individual "repents himself back into himself, back into the family, back into the race, until he finds himself in God. . . . as soon as I love freely and love God I repent" (*E/O*, II, 220-21).[21] But nowhere in *Either/*

[21] Cf. *E/O*, II, 179, 229, 242, 252, 262.

Or—or anywhere else in the pseudonymous literature—does Kierkegaard seriously work out the relation between freedom, love, and repentance as it bears on the social conflict that he found so crucial in *Works of Love*. Kierkegaard also speaks in *Either/Or* of the choice as a "task [that] is principally to order, cultivate, temper, enkindle, repress, in short, to bring about a proportionality in the soul, a harmony, which is the fruit of personal virtues" (*E/O*, II, 267). Nevertheless, it is difficult to find in *Either/Or* an ethical principle according to which the individual repentantly and repressively chooses himself "back into the race," even though the concepts of repentance, harmony, ordering, and repression, as they are used in *Either/Or*, require an ethical principle of some sort if they are to make any sense at all. As we have seen, however, as long as consciousness is the sole origin or ground of freedom, the invoking of any such principle is quite impossible. Of course, Kierkegaard provides such a principle in *Works of Love*: you shall love your neighbor as yourself is the ethical principle according to which any individual is freely to become himself. Indeed, "only law can give freedom" (*WL*, 53). So it is the law that is the condition of the possibility of freedom. This distinctly Kantian move clearly adds something new to the notion of becoming a self developed in *Either/Or* and appealed to in *Works of Love*.

Although the concept of freedom as derived from consciousness creates a difficulty, it is also the ground of a new possibility. Once a detachment in consciousness from one's necessity has been achieved, it is possible not only to choose one's necessity but also to choose it according to a moral law that the individual accepts as binding on the choice.[22] Any such law, if it is to apply to the self, must refer the self to its necessity, since that is what the self *is*, and to its desire to become identifiable and worthy. The law must recognize the nature of human necessity as both social and teleological.

[22] The conditions under which an individual would allow himself to be bound by such a law will be considered below.

That is to say, the law must speak to the condition of human selves, which is the desire to become a self, and to the social context in which each individual tries to complete that goal. As we have already noted, Kierkegaard felt that it is to Christianity's "everlasting credit" (*WL*, 35, 39) that it begins with the presupposition that all human beings love themselves selfishly. Whatever the law is to be, even if it is legislated by God, it must not neglect to presuppose this one fact about human nature. Hence, the acceptance of this law by any individual must begin with the consciousness of himself as one who selfishly loves himself. Thus, freedom derived from the moral law completes the freedom made possible by consciousness. You shall love your neighbor as you love yourself. To keep this law is proper self-love or the condition under which one actually becomes a self. How so?

As we have seen, in the natural sense of becoming the individual wills himself as an end in and through the other. In addition, to will oneself as an end is to will to move from a potential to an actual state of being. Such a transition within the realm of nature occurs through the individual's internal assimilation of the social dimension of his necessity, which involves the granting of special status to certain phenomena—race, sex, cultural heritage—that constitute one's necessity. However, one does not directly confer special status on these phenomena, since they are discovered as already possessing this status within one's necessity. Through internally appropriating their special status as one's own, one tacitly reconfers this privileged status upon them and thereby experiences oneself as having become a concrete, identifiable, and worthy self. This assimilation must also involve a coercive element in the sense that the individual, having imputed this special status to his necessity, will do whatever can be done to guarantee that the thing appropriated does not lose its status (for example, race and sexuality) or that he does not lose the thing that has the special status (for example, wealth), for without the thing and

147

its status he loses his identity. Coercion may take direct or indirect forms; it may be political, cultural, or psychological in nature. In all cases it is the forcible exercise of oneself over the other in the interest of maintaining or securing one's identity. Thus, within nature the other experiences me as a force or a power seeking to realize myself in and through him. (Of course, the predication of identity on power or the lack of identity on powerlessness may be so commonplace to all involved that the oppressive nature of the relation is not directly experienced until it is challenged either internally or externally.)

Within nature, then, one finds a perpetual and universal conflict: every individual seeks to will his finite and particular self as an end in and through the other. It is clear that within the state of nature it is not really possible for anyone to be an end, since to will oneself only as a finite end is to require the other to will himself in the same manner and hence to will the other as a means. One cannot be an end in a world where everyone wills only himself as an end. One can exist as an end only in a community of ends,[23] that is, in a world in which all persons are treated as ends .

For Kierkegaard, to choose oneself as a synthesis of necessity (particularity) and possibility (universality) is to will the existence of a community of ends. One chooses oneself as a concrete and finite being who desires to become something worthy within this world, *and* one chooses the other. As a finite being I am interested in myself, and as a universal self I have an obligation toward the other. I cannot choose myself without choosing the other. But in what sense do I choose the other? I must choose the other as himself a synthesis of necessity and possibility, since that is what all human selves are. To will the other's necessity alone as an end would be to absolutize his particularity and thereby

[23] Kierkegaard does not use this phrase; it is my own. I hope that the following exposition, which attempts to disclose the relation between choosing oneself and loving others, will justify the appropriateness of this phrase in discussing Kierkegaard's ethics.

148

engender the conflict that one is striving to overcome. Thus, to will the other as an end requires not only that I will the other's necessity as an end but also that I will the other equally to will all other selves as ends.

It is apparent that willing the other's necessity as an end is possible by refusing to appropriate it as a means to one's own ends. But how is it possible to will the other as free to will other selves as ends? This is a difficult question for Kierkegaard, for refusing to use the other's necessity as a means and choosing the other as free are not the same thing. For the other to experience me as genuinely accepting his necessity is still not sufficient to motivate him as well to choose other human beings as ends. Nor is it sufficient simply to leave the other alone, to let him go his way while I go mine. In choosing the other, one must exist for him in the sense that one must both value his necessity and strive to lead him to an acceptance of his own freedom. For unless the other accepts his own freedom (universality), just as the ethical individual has done, he will continue to exist egotistically within nature, and under those conditions a community of ends cannot emerge. The issue of how one brings another person to act freely is an important one for Kierkegaard and will be taken up in Chapter Seven.

To will the other as an end, then, requires one on the one hand to cease willing one's own ends in and through the other's necessity and to affirm the other's necessity as a good in itself;[24] on the other hand, it is to will that the other will all other selves as ends. In other words, to will another as an end is both to do something for him and to expect something of him. What one does for the other is to cease coercing him in one's own interest and to begin affirming his necessity as a good in itself worthy of his choosing and developing. What one expects of the other is that he also

[24] Kierkegaard's way of putting this point in *Works of Love* is to say that loving the other "is precisely to give up the . . . immediate" (*WL*, 339). We have already seen that to exist within immediacy is to exist in the state of finite consciousness or in egotism.

149

do the same for all others, since only under these conditions is it possible for anyone to be free. In sum, Kierkegaard claimed that one chooses his necessity properly only if he chooses it freely; that is, at the same time that he chooses himself, he chooses the other. It is for this reason that I must will the other as a synthesis of necessity and possibility, for to will the other as a synthesis is to will that the other allow himself to be bound by the law. This point cannot be over-emphasized. To choose the other is to lead him to the point where he freely allows himself to be bound by the law. According to Kierkegaard, the greatest love that one can show for another is to teach him to love God (*WL*, 133). Again, we should skirt the religious dimension of this issue here, but the passage helps us to see that loving the other is not leaving him alone to develop within his necessity as he chooses; rather, it is leading him to take an action, namely, to love God, or, what is the same thing for Kierkegaard, to allow himself to be bound by the moral law.

It is only in this sense that Kierkegaard conceived of the self as an absolute. For the individual to absolutize himself as a finite end within the limitations of necessity is to invite social conflict and chaos, which prevent the completion of one's goal to become a concrete, identifiable, and worthy self. To love the other is to renounce the natural tendency to become a self through power, force, and manipulation, for one can never become a self in a world in which one wills the other as a means and is also being willed as a means. One can become a concrete, identifiable, and worthy self only in a world where relations between selves are predicated on love. Thus, I must will the existence of such a world, for in willing the other as an end, I will for myself. It is in this sense that ultimately the distinction between oneself and the other dissolves, for I become a self by being for the other. When one conceives of the self as a synthesis of the particular and the universal, it is necessary to say that "one has no neighbor, for the *I* is simultaneously itself and its neighbor . . ." (*JP*, I, 222).

We see now in what sense the choice of oneself entails the choice of all others, for in choosing oneself as a synthesis of necessity (particularity) and possibility (universality), one chooses one's own necessity as well as the necessity of all other persons as a good. Such a choice is also, as we have seen, the choice to exist in a community of ends in which all are free from dependence upon the necessity of others in order to be a self. This freedom is also a freedom for the other in the sense that one wills both the other's necessity *and* his freedom as a good.

Simply to will the existence of a community of ends is not sufficient to produce it, however, for, as we have seen, it cannot exist unless all persons will it equally. It follows, therefore, that one is not fully free until one exists in a community of ends. Outside such a community, one is partially free in the sense that in choosing oneself as a synthesis of necessity and possibility, one no longer needs the other's necessity as a means to the end of becoming a self, what Kierkegaard called "false dependence." Nevertheless, one's own necessity will continue to exist for the other as a means to an end.

The dissolving of this ethical distinction between oneself and the other is a necessary condition for one's becoming a self. But Kierkegaard also realized that it is not a sufficient condition; one does not bring such a world into being by willing it, for it is necessary that all will the existence of such a world in order for it actually to exist. Kierkegaard therefore maintained that while one wills the existence of a community of ends, one must also be related to it in hope. But "no one can hope unless he also loves; he cannot *hope for himself* without loving, for they are eternally insepa-rable . . ." (*WL*, 239; Kierkegaard's italics). One may not hope for oneself unless one loves others; even then, one may only hope for oneself, since one's love is in itself and of it-self powerless to bring into being a community of ends. For Kierkegaard, the biblical proposition " 'Love hopes all things' can mean that the lover hopes all things for himself

151

and it can mean that the lover in love hopes all things for others. But they are indeed one and the same . . ." (*WL*, 242). They are one and the same because only in a community of ends that includes all human beings is it possible for a single individual to become an end.

THE PSYCHOLOGY OF THE ETHICAL SELF

Kierkegaard's psychological profile of persons egotistically existing in the state of nature includes, as we have already seen, anxiety, envy, fear, jealousy, and hatred. The network of exploitive social relations in which the individual establishes himself generates a corresponding internal network of negative feelings and emotions. As we have also seen, the dialectical constitution of human selfhood is not something that is simply grasped conceptually but is experienced directly by individuals existing in those relations. Acting on these negative feelings only perpetuates the conflict that generated them. Kierkegaard believed, for example, that much of the political turmoil in nineteenth-century Denmark was motivated by envy (*PA*, 47-52).[25] Envy, he also believed, motivated the strife within personal relationships, as well as the public hostility directed against him by the Copenhagen population.[26] Actions within the public and

[25] Cf. *WL*, 89-90; *JP*, III, 3219, IV, 4149, 4227.

[26] The strong contempt that the Copenhagen population expressed toward Kierkegaard in the late 1840s was initially provoked by the cartoon caricatures of Kierkegaard appearing in the satirical political and literary journal *The Corsair*. Its editor, Meïr Goldschmidt, had been a great admirer of Kierkegaard. Kierkegaard, though he admired Goldschmidt's first novel, felt that *The Corsair* was a public menace and that Goldschmidt was too far under the influence of the writer Peder Ludvig Møller. In response to an article by Møller, Kierkegaard published an open letter to *The Corsair*, complaining that he alone of Copenhagen's prominent citizens had not been singled out for criticism by *The Corsair*. Goldschmidt, and Møller especially, thereupon launched a steady and merciless series of articles and cartoons ridiculing Kierkegaard's person. The public joined in the ridicule, and it became difficult for Kierkegaard even to walk the streets of Copenhagen without being mocked and scorned by his fellow citizens.

private realms of human life that are motivated by envy merely perpetuate the system that initially generated this psychology. For Kierkegaard, the internal and the external are two sides of the same phenomenon; each generates and nourishes the other, so that an unbroken chain of conflict and exploitation characterizes human relations within the state of nature. The only way in which an individual can free himself from this internal strife and pain is to choose himself as a synthesis of necessity and possibility. In his new self-understanding the individual is freed from his enslavement to the other and the psychological states that such enslavement induces.[27]

Kierkegaard argued that this necessary relation between external relations and actions on the one hand and internal states on the other applies to persons existing within not only the natural but also the ethical sphere of life. The second part of *Works of Love* is devoted primarily to an extended description of the topography of the inwardness that is generated when an individual chooses himself as a synthesis. Kierkegaard characterized this relation between

[27] We have already seen that even though one wills the other as an end, one retains the desire to be willed as an end. Is this desire itself, when unsatisfied, a sufficient ground for envy, so that we may find this negative phychological state even among ethical persons? In response to such a criticism Kierkegaard would say that if one genuinely wills the other as an end, this desire will not become envy. Why? In choosing oneself as a synthesis, one chooses not only the other as an end but also one's own necessity. Indeed, an individual cannot choose the one without the other. Such a choice frees each individual from the other in the development of his own self-understanding. But to choose to accept one's necessity is not sufficient to free it from the exploitive designs of the other. What one therefore desires is not to be like the other but to be free of the exploitation of the other, or, what is the same thing, to have the other will one's necessity as a good. Envy springs from the failure to accept one's necessity as itself a good and expresses itself as opposition to another person or group of persons whom one perceives as in some sense embodying what one desires to be. Though this unsatisfied desire is not the basis of envy in the ethical person, it does ground Kierkegaard's conception of suffering, which will be examined in Chapter Six.

153

external actions and internal states in terms of the concept of reduplication. "When we say, 'Love saves from death,' there is straightway a reduplication in thought: the lover saves another human being from death, and in entirely the same or yet in a different sense he saves himself from death" (*WL*, 262). More explicitly, we should "note the reduplication here: what the lover does, he is or he becomes; what he gives, he is or, more accurately, this he acquires . . ." (*WL*, 262). Much of the second part of *Works of Love* attempts to disclose the substantive character of this reduplication. Although I shall not attempt to analyze fully this part of the book here, it will be instructive to look briefly at a few examples of the inward and psychological reduplication of choosing oneself as a synthesis.

We have already noticed the relation between loving the other and hoping for oneself. The latter is a duplication of the former in the sense that the choice of the other as a synthesis creates a hope for oneself. Kierkegaard described the person who lives without hope as one who cannot conceive the possibility that things as they are can be transformed for the good. Such persons are filled with shrewdness, anger, bitterness, cowardice, fearful small-mindedness, envy, and vanity (*WL*, 240-41). One who hopes for himself overcomes the shrewdness that develops special skills for excelling within the state of nature. One who hopes for himself overcomes with courage the cowardice and fearful small-mindness that are unwilling to hope for anything. One who hopes for himself overcomes with humility the vanity that fears to hope for others for fear of being proved wrong. On the other hand, the lover "hopes all things; for him no indolence of habit, no pettiness of mind, no picayunishness of prudence, no extensiveness of experience, no slackness of the years, no evil bitterness of passion corrupts his hope or adulterates possibility" (*WL*, 241).

A second example of this inward reduplication comes in Kierkegaard's discussion of self-deception (*WL*, 221-30). Within the state of nature, individuals must constantly deceive one another in order to get their way. One must constantly be on guard against the other's discovery of one's real intentions. Nor can one ever make these intentions explicit to another person, for they would reveal one as driven primarily by the desire to advance and protect one's own interests. This deceiving of the other is really self-deception, however, for the attempt to become a self through the use of the other as a means is to be deceived not only about the nature of oneself but also about the way in which one can in truth become a self. The deceiver "does not love, and thereby he has deceived himself out of the highest good and the greatest blessedness" (WL, 225). To choose oneself or to love another person is to advance beyond self-deception and to exist in truth (WL, 224).

As a final example of the way in which inwardness is qualified by the choice of oneself as a synthesis, we might cite self-respect. Kierkegaard did not, as far as I know, use this term, yet it is entirely appropriate to say of an individual who has become a self that he possesses a self-respect. Kierkegaard claimed that "in the world of the spirit this owning one's own soul is the very highest" goal a human being can achieve (WL, 255). And, as we have seen, one cannot own one's own soul without willing that every other individual own himself in the same manner. Such a disposition is surely the ground of self-respect, for in choosing oneself, one affirms the absolute value of oneself and all other selves. Like hope and honesty, self-respect grows out of a positive commitment to all other selves as intrinsically good and valuable. One cannot respect another person when one perceives him as a means, and to perceive the other as a means is to will the existence of a world in which all selves, including one's own self, may possibly be used as means to ends. In a world where no self can in principle be an end it becomes impossible to respect oneself. Thus, the choice of oneself as a synthesis is the condition for the existence of self-respect.

In this abbreviated discussion of hope, honesty, and self-respect we have seen how the choice of oneself as a synthesis not only liberates one from negative psychological states like anxiety and envy but also engenders positive internal states. This concept of choice was important for Kierkegaard, for in his view, even though such a choice cannot in and of itself bring a community of ends into being, it nevertheless transforms a tortured and unhappy inwardness into a more peaceful one.[28]

The main point of *Works of Love*, then, is that one cannot choose what is good for oneself unless one chooses that same thing for all human beings. Over and over again, Kierkegaard maintained that only through love for another person is it possible properly to love oneself. We have seen how this view of love is grounded in Kierkegaard's conception of the individual's choice of himself as developed in the second volume of *Either/Or*. In *Works of Love*, Kierkegaard attempted to expand this conception of choice to include the social nature of human selfhood and the ethical condition that must be met before any such choice can be properly and successfully carried through. In *Either/Or*, the ultimate ethical achievement is the choice of oneself; by the time he wrote *Works of Love*, Kierkegaard had concluded that one can choose oneself or become oneself only in and through the choice of the other.

This idea of becoming oneself through the choice of the other as a synthesis of necessity and possibility may be expressed in another way. We may say that in making such a choice, the individual meets all the conditions that *he must fulfill* in order for him to become an end in a community of ends. By choosing the other's finitude, his neces-

[28] We should note again that, apart from existing in a community of ends, the individual who has chosen himself cannot know an unqualified happiness, since he himself continues to be victimized by the state of nature, even though he has willed its dissolution. Such victimization is the ground of Kierkegaard's conception of religious suffering, which will be discussed in Chapter Six.

sity, as a good, he affirms the other as a material end; by choosing the other's possibility, his freedom, he hopes that the other will also cease relating to his own and others' finitude as means to ends. He recognizes in his choice of the other that he himself can become a material end only by the will of the other. Thus, the choice of the other as free is a condition that must be satisfied before one can exist materially as an end in this world. But even though the other's good will is a requirement for one to become a material end, no such condition need be met in order for the one who chooses himself as a synthesis to become a spiritual end. The choice of the other as a synthesis is sufficient to release one psychologically from this false dependence upon the other. He who chooses himself need no longer coerce or dominate the other in order to accept and respect his own necessity, and in this acceptance he discovers all the possibilities for this life that are for him worth pursuing. Of course, others may not share in that respect; they may even actively deny that one has reason to respect oneself. In Kierkegaard's view, however, it is impossible for others to deprive one of this internal freedom.

What are the necessary conditions, one may wonder, that must obtain before it would ever occur to anyone to choose himself in the Kierkegaardian sense? Why, for example, would the powerful will a community of ends. Given their temporal happiness, security, and well-being, what conditions could conceivably motivate them to choose the good over their personal interests. And one might ask the same question of the disenfranchised, the powerless in both private and public relations. One might assume that they would find the moral law an acceptable form of self-assertion, a means for gaining the power they lack. But under what conditions would the powerless will the good, the existence of a community of ends?

In the first literature, Kierkegaard's answer to these questions is to be found in the advice that Judge William gives to the pleasure-seeking young man who is the author of the papers composing the first volume of *Either/ Or*. The Judge seeks to promote a moment of self-recognition in which the young man will see through his temporal happiness and well-being to the despair that is the reality of one who does not choose himself (*E/O*, II, 212-18). Such a recognition and the acceptance of one's reality are portrayed as dimensions of the choice itself (*E/O*, II, 215).

In the second literature, as we have seen, Kierkegaard expressed the human dilemma not only in terms of despair but also in terms of anxiety and envy. One discovers in the moment of self-recognition that beneath one's apparent temporal happiness (or unhappiness, for that matter) there moves a subterranean stream of what might be called an ontological unhappiness, which flows directly from one's mode of existing in opposition to all others and one's consequent failure to become the self one naturally desires to be. Short of such a recognition, Kierkegaard believed, individuals may in fact be happy in a natural sense. The "spontaneous, immediate person is too happy for the 'neighbor' to exist [*være til*] for him. Anyone who clings to earthly life does not love his neighbor—that is, for him the neighbor does not exist" (*JP*, IV, 4603). The individual is not aware of his egotistical relationship to others or of his own envy and anxiety. In such a situation, Kierkegaard claimed, the individual is not even ethically culpable; he is so entrenched in the natural that the ethical is not in any significant way a dimension of his self-understanding (*JP*, IV, 4603).

If the individual is to change in the direction of the ethical, he must come to a moment of self-recognition in which he perceives both the egotistical nature of his relation to the other and the envy and anxiety underlying his temporal happiness.[29] In the moment of self-recognition,

---

[29] It is interesting to note that *Purity of Heart*, which is a discussion of the good, begins with an examination of remorse, repentance, and confession, which Kierkegaard called "eternity's emissaries to man." The point of the chapter is that the individual must experience remorse

one discovers that one's natural disposition toward self-love, or this desire to be concrete, identifiable, and worthy, is not really fulfilled in the state of nature, that one has failed to become an end in either the material or the spiritual sense of that term. This realization may become a condition under which an individual might be motivated to choose himself or to will the existence of a community of ends.[30]

THE CHOICE AND THE PURE HEART

We should note in closing this discussion of Kierkegaard's ethics that the same theme explored and developed in *Works of Love* is also pursued, though from a different perspective, in *Purity of Heart Is to Will One Thing*. Written a year earlier than *Works of Love* and in many ways anticipating the fuller development of Kierkegaard's ethics in that book, *Purity of Heart* investigates the question: What is a good will? Adopting the Kantian strategy of reserving the unconditionally good to a good will, Kierkegaard explores this philosophical commitment in a way that both aligns him with and distinguishes him from the Kantian position. Kierkegaard's presupposition in this book, as the title suggests, is that a pure heart is one that wills only one thing. Moreover, "if it is certain that a man in truth wills one thing, then he wills the Good, for this

---

about his natural state before it is possible for him to consider what he must do in order to be ethically good. This is simply another way of existentially opening up the possibility of the ethical life. In *Either/Or*, despair is the condition of such a possibility; in *Purity of Heart*, it is remorse.

30 It is worth noting here Kierkegaard's unrelenting emphasis on a Socratic approach to self-recognition. This condition cannot in any way be objectively and directly presented or learned; each must discover it for himself. One must see the human condition *for himself and as his own*, and the Socratic approach is in Kierkegaard's view the only way in which this self-recognition can be disclosed. This issue will be explored in full in Chapter Seven.

alone can be willed in this manner" (*PH*, 55); "he who in truth wills only one thing can will only the Good . . ." (*PH*, 53). This seems to be so for Kierkegaard because the good is itself "only a single thing" (*PH*, 54), and since it is only one thing, it must always be willed for its own sake. Thus, if one is to will only one thing, then he must will the good for its own sake.

Much of *Purity of Heart* is devoted to an analysis of what Kierkegaard called double-mindedness, which is any "act of willing the Good which does not will it in truth . . ." (*PH*, 122). The double-minded person deceptively wills the good because he also "wills one thing that is not the Good" (*PH*, 55). The double-minded person, for example, wills "the Good *for the sake of reward, out of fear of punishment, or as a form of self-assertion*" (*PH*, 122; Kierkegaard's italics); hence, "he does not truly will one thing" (*PH*, 55). Since the good "is only a single thing" (*PH*, 54) and can be willed only for its own sake, it is clear that a double-minded person does not have a good will.

Kierkegaard believed furthermore that the good is not only one but also immutable and unchanging (*PH*, 60). Individuals who will the good are themselves unified by the good that they will such that they are not subject to the internal changes and contradictions characterizing persons who will only temporal or natural ends. Persons who only appear to will the good are disunified and at odds with themselves, since they will not one but many different competing and sometimes conflicting ends.[31]

[31] Kierkegaard's formal analysis of the unconditional good as a good will has been meticulously explored by Jeremy D. G. Walker in his *To Will One Thing*. Walker not only examines all the major arguments in *Purity of Heart* for this conception of the good but also suggests the Platonic, Augustinian, and Kantian roots of Kierkegaard's conception of the good. Since Walker has so thoroughly analyzed *Purity of Heart* in these respects, it does not seem necessary to repeat his efforts here. Jeremy Walker, *To Will One Thing: Reflections of Kierkegaard's "Purity of Heart"* (Montreal: McGill-Queen's University Press, 1972). See also Louis Mackey, "The Analysis of the Good in Kierkegaard's

As stated above, *Purity of Heart* is an anticipation of the arguments in *Works of Love*. Nowhere in the books is this more evident than in the last four chapters (*PH*, 177-219), where Kierkegaard identifies willing one thing in truth with choosing oneself. Although the language of *Either/ Or* has been abandoned, the substance of the concept of willing the good remains firmly tied to the concept of choosing oneself. "For as only one thing is necessary, as the theme of the talk is willing one thing: hence the consciousness before God of one's eternal responsibility to be an individual is that one thing necessary" (*PH*, 197-98). Here Kierkegaard explicitly identifies willing one thing with accepting the responsibility to be oneself; the religious component of the good, which is only vaguely hinted at in *Either/Or*, is recognized. Earlier, Kierkegaard maintained that this consciousness of oneself before God "is the fundamental condition for truthfully willing one thing. For he who is not himself a unity is never anything wholly and decisively; he only exists in an external sense . . ." (*PH*, 184). As we have seen, to be a unity is to choose oneself as a synthesis of necessity and possibility, and here Kierkegaard implicitly identifies this existential unity with willing one thing. To will one thing is to will to be oneself.

Purity of Heart also anticipates the social character of willing one thing, although, again, the book is more suggestive than substantive on this issue. This suggestiveness comes in the form of a series of questions. "Do you now live so that you are conscious of yourself as an individual; that in each of your relations in which you come into touch with the outside world, you are conscious of yourself, and that at the same time you are related to yourself as an individual? Even in these relations which we men so beautifully style the most intimate of all, do you remember that you have a still more intimate relation, namely, that in which you as an individual are related to yourself before

---

Purity of Heart," in T. C. Lieh. ed., *Experience, Existence, and the Good* (Carbondale: Southern Illinois University Press, 1961).

God?" (*PH*, 187). In Kierkegaard's view, this consciousness "does not demand that you withdraw from life, from an honorable calling, for a happy domestic life. On the contrary, it is precisely that consciousness which will sustain and clarify and illuminate what you are to do in the relations of life" (*PH*, 197).

Either/Or identifies the highest good as choosing oneself (*E/O*, II, 228-30); *Works of Love* speaks of the highest good as the "God-relationship" (*WL*, 222) and as loving "in truth" (*WL*, 225); and the subject of *Purity of Heart* is the highest good, which is identified as willing one thing in truth. Though the language and emphasis differ in each book, all three aim to show the reader that the highest good is to will to be oneself, which is also to will to exist in a community of ends.

CONCLUSION

Kierkegaard's second literature develops the position that ethics, not politics, is the way to pass beyond the state of nature. Kierkegaard insisted on an ethical rather than a political solution to the problems posed by existing in the state of nature, because the political solution remains within the state of nature and is therefore infected with the disease it intends to cure. For Kierkegaard, an unsurpassable fact about human existence is that the desire of every individual to become a worthy and concrete end in this world throws each of us into a natural and ethically reprehensible opposition to all other selves. Nothing is more certain about human existence than this natural drive to become a self and the social conflict it generates. Moreover, nothing less than a power that can reach the human core can hope to transform the state of nature into a community of ends. All collective solutions miss the mark precisely because they fail to begin with the recognition that each individual exists egotistically and that collective activity can hope to succeed only when it is grounded itself in the ethical obligation of every individual to love himself properly. Kierkegaard would argue that it would be difficult to imagine either Christ or Socrates leading a revolution in the hope of resolving the fundamental dilemma besetting the human community. Both saw the lack of individual human character as the source of injustice and unfairness within the human community, and both viewed the individual as deviously capable of deceiving both himself and the other into believing that this is not really the case. Collective action aimed at the transformation of the human community is a ruse that simultaneously conceals and perpetuates the problem it ostensibly aims to resolve.

For this reason, the individual must always be the beginning point in all considerations directed toward the resolution of human injustice. The individual must not be allowed to escape his private responsibility, which takes the form of willing others as ends, by slipping into some social movement that allows him to remain in ignorance about himself. To love oneself properly is a necessary condition for the existence of a community of ends, and it is precisely this obligation that is concealed, even ridiculed, by the collective approach to the problem. Kierkegaard saw both Socrates' appeal to the infinite and Christ's appeal to a God who places obligations upon us as ways of thrusting an absolute and uncompromisable ethical obligation upon each individual to recognize and to accept his personal responsibility for all other human selves. Before the infinite and before God, all individuals discover themselves to be lacking in this ethical character, which they are obliged to achieve. It is to this religious ground of Kierkegaard's ethics that we now must turn.

CHAPTER FIVE

Ethical Religion

OUR DISCUSSION of Kierkegaard's ethical analysis of the emergence of the modern Danish state will not be complete until we examine the role of religion in Kierkegaard's later thought. The most important preliminary point to be made is that his understanding of religion is both logically and existentially continuous with his ethical theory. Ethical obligation and religious faith are neither separate and logically distinct categories of understanding nor alternative existential life styles but together constitute a unified vision of human destiny.[1]

Some of Kierkegaard's severest criticisms of nineteenth-century Denmark are directed toward the tendency of Danish Christianity to separate itself from the ethical (*JP*, I, 401, 565). Kierkegaard described this Christianity as a religion of grace without law (*JP*, I, 512, 541), a religion fit for children who in their childish immaturity require everything of God and nothing of themselves, a religion that

---

[1] By now we should understand Kierkegaard clearly when he asserts that "salvation . . . is essentially to seek the ethical, which by qualitative dialectic disciplines and limits the individual and establishes his task" (*AR*, 129). Kierkegaard claimed that "the ethical, and the religious which has the ethical in it . . . would only know how to speak of the universal human tasks . . ." (*AR*, 131-32). In fact, the ethical and the religious are so intimately related that Kierkegaard insisted that "the only medium, through which God communicates with 'man,' the only thing he will talk about with man is: the ethical" (*JP*, III, 2823). Moreover, "this is Christianity's intention. It arranges everything ethically" (*JP*, I, 999). If one doubts this observation, "Let him then take and read the New Testament. No one can deny that the ethical teaching presented here is such that it moves the imagination of every man" (*JP*, I, 513). Cf. *JP*, II, 1348.

nurtures and legitimates the natural tendencies that set persons against one another in perpetual private and public conflict. The ethical vision that requires each individual to love his neighbor as himself is regarded not as the substance of religion but as a perverted and impossible ideal that should be rejected in the interest of prudence and common sense (*JFY*, 170). Ideally, Christianity "takes the absolute requirement seriously" and "maintains that man must be altered to suit the requirement . . ." (*JFY*, 170).[2] Modern Danes, however, "cannot get it through their heads what use there is in having an absolute requirement, what good it can do, seeing that no one fulfils it, that the absolute has become the unpractical, the foolish, the ludicrous, that they (in rebellion or in self-conceit) invert the situation, seek the fault in the requirement, and become themselves the requirers, requiring that the requirement be changed" (*JFY*, 168).[3] Whether in rebellion, self-conceit, or self-deception, the ethical vision that obligates individuals to love one another is abandoned, and religion is linked with human activities that are deemed more prudent and commonsensical.

Common sense is the watchword of the modern liberal state. Common sense countenances the advancement of one's economic and political self-interest, and the shrewd man is one whose morality will in no significant manner interfere with his efforts "to succeed, to win advantages in this world" (*JFY*, 169). The protection of individual rights, the pursuit of human equality, the mediation of human con-

[2] Cf. *JP*, I, 485.

[3] Cf. *JFY*, 169: "Along with the growth of common sense there gains ground a certain sort of human lore, the lore concerning what we men actually *are*, or *are* in these times, the moral situation regarded as the product of natural causes, explained by geographical situation, climate, prevailing winds, rainfall, distribution of water, etc. . . . But how men *ought to be*, about God's requirements, about the ideals—about this less and less inquiry is made in proportion as common sense increases" (Kierkegaard's italics).

flict within the economic realm, and the maximization of happiness all require the abandonment of otherworldly religious speculation and moralizing. To be sure, the modern state must guarantee freedom of religion, but the operation of the state should turn on the balancing of political power among all interest groups. Power, not religious moralizing about human nature and human relationships, must be the practical choice of common sense in all matters pertaining to the organization of human life. Where religion does escape the walls of the church, it serves merely to legitimate particular claims to power within the state itself.

We have seen that Kierkegaard was more than simply suspicious of the modern struggle for freedom within the political realm, for he had seen that liberation from king and country entails a more subtle form of slavery, a slavery infinitely more difficult to overcome.

> We are scarcely aware of the fact that it is servitude we are cultivating: we forget it in our zeal to liberate mankind by overthrowing the dictatorships. We are scarcely aware that it is servitude: how could it be that we are slaves in relation to our fellow-men? Yet we are taught quite rightly, that if a man unfree is dependent on anything he is its slave as well; but our liberty-loving time thinks otherwise, and imagines that when one is not dependent on a ruler, then neither is one a slave, that when there is no ruler neither is there any slave. We are scarcely aware that it is servitude we are cultivating, and this is just what makes it so difficult to tear ourselves away from it. Because this bondage consists not in one man oppressing men (for then we should be aware of it) but in this, that men as individuals, forgetting their relation to God, in their relations among themselves become afraid of one another; that the individual becomes afraid of the group, whether few or many, in which also each man

separately is moved by the fear of man, having forgotten God. . . . (*GS*, 134-35)[4]

In Kierkegaard's view, there is a direct correlation between the emergence of this new form of slavery, which is spiritually grounded in egotism, and the substitution of the state and political power for religion and ethics as the chief principles mediating human relations. This slavery can only be transcended by the reintroduction of religion and ethics into the core of all human relations.

In the preceding chapter we explored the arguments that Kierkegaard developed in his second literature for the primacy of the ethical over the political mediation of human relations. In this chapter we shall examine the religious component of this ethical view of human life. A passage from *Christian Discourses* will serve as an introduction to Kierkegaard's conception of the religious in its relation to the ethical.

> The highest that conceivably can be done for a being, higher than any elevation it might be made to attain, is to make it free. It requires omnipotence for this. . . . But if one will think omnipotence, he will perceive that precisely therein must be involved the distinctive characteristic of being able in the expression of omnipotence to withdraw itself again, and that precisely for this cause what came into existence by omnipotence can be independent. Hence it is that the one man cannot quite make the other free, since he who has the power is captive to the possession of it, and therefore gets a wrong relationship to him he would make free. In addition to this, there is in every finite power (talents etc.) a finite selfishness. Only omnipotence is able to withdraw . . . in giving out, and it is this

---

[4] The same problem obtains in private relations as well. "If love were simply and only a relationship between two, then one person would continually be in the other's power. . . . But when there are three [that is, when God is the middle term in all private relations], one person cannot do this" (*WL*, 283).

relationship precisely which constitutes the independence of the recipient. Hence God's omnipotence is His goodness. For goodness means to give out completely, but in such wise that by withdrawing it makes the recipient free. All finite power makes dependent, only omnipotence can make independent. . . . It is but a worthless and worldly conception of the dialectic of power that it is greater and greater in proportion as it can compel and make dependent. No, Socrates understood it better, that the art of power is precisely to make free. But in the relationship between man and man this cannot be done; although it may need to be emphasized again and again that this is the highest thing, yet it is only omnipotence that can truly do it. In case, therefore, a man had outwardly . . . the least self-substantial existence over against God, He could not make him free. Creation out of nothing is thus an expression for being able to make independent. He to whom I absolutely owe all, whereas He with like absoluteness has retained all, precisely He it is that has made me independent. In case for the sake of creating man God Himself lost a little of His power, He could not make man independent. (*CD*, 187n)

We should add straightway that even for Kierkegaard infinite power is not sufficient to make a being free, for there is no reason not to believe that infinite power, left to itself, would be infinitely corrupting. Kierkegaard must add to his description of God the predicate of infinite love and/or goodness in order to account for the possibility of God's creating free beings. The exclusive emphasis on infinite power in this passage turns no doubt on the supposition that a being that is infinite in power has no need to dominate others. But the need to dominate, as we have seen, grows not so much out of the absence of power as it derives from the desire for identity and from the need of the other in order to satisfy that need. Presumably, God has no such need, since he is "pure subjectivity" (*JP*, II, 1449). That is to say, God has no existential need of others, of objectivity, in order to be whatever it is that he is—hence the capacity of God to create free beings. But absence of need of the other and capacity or power to create free beings are still not sufficient to account for the creating, theologically speaking, of such beings. God himself must love the good, which is freedom; thus, it is out of love for the good that God creates free beings.

It is therefore possible for God to create free beings. "But in the relationship between man and man this cannot be done; although it may need to be emphasized again and again that this is the highest thing, yet it is only omnipotence that can truly do it" (*CD*, 187n). The "highest thing" within human relations is the achievement of freedom; yet this goal is impossible without God. That is the crux of the relation between ethics and religion in Kierkegaard's later thought. As we have seen, to become free requires that one be willed by another as an end, that is, as the particular concrete, identifiable, and worthy self that one is by one's necessity. To become free in this sense is to have satisfied one's natural need to become a concrete and worthy self. But to become free also entails willing the other as an end. Thus, freedom is the realization of the moral law to love one's neighbor as oneself, which is the ethical end that constitutes the perfection of human life. Yet, as the passage from *Christian Discourses* suggests, only God, who is infinite in power and love, can make human beings free. Ethics, left to itself, will inevitably fail. The task of religion, then, is to introduce existence before God as a necessary condition for the fulfillment of the ethical end of human life. We shall see in this chapter how love for and obedience to God are set down by Kierkegaard as necessary conditions for the ethical perfection of human life.

It should be clear from the outset of our discussion that Kierkegaard's conception of religion in his later works cannot be separated from ethics.[5] He was unequivocally explicit about this relation. Christianity "must again be proclaimed unconditionally as imitation [of Christ], as law, so Christianity does not become the conjunctive (which sanctifies all our cherished relationships and our earthly fortune and striving) but the disjunctive: to let go of everything . . ." (*JP*, I, 401).[6] Kierkegaard explicitly identified a relation between Christianity and the notion of the ethical absolute, which we examined in the preceding chapter. He insisted that "Christianity did not come into the world (as the parsons snivellingly and falsely introduce it) as an admirable example of the gentle art of consolation —but as *the absolute*. It is out of love God wills it so, but also it is *God* who wills it, and He wills what He will. . . . He will have nothing to do with man's pert inquiry about why and why did Christianity come into the world: it is and shall be the absolute" (*TC*, 66; Kierkegaard's italics). Indeed, to become a Christian is to stand "*before God, as nothing before Him, yet infinitely, absolutely, under obligation*" (*JFY*, 120; Kierkegaard's italics). We are now in a position to explore much more deeply Kierkegaard's reasons for so closely relating his conception of Christianity with his ethical theory.

CONSCIENCE: INDIVIDUATION BEFORE GOD

As we have seen, for Kierkegaard, ethics is the measure of all things human (*JP*, I, 922), and ethical reflection "is in the last analysis decisive" for all human conduct (*JP*, I, 925). The great misfortune besetting nineteenth-century Denmark was, in Kierkegaard's view, the utter demoralization of human life through what we have previously described as the process of modernization.[7] Modernization

[5] This relation between ethics and religion is also stressed in the earlier pseudonymous works, especially in *Concluding Unscientific Postscript*.

[6] Cf. *JP*, I, 906; II, 1803, 1931, 1939.

[7] For a discussion of Danish modernization, see Chapter One.

demoralizes because it subtly subverts individual ethical autonomy through the political and scientific appropriation of the language of ethics. Terms like *freedom, obligation, God, the good, happiness,* and *truth* are either subjected to reflective and analytical scrutiny to the point where they lose their practical power in human affairs, or they are appropriated by the practical politics of democratic liberalism and made to serve the ends of those for whom the establishment of a democratic state is the ultimate ethical and spiritual end. Kierkegaard believed that the absolutizing of the democratic state had so thoroughly transformed the languages of ethics and religion that they were no longer speaking to and through individual consciences but were sounding only in constitutional conventions, political assemblies, and democratic legislation. Kierkegaard never doubted that political activity can bring about needed quantitative reform, but he refused to believe that ethical and religious reform could be achieved through such activity.[8] And, as we have seen, the unfortunate confusion of his own age about categories stemmed from its failure to make this simple distinction.

This confusion of categories itself became the setting of the ethical dilemma of Kierkegaard's age. The immorality of nineteenth-century Denmark cannot be characterized as rule breaking. Rather, as individuals succumbed to the lure of "the crowd,"[9] they surrendered the clear sense of

[8] "For it is falsehood these times of ours have discovered when they conceived that reforms issue from numbers . . . the crowd, or from the 'highly esteemed' and 'highly esteemed cultured public'—I mean religious reforms, for in the matter of street-lighting and the service of transportation the reform most likely issues from the public; but that a religious reformation might issue from the public is a falsehood, a seditious falsehood" (*FSE*, 44). As we have seen in Chapter Two, Kierkegaard denied the popular Hegelian notion that participation in the state makes one good.

[9] The mode of subjectivity appropriate to the "crowd" or the "public" is aesthetic as opposed to the ethical-religious mode of subjectivity characterizing individual *existence*. This aesthetic subjectivity is acquisi-

personal ethical nature and destiny that makes ethical behavior a human possibility. Thus, identification with the crowd, with its pretensions to ethical sanctity and religious legitimation, is the ethical failure of the individual in nineteenth-century Denmark. Kierkegaard described identification with the crowd as a "ruinous evasion of oneself" (*PH*, 185), as ethical "defiance" (*PH*, 190), as "indolence" and self-indulgence (*JP*, II, 2010). The crowd itself is a "primal forest of evasion" (*PH*, 186), and to identify with it is to sink into the baseness of animality (*JP*, II, 2050), where it is the species and not the particular member of the species that is significant. For Kierkegaard, then, modernization itself is an unethical event, given its tendency to anesthetize and to control the individual's conscience in the interest of the whole. "The sum and substance of the public life is actually, from first to last, lack of conscience" (*JP*, III, 2955).

We must not forget that Kierkegaard was working not as a sociologist like Max Weber, who was interested in mapping the social infrastructure of the modern state. Nor was he a social psychologist, like Philip Slater, who is interested primarily in exposing the loneliness and boredom that modernization generates in the individual psyche.[10] These are legitimate, though from Kierkegaard's point of view aesthetic, approaches to modernization and do not concern Kierkegaard the ethicist, who denounced the entire enterprise as a fraud and a deception.

The preeminent task for any ethicist, according to Kierkegaard, is to confront the individual with the truth about his ethical nature and destiny. If self-deception and self-evasiveness are the real principles or meanings of modern-

---

tive and dominating in nature, and it is cultivated by the liberal spirit that pervades modern Danish life. The conflict between these two modes of subjectivity is discussed in detail in Chapter Seven.

[10] Philip Slater, *The Pursuit of Loneliness* (Boston: Beacon Press, 1970). We have already observed the distinctly moral character of Kierkegaard's psychology in Chapter Four.

ization, then one must attack it by exposing it to the individual as related to his fundamental dishonesty about himself. This Socratic task of educating the individual about himself is, of course, the task that Kierkegaard set for himself,[11] and it is in this context that Kierkegaard understood the significance of religion. We have already discussed Kierkegaard's view that religion had assumed a fundamentally ideological character in the modernizing period of Danish history. Both Mynster and Grundtvig had allied religion with class and political interests and needs so that religion had become a sacred canopy for vying political and class interests. From Kierkegaard's perspective, the consequences of this perversion of religion are profound. Only through religion can the individual be properly educated and continually nurtured with respect to his ethical nature.[12] He will be lost to the lure of the crowd unless he "learns in the reality of religion and before God to be content with himself, and learns, instead of dominating others, to dominate himself, content as priest to be his own audience, and as author his own reader . . ." (PA, 57). In Kierkegaard's Denmark, however, this "religious singling out of the individual before God is ignored" (PA, 53); consequently, the individual remains ignorant of his real nature and destiny as a human self. So sure was Kierkegaard of the power of true religion that he claimed that it alone is "the source and origin of all individuality" (WL, 253).

The purpose of religion, then, is "first and foremost to regard the mass individually, every one by himself as the

[11] We shall explore in detail the relation between this task and Kierkegaard's literary style in Chapter Seven.

[12] The restoring of the true nature and role of religion is therefore a necessary condition for the resuscitation of individual ethical autonomy. For Kierkegaard, of course, the two tasks are inseparable, and in Chapter Seven we shall explore the complexities and subtleties of Kierkegaard's style as an attempt to achieve both ends simultaneously. What is crucial here, however, is an investigation of the role that aesthetic religion plays in the weakening of the ethical conscience.

173

single individual [*den Enkelte*]" (*WL*, 139).[13] Religion fragments the crowd into a collection of individuals by establishing a God-man relationship whose "main point . . . is specifically to preserve [the] individuality" of every single person (*JP*, II, 1451). The essence of this concept of the individual should not be difficult to grasp: to be an individual in Kierkegaard's sense is simply to be related to oneself before God (*PH*, 187). "[B]*efore God* to be oneself" (*WL*, 253; Kierkegaard's italics). One can legitimately regard this call as the watchword of all religion that is genuinely concerned with God's purpose for human beings. We have already seen that, according to Kierkegaard, the ethical task of the individual is to synthesize the finite and infinite dimensions of his self into a concrete and coherent unity—that is, to relate himself to himself. Here Kierkegaard claims that the task of religion is to individuate, to separate, each person from the anesthetizing routine and security of the crowd by setting him before God. So closely does Kierkegaard link becoming oneself with existing before God that he claims that "when one denies God, he does God no harm but destroys himself; when one mocks God, he mocks himself" (*JP*, II, 1349). Self-destruction, then, is the price one pays for remaining securely locked in the political, economic, and cultural interstices of the crowd.

One may legitimately raise questions about the meaning or sense of this notion of existing before God. Indeed, one might justifiably propose that the crucial distinctions and similarities between the religions of the world can be accounted for in terms of the various ways in which the God-relationship is symbolically understood and ritually expressed. The sense of Kierkegaard's notion of the God-relationship can be glimpsed in his description of its purpose as bringing individuals to a consciousness of themselves as distinct from the crowd. This claim is itself prob-

13 Cf. *JP*, II, 2030: "But for God, the infinite spirit, all these millions who have lived and are living do not form a mass—he sees only single individuals."

lematic, however, since there are a variety of ways in which individuals might perceive themselves as distinct from the social groups in which they live. In fact, it would not be difficult to discover in human history religious justifications for almost every form of antisocial and extrasocial behavior. Left undeveloped, the claim that religion individuates is too ambiguous and vague to be very helpful in disclosing the nature and purpose of religion.

Fortunately, Kierkegaard did not abandon the discussion of religion in his second literature to such vague meanderings. Central to the sharpening of this notion of existing before God is the concept of conscience. According to Kierkegaard, "to relate oneself to God is precisely to have a conscience. Therefore a man could not have anything on his conscience if God were not present, for the relationship between the individual and God, the God-relationship, is conscience; for that reason it is dreadful to have even the least thing on one's conscience, because one is immediately involved in the infinite gravity of God" (*WL*, 143). Conscience is a "privy confident which follows man everywhere [and] is in league with God . . ." (*FSE*, 19). Metaphors abound in Kierkegaard's references to conscience. It is not only a "privy confident" that is in league with God but also God's voice "forever installed with its eternal right to be the exclusive voice" (*PH*, 186). Again, "in the conscience it is God who looks upon a human being so that the human being now must look to him in all things. In this way God educates" (*WL*, 346). As if to underscore the priority of conscience as the source of the God-man relationship, Kierkegaard claimed, "In the conscience—there God has the power. Let a man have all the power in the world—God is still the master there" (*JP*, IV, 4431).

For Kierkegaard, then, the God-relationship is a relation of conscience. It would be mistaken, however, to interpret this position as a clear and unambiguous example of the divine command theory of ethics or of ethical heteronomy. In Kierkegaard's view, God does not function as an ethical

175

authority who commands individuals through their consciences to obey specific and particular social conventions, rules, and moral laws. It is also important to dismiss the notion that for Kierkegaard conscience is the internal appropriation of social norms, rules, and practices that are culturally legitimated by grounding them in the will of God. Nor was Kierkegaard following the romantics, who portrayed conscience as natural and socially uncorrupted feelings and inclinations urging the individual to perform the good. Rather, for Kierkegaard, conscience is a call to actualize one's selfhood or one's individuality, and it is through conscience that God appeals to each person to become the individual that he authentically can become.

Throughout his second literature, Kierkegaard repeated this notion of conscience as the means to individuation. "Eternity seizes each one by the strong arm of conscience, holding him as an individual. Eternity sets him apart with his conscience" (*PH*, 192). Within "the temporal order conscience is prepared to make each person into an individual" (*PH*, 186). Moreover, conscience is inescapable, for "it continues to belong to him, or more accurately, he continues to belong to it" (*PH*, 186). Unlike the parson who speaks to the masses "in general terms," conscience speaks "solely and alone about thee, to thee, in thee" (*FSE*, 20). In fact, so closely does Kierkegaard identify conscience with the process of individuation that he asserts that to become an individual "is to have and to will to have a conscience" (*JFY*, 109). As an individual, "you and conscience are one" (*PH*, 189).

Those who have a conscience in Kierkegaard's sense have been individuated by seeking to become existentially a unity of particularity and universality. That Kierkegaard conceived of the development of conscience in religious terms is very significant, because his insistence on the religious character of conscience is based on the view that conscience and self-consciousness are necessarily related by virtue of their mutual dependence upon the self's social nature. Without the other, the self can neither be self-conscious nor have a conscience. Kierkegaard never expressed this relation so succinctly, though the implication is clear in a journal entry. "After all, to have a conscience before men does not reach much farther than having a conscience (con-sciousness) with men. Thus, even taking an oath—look more closely and you will see what creeps in: Well, I'll swear in the same way, with the same implications, as all the others. How many people really have a conscience with God?" (*JP*, I, 688). If the self is constituted by the other in its being and its self-consciousness, then it is no less reasonable to conclude that its conscience is also formed by the other. Such a view means that conscience may have both egotistic and nonegotistic expressions. Within the state of nature, the consciences of those who possess power and those who strive for power will be formed in the social struggle for dominance. By the same token, the consciences of those who are enslaved and do not actively seek power will be shaped by envy, resentment, and anxiety. Kierkegaard would argue, then, that within nature conscience can take both ideological and resentful forms.

In these cases, conscience is alloyed with either self-interest or envy and resentment and therefore cannot be regarded as a legitimate expression of the good. As Kierkegaard explains, "Just as gold in its original state is found alloyed with all sorts of worthless and miscellaneous components, so it is with conscience in its immediate state, which contains elements which are the very opposite of the conscience. Herein lies the truth of what Hegel says about conscience being a form of the evil" (*JP*, I, 684). Though Kierkegaard agreed with Hegel that immediate expressions of conscience are evil,[14] he took exception to Hegel's way of mediating this immediate conscience. Kierkegaard imputed to Hegel the view that the immediate

[14] G.F.W. Hegel, *Philosophy of Right*, trans. and ed. T. M. Knox (Oxford: Oxford University Press, 1967), pp. 86-104.

conscience erroneously pursuing its private or public vision of the good will be corrected by recognition of the moral correctness of the conscience of the whole expressed in and through the state. Kierkegaard, of course, strenuously resisted this notion, arguing that the crowd is "from first to last, lack of conscience" (*JP*, III, 2955), and cannot by definition be a guide to anyone's conscience. "It is absolutely true," Kierkegaard observed, "isolated subjectivity as the age understands it is evil, but restoration to health by means of 'objectivity' is not a hair better. Subjectivity is the way of deliverance—that is, God, as the infinitely compelling subjectivity" (*JP*, IV, 4555). The possibility of conscience must lie in a subjectivity that transcends the crowd or the public and can therefore be known only by the individual. To be self-conscious before the other is, then, to have a conscience before and with the other, which is to have no conscience at all.

At this point, Kierkegaard's question about how many persons really have a conscience with God becomes pertinent. Kierkegaard agreed with Hegel that the immediacy of conscience must be mediated and that the mediation is social in nature. He accepted the unsurpassability of the social nature of the self in its constitution, self-consciousness, and conscience. But he diverged from Hegel at the point where the state is stressed as the mediating entity. As completely as can the individual, the collective can be the expression of egotism, and it is therefore ethically imprudent to rely upon either the subjectivity of the other or the objectivity of the state in order to overcome the immediate conscience. Rather, the individual cannot escape the immediate modes of self-consciousness and conscience until he is "known by God in the possibility of conscience" (*JP*, III, 3214). Wherever conscience is present, there also exists "consciousness of being an individual [which] is the primary consciousness in a man, which is his eternal consciousness" (*PH*, 193). To be known by God is the ground of both one's eternal consciousness and one's conscience; in other words, "God's shared knowledge [*Guds Samviden*] is the stabilization, the confirmation" of consciousness and conscience (*JP*, III, 3214). Personhood "is an individual determinateness confirmed by being known by God in the possibility of conscience" (*JP*, III, 3214).

What is crucial here is Kierkegaard's claim that the religious relation is a social relationship in which the individual comes to know both himself and his ethical obligation as they are known by God. The individual's self-consciousness and conscience are grounded in the divine other. To be known by God, then, is both to discover oneself as a synthesis of particularity and universality and to know oneself as ethically obliged to actualize that synthesis existentially. This knowledge of oneself and one's obligation—conscience—is made possible in a religious relation with the divine other. It is important to remember that this religious relation is social in nature. And since love is the ground of all social relations, the religious relation must also be grounded in love. In examining conscience, then, we have returned to our discussion of love, and we must now explore the nature of the love that grounds the religious relation.

LOVE FOR GOD

Just as love is the foundation of Kierkegaard's ethical theory, it is also the center of his conception of religion. In fact, for Kierkegaard, both self-love and love for one's neighbor are grounded in love for God. Kierkegaard argued that one can love neither oneself nor one's neighbor without loving God; conversely, love for God makes possible both self-love and love for the neighbor. Kierkegaard's conception of religion necessarily unites the self, the neighbor, and God in the power of love. It is the egotism and the nobility of love that make possible such an intimate and complex unity. And the many often con-

179

flicting dimensions of this unity are paralleled by the simplicity and the power of the love that permeates it.

Caution is necessary in approaching Kierkegaard's conception of religion. Kierkegaard does not, for example, conceive of love for God as a mystical or otherworldly activity that expresses itself in a rejection of the aesthetic and ethical relations that constitute the individual's finite and temporal existence.[15] Indeed, love for God expresses itself

[15] Such a claim immediately brings to mind the early pseudonymous work, *Fear and Trembling*, as well as late works like *Judge for Yourselves*, the articles published in 1854-1855 in *The Fatherland* and *The Instant*, and the accompanying journal entries from the same period. These writings all proclaim the heterogeneity of the Christian who loves God. Johannes de Silentio writes of Abraham's teleological suspension of the ethical, and Kierkegaard himself in his late works frequently speaks of the necessity for the Christian to hate the world. In Chapter Seven, in the section entitled "Direct Communication as Direct Attack," I argue that these late writings must be understood polemically. They reflect both Kierkegaard's frustration at failing Socratically to awaken Christendom and his calculated strategy to launch a direct attack to make clearer the implications of his earlier indirect communications. As for *Fear and Trembling*, I am convinced that it must also be read polemically, although I do not believe that we can leave the matter so simply in the lap of polemics. It is well known that this book is an attack on the nineteenth-century philosophical ploy to reduce religion to morality. However, more needs to be said about its positive implications for understanding the relation of ethics and religion. I am convinced that Kierkegaard's remark in *For Self-Examination* that *Fear and Trembling* attempts to illuminate God's attack on selfishness is extremely significant for getting at the positive implications of *Fear and Trembling* for our understanding of the relation of religion and ethics:

here we have an example of what it is to die (*afdø*). For not to see his wish, his hope, fulfilled, to be deprived of the object of his desire, his beloved—that may be very painful, selfishness is wounded, but that does not necessarily mean to die. No, but to be obliged to deprive oneself of the object of desire of which one is in possession—that is to wound selfishness at the root, as in the case of Abraham, when God required that Abraham himself, that he himself—frightful!—with his own hand—oh, horror of madness!—must sacrifice Isaac, the gift so long and so lovingly expected, and the gift of God, for which Abraham conceived that he must give thanks his whole life long and

in and explains both the egotistical and ethical character of human relationships. Kierkegaard would have us look deeper into the finite and temporal dimension of human life in order both to understand and to express love for God. His discussion of love is reflexive in the sense that he begins with its immediate expression as egotism and then moves reflexively or dialectically to its mediate expression in the ethical-religious sphere of life. Kierkegaard's ethical-religious conception of love mediates egotism by explaining it as an immediate and contradictory expression of life. It is immediate because it is prior to reflection; it is contradictory because it culminates in its own negation, both materially and psychologically. We have already seen the ethical dimensions of this mediation of egotism. In discussing Kierkegaard's conception of religious love as love for God, we must consider the relation of love for God and love for neighbor, the relation of self-love and love for God, and, finally, the relation of religious love and conscience.

Love for God and Love for Neighbor

By so closely linking love for God with love for neighbor, Kierkegaard raises the issue whether neighbor love exhausts the material content of love for God. The referential status of the term *love* in these two phrases comes into question, for it is not immediately clear in Kierkegaard's thought whether the term in both phrases is univocal or equivocal in its function. Within Christian theology there has always existed a strong overlap, especially in the Protestant tradition, between love for God and love for neighbor. This overlap, it has been argued, sug-

---

would never be able to give thanks enough—Isaac, his only son, the son of his old age, and the son of promise. (*FSE*, 98)

It is possible to argue that the teleological suspension of the ethical in *Fear and Trembling* refers not to the negation of ethics but to the purgation of its religiously unmediated erotic dimension. If such an interpretation, which obviously cannot be developed here, stands up, then *Fear and Trembling* need no longer be understood as a radical negation of ethics and community.

gests that the principle of neighbor love is all the content that love for God possesses. Kierkegaard himself often appears to take this position in his later works. In discussing the character of love for God, Kierkegaard approvingly quotes I John 4:20: "He who does not love his brother whom he has seen, cannot love God whom he has not seen" (*WL*, 158). He also criticizes those who want "to love only the unseen or that which one has not seen" (*WL*, 159), arguing that such love is unreal, illusory, and an escape from the demands of neighbor love (*WL*, 158-59).[16] It is in fact a misrepresentation of God to perceive him as one who has his own interests (*WL*, 158) and causes (*JP*, II, 1449)[17] that ought to be served by human love. Moreover, "God is too exalted to be able to accept a man's love directly . . ." (*WL*, 158).[18] Kierkegaard admitted that it "may seem so natural that in order to love God one must raise oneself to heaven where God dwells: the best and surest way, however, to love God is to remain on the earth" (*CD*, 197). Christianity has correctly expressed this perception of proper love for God in its principle that "to love human beings is to love God and to love God is to love human beings . . ." (*WL*, 351-52). In other words, "Love to God and love to neighbor are like two doors that open simultaneously, so that it is impossible to open one without opening the other, and impossible to shut one without also shutting the other" (*JP*, III, 2434). These passages reflect a strong and persistent tendency in the second literature to give a univocal interpretation to the concepts of neighbor love and love for God; that is, the material content of the

---

[16] Cf. *WL*, 159: "The most dangerous of all escapes as far as love is concerned is wanting to love only the unseen. . . ."

[17] Cf. *JP*, II, 1450.

[18] Cf. *WL*, 159: "God is not a part of existence in such a way that he demands his share for himself; he demands everything, but as you bring it you immediately receive, if I may put it this way, an endorsement designating where it should be forwarded, for God demands nothing for himself, although he demands everything from you."

religious love for God appears to be reducible to the ethical obligation to love one's neighbor.

Kierkegaard's position, however, is not quite as unambiguous as it may appear. Other passages imply an equivocal function for the term *love*. For example, "everyone as an individual, before he relates himself in love to a beloved, to a friend, to lovers, to contemporaries, must first relate himself to God and the God-demand" (*WL*, 117). The character of this relationship to God, moreover, could never qualify ethically sound human relationships, for "a man should love God in unconditional *obedience* and love him in *adoration*. It would be ungodliness if any man dared love himself in this way, or dared love another person in this way, or dared to let another person love him in this way" (*WL*, 36; Kierkegaard's italics).[19] Kierkegaard seems to claim that love for God is in some sense prior to love for neighbor and that this love is distinguished from love for neighbor by God's claim to unconditional obedience and adoration. Thus, Kierkegaard seems also to insist on an equivocal meaning for the concept of love in these two modes of loving.

This tension within Kierkegaard's second literature presents us with at least two interpretations. We may simply claim that Kierkegaard developed two separate and incompatible positions with respect to this issue and carelessly fell into a contradiction. Kierkegaard did in fact believe that love for God entails unconditional obedience and adoration and must therefore be distinguished from neighbor love, since no one human being ought ever to love another in this manner. This religious love for God is not an end in itself, however, but the necessary grounding of neighbor love. That is to say, love for God is a necessary condition for making correct ethical judgments about one's relation to one's neighbor. Only in this sense may one legitimately

19 Cf. *CD*, 335: God "demands obedience, unconditonal obedience. If thou are not obedient in everything unconditionally, then thou loves Him not. . . ."

speak about love for God. The distinctness of love for God is preserved while at the same time it is given an essentially ethical value in Kierkegaard's ethics of neighbor love.

Love for God and Self-Love

The second of the two central issues that come up in this investigation of Kierkegaard's conception of religious love concerns the relation between self-love and love for God. We have seen how individuals are necessarily social-ized by self-love, and we have also seen that self-love socializes individuals in both egotistic and nonegotistic ways. Religion introduces a third party into the social character of the self. Religiously conceived, the self is con-stituted not only by its relation to another self but also by its relation to God. Kierkegaard conceived of the God-rela-tionship as one in which the self stands related to God, and he did not forget that since the self is social in nature, it is not possible for it to relate to God without simultaneously relating to others. Thus, the God-relationship can never preclude one's relation with another self, and one's rela-tion with the other may be either prudentially or ethically defined. A religious dimension may be discerned within both social modes of selfhood. Moreover, the character of the religious dimension of the self will not be inconsistent with the character of one's relation to the other. It is there-fore possible to discover in religion both egotistic and non-egotistic God-relationships.

Kierkegaard's later works are filled with references to the egotistic complexion of much of nineteenth-century religion.[20] In this sort of religion God is more often than not conceived as a divine ally whose purpose is to facilitate human self-development as egotistically conceived, that is, by assisting individuals to secure satisfaction of personal

[20] For example, "We human beings have now ventured almost ego-tistically to take over Christianity. We do not bear in mind (what An-selm and the ancients remembered) that Christianity is God's invention and, in a good sense, God's interest" (*JP*, I, 532).

184

material and psychological needs. The Danish religious imagination had been captured by the subtle and pervasive undercurrent of egotism that grounded the social, political, and economic life of this turbulent period. Kierkegaard believed that the marriage of liberalism and cultural Christianity in nineteenth-century Denmark falsely authorized and legitimated an essentially egotistic way of life. To speak of loving God in this manner is neither more nor less than selfishly to exploit religion for one's private ends. Moreover, this egotistic religion actually prevents the attainment of knowledge of oneself as a synthesis of particularity and universality. Those who love God egotistically cannot possibly know and respect the other as a synthesis of particularity and universality. And because one's knowledge of and respect for the other is based on self-knowledge and self-respect, a religion, that fails to cultivate love for the other as an end simultaneously obscures a knowledge of and respect for oneself as a synthesis of particularity and universality.

Even though Kierkegaard rejected egotistic religious consciousness on the grounds that it is a specious mode of self-consciousness, he nevertheless maintained that religious love for God is grounded in human need. The "prime condition at the basis of a man's love for God is to understand effectually that one needs God, to love Him simply because one needs Him. The man who most deeply recognizes his need of God loves Him most truly. Thou shalt not presume to love God for God's sake; thou shalt eternally understand that thy life's welfare eternally depends upon this, and for this reason thou shalt love Him" (*CD*, 197). This passage implies that life's welfare depends upon the divine satisfaction of some need, the provision of something that is lacking. Psychologically and materially, we, for example, speak of the need for affection, food, and shelter. Satisfaction of these sorts of needs is not what should motivate love for God, however. To speak of God in these terms amounts to placing the con-

185

cept under aesthetic categories, and Kierkegaard obviously had no such intentions. The need referred to here is an ontological one. In Kierkegaard's view, each individual within nature lacks selfhood. This existential incompleteness is itself based on a lack of self-knowledge and eventuates in lack of self-respect. The need for God is rooted in this incompleteness, and, in Kierkegaard's view, it is by means of love for God, properly conceived, that the individual overcomes this lack of self-knowledge.

Kierkegaard, then, maintained that love for God is a necessary condition for overcoming one's existential incompleteness and corresponding lack of self-respect: the "discovery of God is an *inland journey*" in which one discovers oneself (*JP*, II, 1451; Kierkegaard's italics). It is in this sense that love for God and self-love are identified in Kierkegaard's thought. To love God is the necessary condition for coming to know oneself and for realizing the possibility of achieving self-completeness and self-respect. In order to make this claim clearer, we must first briefly look at Kierkegaard's conception of God.

According to Kierkegaard, it is mistaken to conceive of God as a being who identifies with historical plans, projects, and goals that are established by human reason. In fact, history is a function of the spiritual desire to become concrete, identifiable, and worthy. The self strives to overcome its subjective incompleteness by objectively constituting itself in and through the completion of historical projects. God, on the other hand, is not ontologically incomplete and therefore has no need to objectify and complete himself in and through the historical realization of divine and/or human projects of any sort. It is in fact a degradation of God's majesty to conceive of him as one who makes use of individuals in the completion of goals that he has set for himself in and through history (*JP*, II, 1449). God is essentially "pure subjectivity, has nothing of objective being in himself which could occasion that he has or must have intentions. Whatever is not purely transparent

186

subjectivity has at some point or other in its objective being a relationship to an environment, a relationship to an other and therefore has, must have, intentions. Only that which infinitely subjectively has its subjectivity infinitely in its power as subject, only that has no intentions" (*JP*, II, 1449). Simply summarized, God cannot possibly enter egotistically into human history, given the ontological completeness of his being.

Moreover, it is mistaken to identify any human activity as essentially a means to God's end (*JP*, II, 1449).[21] Kierkegaard is quite straightforward in claiming that "God does not have a cause in the sense that there is something which has not been fought out, something of concern to him but of doubtful outcome in the cause of the Almighty One . . ." (*JP*, II, 1431). Kierkegaard admitted that "this idea has in its time inspired many people and made it easy for them to sacrifice everything" (*JP*, II, 1431). In fact, this is "the idea which Christianity, especially Protestantism, has pursued, and thereby God has fallen from being the infinite Majesty, who humanly speaking has no cause, to the level of a Majesty who [like a king] must make use of men" (*JP*, II, 1447). To believe that God has a cause in this sense is "childlike," both "a flight of fancy" and "a frightful conceit" (*JP*, II, 1431).

It does not follow from Kierkegaard's theological view that God is either uninterested in or ignorant of human history. It merely follows that one may not identify human and divine purposivity. God's infinite majesty and pure subjectivity enable him to transcend the realm of becoming and its essentially egotistic nature. It also follows that religiously selfish self-love is both fanciful and conceited in providentially interpreting its own historical activity. Precisely God's transcendence over the realm of becoming

21 Cf. *JP*, I, 532: "We forget that egotism [*Egoisme*] is one thing and I-ness or subjectivity [*Egoitet*] is another, and that although God is infinitely far from being an egotist, he nevertheless is infinite subjectivity (he cannot be otherwise)."

is the point of reference that makes possible the ethical-religious transformation of the self's egotistic nature.

We have seen that Kierkegaard conceived of the self as desire to be concrete, identifiable, and worthy and that this desire is the essential motivation of all human activity.[22] When the self enters into relations with others, it is for the purpose of satisfying this ontological desire. Given the finite dimension of the self, that desire always expresses itself concretely; and given the necessity of the other, it always expresses itself socially. Thus, concrete social relations are the medium through which the desire to be a self is expressed. Neither finitude nor the other transforms or alters this desire; they are both merely necessary conditions for its fulfillment. All social relations within nature, then, can only be expressions of the desire to become a self. Kierkegaard never avoided these ontological facts about the self or regarded them as essentially perverse. Without ethically condemning the self, Kierkegaard recognized that unmediated desire culminates in its own contradiction: so long as the self remains within nature, it can never become a concrete, identifiable, and worthy self.

Mediation of this desire, in Kierkegaard's view, cannot be achieved by reason, because the self is desire that precedes reason. The self both expresses and seeks to satisfy itself as desire in a finite and historical situation, and it also requires the other as a necessary condition for its fulfillment. This matrix of desire, finitude, and otherness constitutes a reality that is both prior to and inaccessible to reason. This reality is prior to reason in the sense that desire, finitude, and the other are not ontologically constituted by reason. It is inaccessible to reason in the sense that reason is powerless to transform it.

Since this reality is unsurpassable, the issue becomes one of transforming its egotistic expression so that it ceases to be self-contradicting. As we have seen, Kierkegaard

[22] See Chapter Three for a discussion of the self as desire to be concrete, identifiable, and worthy.

believed that what is required for this transformation is the ethical disposition to will the good of all. Although a necessary condition for the actualization of the desire to be a self, this ethical disposition is itself problematic. How is it possible for such a disposition to transform the self as it is egotistically constituted in nature? In Kierkegaard's view, the social character of the self cannot be ignored at this point. Since the individual is always existentially constituted by the social relations into which he enters, he must enter a relationship that existentially makes possible such a disposition—namely, the God-relationship. It is this religious relation that makes possible existentially the constitution of an ethical disposition.

Now we are in a position to bring together Kierkegaard's conception of God as pure subjectivity and his conception of the self as social in nature in order to illuminate the assertion that self-love and love for God are univocal. In the social relationship with God, each individual is constituted as a synthesis of particularity and universality, and he discovers that his self is not an abstract self but a concrete and identifiable reality that is loved and valued by God as intrinsically good. The desire to be identified as a concrete and worthy self is satisfied in this relationship. Because God does not enter egotistically into a relation with the individual—since God has no particular historical ends of his own—the individual discovers in the religious relation no threat to the intrinsic value and goodness of his particularity. The unintentional character of God's nature also makes it impossible for the individual to enter egotistically into this relation. One can relate to God egotistically only under the condition that it is possible to identify one's own ends as also God's ends. But since God is pure subjectivity and wills for himself no particular ends, it is impossible for individuals privately or publicly to enter egotistically into a genuine relationship with God. In this social relation, God wills particularity as an end and as a good in itself, but never as his end or his good.

It is important to recognize that God's willing one's particularity as an end is not sufficient for it to become an end, for all others must will it as well. Even though one experiences God as love, one's particularity may still be coerced by others. God's love is psychologically, but not materially, satisfying, and therefore the desire to be a self is not completely realized.

It is also crucial to note that God's affirmation of particularity as intrinsically good and valuable has universal applicability. To be loved by God is to be affirmed as intrinsically worthy as the particular being that one is. But God wills all particularities as goods in themselves. Since no particularity is his own, all can be willed equally. This universal willing of the goodness of particularity is the ground of the universal dimension of selfhood, which is established in the form of the law to love others as one loves oneself.[23] It is precisely in my relationship to God as one who affirms my particularity and demands my obedience to the law that I am constituted as a self that is a synthesis of particularity and universality. Indeed, it is only in such a relationship that this sort of self can come into existence. No other social relation can provide logically and existentially the ground of my obligation to the other. To love God is to enter the universal dimension of selfhood.

The individual is, as we have seen, constituted by the sorts of social relations into which he enters. Thus, to enter into a relationship with a God who makes demands is existentially to be constituted as a self defined by the law. And to be defined by the law is not to cease to love one's particularity but to love one's neighbor's particularity as one loves one's own. Finally, to love one's neighbor in-

[23] The religious justification of the view that the recognition of the value of one's own particularity entails the affirmation of the value of the particularity of all other selves is clearly stated in *Works of Love*: "To have individuality is to believe in the individuality of every other person; for individuality is not mine but is God's gift by which he gives me being and gives being to all, gives being to everything" (*WL*, 253).

volves not only accepting the intrinsic value of his particularity but also teaching him to love God and his fellows.

Love for God and the Maieutic

Kierkegaard occasionally described the God-relationship in Socratic terms. For example, "God is like a maieutic in relation to the learner" (*JP*, II, 1450). God is a Socratic teacher who draws out of the individual an understanding of himself that is not possible outside of this religious relation. To emphasize the maieutic character of the relationship, Kierkegaard described God as an "examiner" who "has not the slightest thing in common with one who, humanly speaking, has a cause" (*JP*, II, 1447). As pure subjectivity, God seeks not providentially to constitute human history but maieutically to make possible the individual's discovery of himself as a synthesis of particularity and universality. There is, then, an epistemological dimension to the individual's love for God in that it makes self-knowledge possible. One learns something about oneself in the religious relation that one cannot possibly learn in religiously unmediated relations with others.

It is important to note that the character of this self-knowledge is not strictly propositional, for knowing oneself as a synthesis of particularity and universality is commensurate with existentially striving to become that self. The knowledge of which Kierkegaard speaks is a transforming knowledge in the sense that it is not possible to separate knowing and being. One cannot know something without simultaneously being, or at least striving to become, what one knows. Kierkegaard captured the transforming character of self-knowledge in the term *obedience*: "There is no question of the capacity of the teacher to instruct, for God is the Teacher. Only this one thing is taught: obedience" (*GS*, 57). One learns in the religious relation that one ought to love one's neighbor as one loves oneself. To know oneself as one is known by God is to discover oneself in a relationship in which one is required by God to keep the

191

law.[24] Obedience to the law is the existential content of the religious relationship with God. Thus, to know oneself as one is known by God is existentially transforming in the sense that it is a knowledge that entails the ethical act of loving one's neighbor as one loves oneself.

Conclusion

We are now in a position to understand the manner in which religion, understood as existing before God, grounds Kierkegaard's conception of the ethical life. In order to fulfill the moral law to love one's neighbor as one loves oneself, it is necessary to exist before God in such a manner that one comes to understand that one is both loved by God and obligated by God to love one's neighbor. Existing before God is a necessary condition for both recognizing one's concrete self as worthy and acknowledging and accepting one's ethical responsibility for others. Kierkegaard recognized that the individual's coming to exist before God in this manner would necessarily set him in a polemical relation to his contemporary Denmark. In Kierkegaard's view, to strive to become a Christian in Denmark was to set oneself, on religious grounds, in opposition to the modern state. It is, then, important for us to turn to an investigation of the polemical character of Kierkegaard's understanding of religion.

[24] Despite Kierkegaard's statements, he must admit that God is intentional at least in the abstract sense that he wills that all persons should keep the law. The particular content of willing the law depends, of course, upon the concrete situation in which the individual exists. It is in this sense that the individual's intention is different from God's, since God is not a subject existing in a particular situation.

CHAPTER SIX

Polemical Religion

IN TURNING to a discussion of Kierkegaard's polemical religion, we must focus on what Walter Lowrie called Kierkegaard's "attack upon the established order" (AC, xiii). As we have seen, the religiously legitimated modern liberal state is what Kierkegaard meant by the term "Christendom." It is important to note that Kierkegaard used a religious term to identify modernization and the new established order. Religious leaders like Mynster and Grundtvig tended to identify modernization as essentially religious, because they viewed it as either the will of God or an ethical achievement. Kierkegaard correctly perceived that religious legitimation of modernization in these terms requires an equally and essentially religious attack. Such an attack must necessarily include a redefinition of key Christian categories, a demonstration of the polemical character of the Christian life lived under these categories, and the discovery of a way to reintroduce Christianity into a culture that is already intimately, though mistakenly, familiar with it. The substance of Kierkegaard's religiously polemical analysis of Christendom is determined by this three-pronged task.

In discussing one or more of these aspects of his polemical analysis of modern Denmark, Kierkegaard often described his task as "re-introducing Christianity into Christendom." The polemical force of this phrase has not been fully understood. The idea of reintroducing Christianity into Denmark involves not simply correcting misconceptions that Danes have about the nature of Christianity but also challenging both the secular and the ecclesiastical structure of modernization. Theoretical evaluation of religious beliefs is a necessary dimension of this reintroduction; equally crucial, however, is practical reorientation of the way in which Danes live. We have seen how the individual is psychologically, ethically, and politically reconstituted by the structures of modernization, and it is precisely this religiously legitimated reconstitution of the self that Kierkegaard intended polemically to assault. The polemical character of Kierkegaard's later books is not directed simply to a theological rescue of Christian categories from Martensen, Mynster, and Grundtvig. It is true, of course, that one must know what Christianity is in order to become a Christian, and Kierkegaard attended to this question throughout his second literature. But he carefully avoided making intellectual elucidation of Christianity an end in itself. Rather, the intellectual activity is a means to the end of existentially becoming a Christian. This existential transformation of the self by the process of becoming religious has already been made clear in the discussion of Kierkegaard's ethical religion. What remains to be explored is the polemical dimension of Kierkegaard's conception of becoming a Christian.

In turning to this task, we shall range throughout the second literature but pay special attention to *Training in Christianity*.[1] In this book Kierkegaard most successfully developed the polemical character of Christianity on the theoretical and practical levels of activity.[2] We shall also inves-

---

[1] The Hongs' new translation of *Indøvelse i Christendom* for Princeton University Press's edition of *Kierkegaard's Writings* is entitled *Practice in Christianity*. Since the new translation is not yet available, the earlier Lowrie translation is quoted here.

[2] Whereas Kierkegaard's polemical attack on Christendom is of an indirect nature in the second literature up through the publication of *Training in Christianity*, it becomes direct after 1850 in *For Self-Examination*, the posthumously published *Judge for Yourselves*, and *Attack upon Christendom*. Much of the material in these three works is lifted directly from his pre-1850 journals. Thus, the direct attack was being developed privately in Kierkegaard's journals while he was publicly carrying out his indirect polemic from 1846 to 1850. The sup-

tigate his redefinition of key Christian categories and the polemical character of the life that is lived under these categories. The issue of communicating Christianity to those who are already intimately familiar with it is the subject of the following chapter.[3]

CHRISTIANITY AND CHRISTENDOM

In a journal entry from late 1849 Kierkegaard referred to his "latest books"—which surely include *Training in Christianity*, *The Sickness unto Death*, *Works of Love*, and *The Present Age*—as a "judgment upon Christendom" (*JP*, VI, 6317). Kierkegaard was not always this clear in his journals and elsewhere about the relation of his books to the established order. Concerning *Training in Christianity* in particular, Kierkegaard seems to have regarded it with some ambiguity. At times, he clearly conceived of it as representing an attack on the established order, speaking of it as partially carrying out his task "to oppose the reformers" (*JP*, VI, 6721). This 1851 entry is supported four years later in *Attack upon Christendom*, where he affirmed that "*Training in Christianity* is, Christianly, an attack upon the Establishment . . ." (*AC*, 55). Other journal entries, however, refer to this book as a defense of the present order of society. Kierkegaard observed in 1850, "It is tragic that the established order (the majority of those in it, at least) know so little about governing that they promptly mistake *Practice in Christianity* for the opposition, although it is as different as possible from that, indeed, is diametrically opposed to that" (*JP*, VI, 6699). And in an 1854 journal entry

pression of this journal material until 1850 is significant and will be discussed in Chapter Seven.

[3] *Training in Christianity* takes up in serious detail the issue of communication; see pp. 132-45. The point is made here in order to show the completeness of this book as an attempt to reintroduce Christianity into Christendom. More than any other in the second literature, this book captures the spirit and intent of Kierkegaard's Christianity.

Kierkegaard tried to account for his disagreements with Bishop Mynster as fundamentally concerned with "how the established should be defended . . . I was in agreement with him that it had to be defended as vigorously as possible" (*JP*, VI, 6854).

Kierkegaard was not unaware of the ambiguous character of *Training in Christianity*, and in an 1850 journal entry he admitted that "no one can see directly whether it is primarily radical or primarily conservative, whether it is an attack on the established or in fact a defense" (*JP*, VI, 6690). This ambiguity stems in part from Kierkegaard's ironic delight in making the meanings and purposes of his books difficult to comprehend. From Kierkegaard's perspective, of course, there is a legitimate Socratic justification for this ambiguity. A "consideration of piety towards the old bishop . . ." (*AC*, 55) also motivated this ambiguity. In fact, however, *Training in Christianity* and most of the other books in Kierkegaard's second literature were intended simultaneously to defend and to attack the established order. Kierkegaard conceived of himself as a defender of the established order to the extent that it represents a link with a past that had an ethical and religious understanding of self and society. But to the extent that the ethical and religious beliefs and practices of the established order had been deformed into a "monstrous illusion" (*AC*, 139)[4] and their meanings distorted by reformers' attempts to identify the new political and scientific order with the essential content of the Christian religion,[5] the religion of the established order must itself become an object of attack. Kierkegaard lamented that "Christianity continues to survive after it has been made into the opposite of what it is to be Christian (especially in Protestantism, especially in Denmark)" (*JP*, I, 405).

That Christianity had been converted into the opposite

---

[4] Cf. *JP*, I, 389, 516; V, 6070; VI, 6228, 6780.

[5] In one of his three prefaces to *On Authority and Revelation*, Kierkegaard identifies politics as a "surrogate for religiousness" (*AR*, lvi).

of its essential nature stemmed in part from the Danes' convenient neglect of the truth that the "navigation marks" that point toward the intelligibility and practicality of Christianity are all located in the individual's ethical resolve and struggle to love others as he loves himself. With the abrogation of this task by modernization's emphasis on the collective, Christianity disappears and is replaced by an established Christendom. This is confusing, according to Kierkegaard, "because it is really impossible to be a Christian in this way, since an establishment as the true arena for religiousness gives all Christian qualifications as unchristian, conciliatory perspective upon the temporal; whereas the true Christian perspective for every Christian qualification is polemically oriented toward finitude . . ." (*ANOL*, 34).[6] From Kierkegaard's perspective, "Christianity relates to the single individual [*den Enkelte*] and exists only where it is primitive. Nowadays we have gotten the whole thing turned around: Christianity is supposed to be related to the race. . . . From this one can also see to what extent the Grundtvigian position misses the point of Christianity" (*JP*, II, 1646). Kierkegaard attempted to defend Christianity "against the numerical, parties, etc. by means of ideals" (*JP*, VI, 6778). The "ideals," of course, are related to the ethical life as a resolve to love others as one loves oneself. Without such an existential foundation, Christianity quickly loses its polemical thrust, becomes established, and provides a "conciliatory perspective upon the temporal."[7]

---

6 Cf. *JP*, I, 510: "The deepest confusion of Christianity is the profane, frivolous way in which Christianity has been identified with the world and all are made Christians as a matter of course—in short, the greatest deterioration has been the concept 'Christendom,' which in our time is simply synonymous with mankind."

7 Gregor Malantschuk has nicely expressed this relationship between the disappearance of Christianity as essentially related to the individual and its appropriation by the established order. "The polemical stance of Christianity toward the world is forgotten. In this way the tension between the single individual and the world vanishes. The result is the idolization of the *status quo*, leading to relaxation and to excluding

Replacing the polemical relationship between Christianity and society with a conciliatory one has, as we have seen in Chapter Two, the effect of religiously legitimating the existing social order. In Christendom, Christianity has "become the conjunctive (which sanctifies all our cherished relationships and our earthly fortune and striving) . . ." (*JP*, I, 401). In fact, being a Christian in Christendom is "plain and simple conformity" (*JP*, I, 409). This conjoining of the Christian and the secular in such a way that the latter is legitimated by the former is nowhere more apparent than among the Grundtvigians, who had come to represent "precisely what Christ came to supersede" (*JP*, VI, 6876). Symbolic of the Grundtvigians' religious capitulation to the established order are their positions on marriage, the struggle for political freedom, and Danish destiny. Their simple-minded identifications of the Peasant party's struggle for political freedom with Christian hope (*JP*, VI, 6735), of marriage with religious obligation (*JP*, VI, 6876), and of Danish destiny with divine providence (*JP*, VI, 6876) are distortions of the polemical nature of Christianity. Through identification of the essence of Christianity with innovative political movements and with democratic social institutions, the dialectical elements of Christianity, which is identified with the eternal and ideal component of the self, is lost, and religion is domesticated by those very phenomena that should legitimately be the object of a religious polemic.[8]

---

internal struggle within oneself and external struggle with the world. . . ." See Malantschuk's background essay for the Hongs' translation of *ANOL*, 129.

[8] "Everything has become reversed. There was a time when the world wanted to fight—then Christianity fought. Now the world is in fraudulent possession of Christianity, and its tactics therefore are: with all its power, at any price, to prevent a showdown. It is as when a swindler has misgivings—if the matter goes to court, he has lost—and therefore all his tactics are directed toward keeping it from going to court. In the realm of the spirit this is far easier than in the actuality of civil life, for the technique consists in continually counterfeiting the

Kierkegaard portrayed Christianity within Christendom as being "served by human fear, by mediocrity, by temporal interests . . ." (*AC*, 102) and as knitting "natural intimate relationships more intimately together . . ." (*JP*, III, 2893). Those living in modern Denmark are made to feel spiritually secure and comfortable in the private and public relationships constituted by the new order. Having been taken over egotistically (*JP*, I, 532), Christianity is "employed as a stimulant oriented toward enjoying life. . . . Therefore, Christendom is: refined life-enjoyment, dreadfully refined, for in paganism's enjoyment there was always a bad conscience. But in Christendom an attempt has been made to eliminate conscience by introducing atonement in the following manner: You have a God who has atoned—now you may really enjoy life" (*JP*, I, 534). But, Kierkegaard asks, "where have they found the text which is now orthodox Christianity—that Christianity is the enjoyment of life (which both Mynster and Grundtvig have, each in his own way)?" (*JP*, II, 1860).[9] Kierkegaard accused both Grundtvig and Mynster of converting Christianity in Denmark into something that "might thoroughly please and appeal to the natural man, almost as if it were his own invention . . ." (*AC*, 150).[10] Kierkegaard was not surprised that the natural man found this sort of Christianity so appealing, for it maintains that "the enjoyment of this life becomes the worship of God" (*JP*, VI, 6876).

Nevertheless, this sacralization of the natural order cannot be so complete as to succeed in banishing pain and death, although it can provide sedatives for both. When psychological pain and misfortune occur, Christianity is

---

other party's position so that to a certain extent they are saying the same thing—but good God, then we are agreed!" (*JP*, I, 516). "Here Christian scholarship has its place. Christian scholarship is the human race's prodigious invention to defend itself against the N[ew]. T[estament]., to ensure that one can continue to be a Christian without letting the N[ew].T[estament]. come too close" (*JP*, III, 2872).

9 Cf. *JP*, VI, 6845.   10 Cf. *AC*, 122.

applied as a consoling assurance "that in earthly respects things will surely get better, etc." (*JP*, I, 541).[11] Even in the most completely sacralized of natural orders "there is still the question of eternal life [and] a prudent man does something about it for safety's sake; he insures himself and pays a certain percentage a year" (*JP*, I, 516). Protestants could not buy indulgences in nineteenth-century Denmark, but they could conceive of religion as a means toward immortal life. It is clear, then, that from Kierkegaard's perspective Danish Christianity, and Protestantism in particular, had become a cultural sedative that tranquilized the pains of misfortune and the fear of death and legitimated the human quest for power, authority, and comfort. Kierkegaard found it difficult to avoid drawing the conclusion that Danish Christianity had fallen victim to the natural egotistic impulses of the self in the new liberal order.

As we have seen in the first three chapters, Danish life assumed the liberal spirit of the democratic revolutions engulfing western Europe. Its economic, political, and social institutions, as well as its culture and science, were all essentially formed by the beliefs and practices of liberalism. As we have also seen, the rise of liberalism in Denmark took a religious form and justification. Both Mynster and Grundtvig chose, though for different reasons, to represent the new order as spiritually consistent with the highest ideals and values of the Christian religion. This lending of religious authority to the new order was aided by the transformation of the essential character of Christianity by philosophy, science, and biblical scholarship. Kierkegaard argued that all three modes of reflection had shifted the subjective task of becoming a Christian as the highest human achievement to an objective one of understanding the nature of Christianity. Once Christianity had been removed from the arena of subjectivity, it could more easily be appropriated by the new liberal order. This "shifting of the

[11] Cf. *JP*, I, 516, III, 2920; *FSE*, 99.

essentially Christian back into the esthetic" (*JP*, VI, 6466)[12] had, in Kierkegaard's view, two significant consequences. First, "Christianity has halted in secular prudence which says goodbye to ideals and regards striving after them as fanaticism. What we are living in is this secular prudence. But this secular prudence finds it very advantageous to have the religious represented solely by the Sunday ceremony" (*JP*, VI, 6694). The ideal of constituting a community of ends through the ethical resolve of each individual is regarded as a delusion, something utterly impossible to achieve. The species should aim at what is more probable, namely, the creation of a society in which individuals are allowed by right to pursue their private and public interests through the mechanisms of political and economic activity. The second consequence of shifting the essentially Christian back into the aesthetic derives from the first. Kierkegaard claimed, "The defect in the life of Christendom is neither in the form of government nor in anything of this sort—no, the error is that people on the various levels of that life live too remote from one another. In the absence of close acquaintance with others, everything becomes too much a matter of comparison and too rigid in its comparativeness" (*JP*, I, 377).[13] The prudential pursuit of one's private and public interests sets one in competitive and comparative opposition to others. We have seen that envy, fear, and anxiety are the prominent psychological features of such a society. Ironically, Christianity in this situation becomes the ally of prudence and social stratification and comparison. From Kierkegaard's perspective, it is

12 Cf. *JP*, VI, 6475.

13 Cf. *ANOL*, 91: "In Christendom life is completely unchristian also in terms of what it means to live together with the common man and what this involves. . . . It is unchristian and wicked to base the state on a substructure of men who are totally ignorant and excluded from personal association—even though on Sunday there are touching sermons about loving one's neighbor."

difficult to imagine how Christianity could have been converted into anything more completely its opposite.

The practical consequences of this coalescing of "the finite and the infinite, the eternal and the temporal, the highest and the lowest" (*JFY*, 138) are most tragic. The task for anyone in nineteenth-century Denmark who is seriously intent upon reconstituting this distinction will entail both a theoretical and practical separation of Christianity from Christendom. More specifically, the task will include the resuscitation of Christianity as a religion that is polemically ordered against the new liberal order.

THE OFFENSE AND CHRISTENDOM

One of the central themes of *Training in Christianity* is that the "possibility of offense then becomes that which is to judge Christendom" (*JP*, I, 691). As an offense to reason, Christianity can become an instrument of attack against Christendom. Kierkegaard's opposition to a reliance upon reason in matters of faith is well known. The pseudonymous authorship may be understood as a sustained objection to the attempt of Danish Hegelians to provide a theoretical defense of the truth of the Christian faith. Kierkegaard's criticism of this rationalizing strategy includes criticism of the standard proofs for the existence of God. In both *Philosophical Fragments* and *Concluding Unscientific Postscript*, Kierkegaard argued for the logical impossibility of proving the existence of God. This objection to one of the main components of rationalist theology appears again in the early pages of *Training in Christianity*. Here, however, the proof to which Kierkegaard objects is a so-called historical proof for the divinity of Christ. Grundtvig maintained in his *Nordic Mythology* that the "unmatched and blessed consequences" of Christ's life over the past 1,800 years constituted proof of Christ's divinity.[14]

14 *N.F.S. Grundtvig*, trans. Johannes Knudsen, Enok Mortensen, and Ernest D. Nielsen, ed. with an intro. by Johannes Knudsen (Philadelphia: Fortress Press, 1976), p. 23.

For Kierkegaard, however, that "He was God, that He will come again in glory—this is considerably beyond the comprehension of history . . ." (*TC*, 34).[15] Kierkegaard found it "strange" that people are "eager by the help of history, by considering the consequences of His life, to reach by logical inference the *ergo, ergo* He was God—and faith's contention is exactly the opposite . . ." (*TC*, 32).[16] Kierkegaard never for a moment saw such reasoning to be anything but the logical absurdity it is. "Is it possible to conceive of a more foolish contradiction than that of wanting to prove . . . that a definite individual man is God?" (*TC*, 28). The only aspect of Jesus' claim to divinity that can be proved is that it "is at variance with reason" (*TC*, 29). A logical consideration of the consequences of Jesus' life leads to the sole conclusion that "Jesus Christ was a great man, perhaps the greatest of all; but that He was . . . God—nay, stop there! The conclusion shall by God's help never be drawn" (*TC*, 29). In fact, the claim that a particular man is God is so repellant to reason that one must either believe it or be offended by it. Kierkegaard claimed that "the God-Man exists only for faith . . . the possibility of offense is just the repellant force by which faith comes into existence—if one does not choose instead to be offended" (*TC*, 122). In Kierkegaard's view, "one can 'know' nothing at all about 'Christ'; He is the paradox, the object of faith, existing only for faith" (*TC*, 28).[17] Faith, and not knowledge, is the way toward Christ. Being a Christian is not a life style based on propositions that can be rationally deduced and defended. The way of Christianity is a subjective and ethical path, not an objective and theoretical one.

From this small sampling of the early pages of *Training*

---

15 Cf. *TC*, 26: "He is not, and for nobody is He willing to be, one about whom we have learned to know something merely from history. . . for from history we can learn to know nothing about Him, because there is absolutely nothing that can be 'known' about Him."

16 Cf. *TC*, 29.   17 Cf. *JP*, II, 1635.

in Christianity it is easy to see that in one sense the book may be understood as a continuation of Kierkegaard's earlier criticisms of the theological and philosophical pretensions to prove the existence of God. More broadly, these pages should be seen as an extension of the earlier pseudonyms' criticisms of the reflective and rationalizing spirit of the age. Philosophical reasoning in the Danish Hegelian mode and theologies of history of the Grundtvigian sort are rejected outright. But although Kierkegaard brings into question the logical soundness of these modes of reasoning about religion and objects to their tendency to remove religion from the subjective realm, he is more concerned in *Training in Christianity* with what might be called the ideological character of reasoning about religion. In his view, practical reasoning is always egotistic when it is not disciplined by ethics and religion, and when reasoning is elevated to supremacy in practical matters, human beings will always choose to behave in such a manner as to maximize their own private interests. In this respect, the modern liberal state, which cultivates and legitimates the egotistic dimension of the self, represents the triumph of reasoning with regard to the practical question of how one shall live. "When a man so lives that he recognizes no higher standard for his life than that provided by the understanding, his whole life is relativity, labour for a relative end; he undertakes nothing unless the understanding, by the aid of probability, can somehow make clear to him the profit and loss and give answer to the question, why and wherefore" (*TC*, 118).[18] When human reasoning falls so com-

[18] Under the influence of this egotistic rationality, the Christianity of Christendom loses those category distinctions that prevent conceptually the subjection of Christianity to reason. "Our Christianity therefore, the Christianity of 'Christendom' . . . takes away from Christianity the offense, the paradox, etc., and instead of that introduces, probability, the plainly comprehensible. That is, it transforms Christianity into something entirely different from what it is in the New Testament, yea, into exactly the opposite; and this is the Christianity of 'Christendom,' of us men" (*AC*, 162-63). The Christianity of Christendom is categorical-

pletely under the sway of egotism, it is unreasonable to expect that it will develop politically or religiously in a non-egotistic manner. Kierkegaard's purpose in criticizing the glorification of reason in science, philosophy, and politics was not to glorify an untrammeled subjectivity so much as it was to counter polemically the rise of an egotistic rationality in these dimensions of the modern state. *Training in Christianity* is especially crucial in this respect; nowhere else does Kierkegaard more persistently attack the egotistic character of theological reasoning in nineteenth-century Denmark.

The proof for the divinity of Christ is a good example of theological egotism. Kierkegaard argued that this proof is unsound and invalid because it is based on the erroneous premise that the claim that Christ will return was made by God. In fact, the claim that Christ will return was uttered by a mere man; at least, this is how humans must perceive it. "From the seat of His glory [God] has not spoken one word. Therefore it is Jesus Christ in His humiliation, in the state of humiliation, who spoke these words" (*TC*, 26). About Christ's coming again in glory, "nothing can be known; in the strictest sense, it can only be believed" (*TC*, 27). In Kierkegaard's view, it is untruthful to represent Christ as essentially different from what he was when he spoke these words (*TC*, 27). It pleases God to assume "an incognito impenetrable to the most intimate observation," namely, the incognito of a lowly, humble, and human servant (*TC*, 27-28). When "somebody repeats exactly the words he uttered, but makes it appear as if it was God that said them, the thing becomes untrue, for it is untrue that He uttered these words" (*TC*, 28). Kierkegaard warned that "history must not incommode itself to do Him

---

ly transformed by egotistic and prudential reasoning. In the first part of *Judge for Yourselves*, Kierkegaard returns to this discussion of reason, emphasizing its prudential character in the modern state and Christianity's complete capitulation to egotistic reasoning (*JFY*, 113-57). Cf. *JP* I, 536.

justice, nor must we with impious heedlessness fancy presumptuously that we know as a matter of course who He was. For no one *knows* that, and he who *believes* it must be contemporary with Him in His humiliation." (*TC*, 36; Kierkegaard's italics).[19] The claim to *know* the identity of Christ is revealed as an attempt to identify Christ with something knowable, such as national identity, political ideology, or private and class interests. Kierkegaard saw the claim to *knowledge* of Christ's identity as a theological disguise covering the attempt of egotistic rationality to achieve supremacy in the modern state.[20]

Who, then, is guilty of claiming to know the true identity of Christ, and who speaks for him in his glory? From Kierkegaard's perspective, it is those who want to prove the divinity of Christ from the historical consequences of his life. These same persons see the present moment of Danish history as a consequence of the life of Christ, and the greatness of this moment they in turn interpret as evidence for the deity of Christ. For Kierkegaard, "these brilliant consequences are surely not His return in glory! But this is really about what they mean by it: it appears here again that they make out Christ to be a man *whose return in glory can be nothing more than the consequences of His life in history*—whereas Christ's return in glory is something entirely different, something that is believed" (*TC*, 33; my italics). In fact, Christendom "would like to inherit Him and His great name, to gain advantage from the immense consequences of his life, coming pretty close to appropriating these consequences as its own meritorious achievement and making us believe that Christendom is Christ" (*TC*, 109).[21] Christendom, Kierkegaard argued, speaks not only

[19] The identity of belief and contemporaneity will be taken up later in this chapter.

[20] Kierkegaard elucidated this point through a series of examples in *TC*, 44-56.

[21] Cf. *JP*, I, 516: "These 1,800 years are so far from being a proof of the truth of Christianity that one could . . . rather convert it to an

for but also *as* Christ in his glory; it claims that the "veritable Expected One will therefore appear totally different; He will come as the most glorious flower and the highest unfolding of the established order" (*TC*, 50). This is the sum and substance of the historical proof for the divinity of Christ. Such reasoning is clearly ideological by any standard of judgment, and it can begin to make sense only if one circumvents the obviously scandalous and paradoxical character of the claim of a man to be God. Those who embrace such a claim blindly ignore its logic because they are intent on securing a divine legitimation for their own misperception of the logic of history as it works itself out in the modern liberal state.

Kierkegaard believed that theological egotism is "the invention of the indolent worldly mind, which would put itself at rest and imagine that all is sheer security and peace, that now we have reached the highest attainment" (*TC*, 89). This ideological perversion of religion is accomplished by overlooking the origin and truth of religious consciousness. "But that the established order has become something divine or is regarded as divine constitutes a falsehood which is made possible only by ignoring its origin. When a *bourgeois* has become a nobleman he is eager to make every effort to have his *vita ante acta* forgotten. So it is with the established order. It began with the God-relationship of the individual; but now this must be forgotten, the bridge hewn down, the established order deified" (*TC*, 89). The secret of Christendom's success is the establishment of "a complete commensurability as between the outward and the inward—so complete that the inward [has] fallen out. It is just by this one can recognize that the established order is on the point of deifying itself . . ." (*TC*, 89).

Inwardness is the consciousness before God of one's ethical obligation to will the existence of a community of ends.

---

argument against Christianity—that providence has allowed Christianity to sink so far down in an illusion.

When this consciousness is allowed to languish, the ethical and religious distinction between the inward and the outward itself languishes, with the result that the individual comes to identify himself exclusively with the external political, economic, and social relations in which he exists. The priests of modernization perceived these historical changes as religious in nature. Kierkegaard understood more clearly that in the end Christendom "secularizes also the God-relationship" by insisting that "this shall be congruous with a certain relativity, not essentially different from one's station in life . . ." (*TC*, 92).[22] Kierkegaard anticipated that Christendom, as the religious form of the modern state, would itself quickly expire once the modern state learned to stand on its own without the prop of divine legitimation. Christendom is a quick step into a totally secularized order in which atheism and identification of the internal and the external prevail.

Kierkegaard also understood that in order to combat this attempt to "abolish God, and through fear of men cow the individual into a mouse's hole" (*TC*, 91), it would be necessary to revive the God-relationship in its pristine form.[23] Only the God-relationship can "provoke the established order out of its self-complacency" (*TC*, 91) and put it in suspense (*TC*, 92). To counter the challenge of the established order, Kierkegaard hoped to reintroduce Christianity into Christendom through the categories of offense and contemporaneity.

With the possible exception of Tertullian, the Christian church has never known such a radical advocate of the logical and ethical disparity of the relation of faith and

[22] Cf. *TC*, 92: "The deification of the established order is the secularization of everything."

[23] Cf. *TC*, 92: "The established order desires to be totalitarian, recognizing nothing over it, but having under it every individual, and judging every individual who is integrated in it." Moreover, "he who disparages such an established order is regarded as one who makes himself more than man, and people are offended in him, although in reality he merely makes God God and man man" (*TC*, 93).

reason. But there can be no doubt that historical circumstances led Kierkegaard to emphasize the offensive character of Christianity. The appearance of the modern state in a religious form, Christendom, represented for Kierkegaard the complete identification of the sacred and the profane, the inward and the outward, religion and secularity, faith and reason. Such a commensurability between heaven and earth entails, as we have seen, the dissolving of the ontological and ethical distinctions between these disparate phenomena. It is this homogeneity, historically reaching its apex in Christendom, that led Kierkegaard to emphasize the offensive character of the Christian religion. Indeed, Christianity, as Kierkegaard understood it, derives its offensive and scandalous character in part simply from its refusal to recognize the ethical legitimacy of Christendom.[24]

In his second literature, however, Kierkegaard vacillated between conceiving of the category of offense polemically and normalizing it as an essential category of Christianity for all historical epochs. This vacillation is problematic for determining Kierkegaard's view about the possibility of giving a universal definition of Christianity. It is nevertheless correct to say that Kierkegaard was not cutting a polemical Christianity out of whole cloth, for it is abundantly clear that polemical elements inhere in Christianity's proto-biblical and biblical forms. It is also possible to see that there is no ambiguity in Kierkegaard's insistence that the category of offense be considered a primary one for developing a normative understanding of Christianity in Christendom. This insistence is based on Kierkegaard's perception of Christendom as the homogenizing of the sacred and the profane and his recognition of the necessity to demonstrate that such a complete identification of these two

[24] The historical nature of Christendom is not clear in Kierkegaard's journals. Sometimes it appears as an isolated and historically discontinuous phenomenon; at other times, it appears as historically continuous, beginning almost with Christianity's origins and culminating in the nineteenth century. For examples of this ambiguity, see the "Christendom" entries in *JP*, I.

modes of being is both logically mistaken and ethically wrong.

Kierkegaard's decision to intensify the polemical dimension of Christianity through the category of offense was intended to make it *rationally* inaccessible to thinkers like Martensen and Heiberg who tried to demonstrate a speculative unity of Christianity and philosophy and to social innovators like Grundtvig who attempted rationally to justify contemporary historical trends as providentially significant. The emphasis on offense also had the practical intent of presenting an ethical interpretation of Christianity that would provide both a challenge and an alternative to the interpretation of the triumph of liberalism as an ethical imperative.[25] Finally, the offensive character of Christianity would have the psychological impact of shaking Danes out of their complacent and self-assured life styles in the new liberal order.

It is important to note that the category of offense is anchored in the person of Christ. It is Christ who offends the contemporary Dane. More specifically, he offends by his actions and his claims about both himself and the ethical life. Christ is offensive if only because he "makes the truth a heart-felt matter of inwardness" (*TC*, 88). To make truth a matter of inwardness for Christ is to present him as one who is "unwilling to subordinate himself to the established order" and as one who "protests against its claim to be the truth . . ." (*TC*, 87). Christ is also a "teacher" who "insists upon inwardness in contrast with all empty externalism, a teacher who transforms externalism into inwardness" (*TC*, 87). The teacher of inwardness espouses the individual's task of willing the existence of a community of ends as the highest ethical responsibility. Christ both represents this inwardness and attempts dialectically to teach others to live

[25] We examined the ethical dimension of Kierkegaard's religion in Chapter Five. We shall return to this issue below when we take up the discussion of contemporaneity, in which we shall assess the relationship between Kierkegaard's ethical and polemical religion.

in the same manner. This ethical stance of inwardness inevitably establishes a "collision of pietism with the established order." (*TC*, 87). In Christendom, then, even simple piety is regarded as an offense. That an individual would lay claim to a private inwardness that establishes a psychological and especially an ethical and spiritual reality distinct from the conventional and public mode of being constituted by the modern state is a matter of offense. The public order is threatened not only by the inaccessibility of this private inwardness but also by its claim to constitute an ethical and spiritual challenge to the prevailing view of ethical goodness and happiness implied in modern liberalism.

Christ most essentially offends modern ethical and religious sensibilities not as a teacher or as a pious man but as the God-Man. Kierkegaard's discussion of the *"possibility of the essential offence"* (*TC*, 96; Kierkegaard's italics) in *Training in Christianity* constitutes a return to the theme of the *sensu strictissimo* paradox developed earlier in *Philosophical Fragments* and *Concluding Unscientific Postscript*.[26] In these two works, Kierkegaard speaks of the nature of Christ as a synthesis of the temporal and the eternal that offends human reason's principle of contradiction as an inviolate rule of thought. Kierkegaard continued to emphasize this dimension of the *sensu strictissimo* paradox in *Training in Christianity*, though he added that the "essential offence" is also constituted by Christ the man's exaltation and humiliation. The essential offense depends on two contradictory facts: that *"an individual man speaks or acts as though he were God"* (*TC*, 96; Kierkegaard's italics) and that the *"one who gives Himself out to be God shows Himself to be the poor and suffering and at last the impotent man"* (*TC*, 105; Kierkegaard's italics).

In *Philosophical Fragments* and *Concluding Unscientific*

[26] *CUP*, 188ff.; *PF*, 61ff.; Per Lønning, "Kierkegaard's Paradox," in Steffen Steffensen and Hans Sorensen, eds., *Kierkegaard Symposium* (Copenhagen: Munksgaard, 1955), pp. 156-65.

Postscript, the contradiction appears as a bold dogmatic proposition: "Jesus is God." It is the contradictory character of the proposition that is offensive. In *Training in Christianity*, however, the offense is not so exclusively propositional in nature; rather, the words and actions of a human being constitute the offense. Here Jesus is presented as a man "who is like other men, [and] in whom there is nothing *directly* to be seen . . ."; nevertheless, he acts "in a way suggestive of being God" (*TC*, 99; Kierkegaard's italics). This man claims to perform miracles and to forgive sins, neither denies nor affirms that he is the Expected One referred to by John the Baptist, and symbolizes through the breaking of bread and the drinking of wine God's presence in him. These words and actions signify Jesus' exaltation, "that this individual man makes himself out to be more than man, makes himself out to be something pretty near to being God" (*TC*, 99). Kierkegaard correctly saw that such behavior, which is suggestive of self-exaltation, must be offensive to reason since it implies a claim that can in no way be rationally justified. Moreover, Kierkegaard correctly argued that contemporaneity with Christ in no way relieves the tension of the offense, since miracles and prophecies are compelling only if one already believes that this man is in some sense divine.

Part of the problem with Christendom is that it has mitigated the offense by virtue of two thousand years of specious philosophical and historical justifications of the divinity of Christ. The result, according to Kierkegaard, has been the creation of a "fantastic picture of Christ" (*TC*, 103) as one who unambiguously presented himself and was unambiguously received as God. Kierkegaard correctly labeled this conception of Christ as paganism (*TC*, 103) and claimed that Christendom had become pagan by virtue of its mitigation of the offensive character of Christ's actions and words. A proper reading of the New Testament, Kierkegaard argued, would quickly and decisively disabuse Christendom of this foolishness, because the offense is a central theme of the book. Even though one may find direct references to Christ as an offense to reason in only a few passages,[27] "the offence was present every instant when He (the God-Man), this individual man, spoke or acted in a way suggesting the qualification God" (*TC*, 103).

One might argue that Kierkegaard could have an easily, if not more appropriately, emphasized Christ as teacher, healer, and apocalyptic prophet. There is, in fact, more evidence in the New Testament for these views of Christ than for the view of him as an offense to reason. But this objection rests on the failure to recognize Kierkegaard's historical situation, which both motivated and justifies his emphasis. When Kierkegaard represents Christ as essentially an offense to reason, he does not conceive of the conflict in abstract terms, as have most of the scholars who attempt to interpret Kierkegaard's thought.[28] Kierkegaard was not conducting a philosophical debate *in vacuo* about the nature of Christ and the relation of reason and faith. On the contrary, he was struggling to prevent the ideological use of the name of Christ in the name of specific modes of reasoning by speculative theologians and social innovators in nineteenth-century Denmark. It is mistaken to assume that Kierkegaard was as politically unengaged as most theologians and philosophers have thought themselves to be. His purpose was to place the actions and words of Christ on such a paradoxical footing that all attempts rationally to comprehend and justify them for speculative and practical purposes would be rendered impossible. His radical emphasis on the self-exaltation of the man Jesus rendered the Christian religion useless to those committed to the modernization of Denmark.

It is also crucial to recognize that Kierkegaard's emphasis on Jesus' self-exaltation was intended to emphasize individual inwardness as a necessary condition for the presence of

[27] Matthew 11:6; Luke 7:23; John 6:61.
[28] With the exception of German idealism, the historical context of Kierkegaard's thought has been little studied.

213

God in history. Kierkegaard insisted that the "God-Man is not the unity of God and mankind. Such terminology exhibits the profundity of optical illusion. The God-Man is the unity of God and an individual man" (*TC*, 84). This claim offends those who argue either for the speculative unity of the God-Man (*TC*, 22, 123) or the unity of God and man through the historical developments of Western culture. In Kierkegaard's view, God acts neither through his eternal unity with the species nor through its historical developments but through those who choose as individuals to exist contemporaneously with him. This conception of the unity of the divine and the human lays the responsibility for fulfilling the divine imperative to love all as one loves oneself upon individuals rather than upon revolutionary groups and political assemblies. The emphasis on the first aspect of the essential offense—the exaltation of an individual man as God—was intended, then, to make Christianity inaccessible to those theological modes of reasoning in nineteenth-century Denmark that in Kierkegaard's view functioned practically to legitimate the emergence of the modern liberal state. Kierkegaard's emphasis on this aspect of the offense was also intended to identify the individual as the potential locus of the expression of the divine.

In the second form of the strict offense, "one is not offended by the claim that He is God, but by the observation that God is this man . . ." (*TC*, 105). Again, relying upon scant biblical evidence, Kierkegaard argued that Christ's contemporaries were equally offended by his lowly origin and his powerlessness and humiliation before the political authorities in Jerusalem. Those who interpret the emergence of the modern state as symbolic of the continuing triumph of Christ completely ignore his powerlessness, poverty, humiliation, and death. Kierkegaard, however, chose to emphasize this aspect of Christ's life, because he perceived the contemporary religious vision of the world as completely lacking in any serious conception of suffering.

214

Kierkegaard countered this view by arguing that if one can love Christ only in his exaltation, "It signifies that [one] can love the truth . . . only when it has conquered, when it is in possession of and surrounded by power and honour and glory" (*TC*, 154). "In Christendom they preach perpetually about what happened . . . after Christ's death, how He triumphed, and how His disciples made a triumphal conquest of the whole world—in short, one hears only sermons which might properly end with Hurrah! rather than with Amen" (*TC*, 109). Such a conception of Christ can be maintained only at the expense of forgetting that Christ endured "every possible sort of derision and insult," stood impotent and powerless before political authority, and suffered an ignominious death as a criminal (*TC*, 108). According to Kierkegaard, the apostle Peter stood offended by precisely this powerlessness and humiliation. "That a man falls into the power of his enemies is human. But that He whose almighty hand had wrought signs and wonders now stands impotent and paralysed—precisely this it is that brings Peter to the point of denying Him" (*TC*, 106). For Kierkegaard, however, there is more integrity in Peter's denial of Christ than in his own contemporaries' choice to ignore his suffering by identifying him as triumphant in and through power struggles within human history.

Kierkegaard is too much the dialectician to accept any one-sided vision of Christ. The exaltation of Christ is even more mistaken, he believed, because it rests on a fundamental religious misunderstanding of what it means for a man to be exalted by virtue of his unity with the divine. Divine presence and the exaltation it bestows upon those who legitimately claim it cannot be found in either the political pursuit of equality or the scientific penetration of nature and the power that flows from it. If at all, divine presence is to be found in each individual's resolve to love his neighbor as himself and his willingness to endure— indeed, to expect—the suffering that is essentially related to this ethical resolve.

215

Closely allied with Christ's powerlessness and humiliation is the religious character of compassion and his conception of human misery. Kierkegaard believed that both the nature of Christ's compassion and his conception of what constitutes true human misery also offend human beings. It is only our poetic and philosophical conceptions of compassion, not our practice of it, that closely resemble Christ's compassion. On the level of human practice, compassion has a very provincial nature. Beginning with the assumption that "everybody is for his own class"(*TC*, 63), Kierkegaard claimed that this "partiality constitutes a fixed point, which explains why *human* compassion never goes beyond a certain degree" (*TC*, 63; Kierkegaard's italics). "The greengrocer's compassion is entoiled in one sole reference, a reference first of all to the other greengrocers, and then to the alehouse keepers" (*TC*, 63). And so it is with every class. If one seeks to express compassion for those of a lower class, one does so without sacrificing one's economic and psychological identity with one's own class (*TC*, 61-62). As an example, Kierkegaard derided those "journalists who live off the pennies of the poor, under pretence of asserting and defending their rights . . ." (*TC*, 63). In all cases, human compassion is unwilling to sacrifice an egotistic and prudential identification with class position.

If one is to be compassionate in a genuine sense, Kierkegaard asserted, one must "give up this [class] distinction and seriously seek his society among the poor . . . and the like!" (*TC*, 62). Unlike human compassion, which is always "only to *a certain degree*" (*TC*, 64; Kierkegaard's italics), genuine compassion is divine, because it represents a "limitless *abandon* in its concern for the sufferer alone . . ." (*TC*, 62; Kierkegaard's italics). The religiously compassionate person challenges the legitimacy of class boundaries by asserting that compassion must be neither selectively offered nor expressed with one's own class interests and identification in view. Genuine compassion is "unconditionally a sacrifice" (*TC*, 64) in that it is an expression of limitless care for the well-being of the other without seeking egotistically to protect oneself.

It does not follow from this view that genuine compassion entails a lack of concern for one's own well-being. An individual cannot not love himself, and this self-love is, as we have seen, a desire to be willed as an end, an ultimate value and good. We have seen also that to will oneself as an end is to will others as means to that end, and to will others as means is to invite, indeed compel, others to will themselves as ends and others as means. This practical contradiction can be broken only by an act of religious compassion in which one wills not oneself but the other as an end with the hope that others will so will oneself. This religious conception of compassion is offensive because it requires the limitless abandonment of the psychological and economic walls of security guaranteed by class distinctions. Such an act is offensive not only because it is imprudent but also because it is impractical, since its results can in no way be predicted or guaranteed.

This dissolving of class boundaries through the religious act of compassion is possible not only in the sense that the high may join the low. That the poor may show compassion for the rich sounds strange only when it is assumed that human misery is essentially material in nature. In Kierkegaard's view, however, the essential human misery is not material but spiritual in nature (*TC*, 64), encompassing anxiety, despair, envy, jealousy, hatred, and resentment. These are the constituents of what we have earlier described as the psychological dimension of egotism.[29] Genuine compassion is directed toward the healing of this

29 See Chapter Three, pp. 108-14. An excellent example of the spiritual nature of human misery and of the capacity of the poor to show compassion for the rich is Leo Tolstoy's short story *The Death of Ivan Ilych*. In the last days of Ivan Ilych's life, he found in his peasant servant, Gerasim, the only person who understood and compassionately responded to his despair over the way he had mistakenly lived his life.

217

spiritual sickness as well. This view of compassion is even more offensive when it is claimed that sin—egotism—and not hunger is the most essential human misery and the object of genuine compassion.[30] Nor should one forget that what Kierkegaard calls sin is itself the ground of material misery. Kierkegaard viewed class conflict as a function of egotism, and so long as egotism prevails, so will the class society and its material misery. Thus, religious compassion aims essentially at the eradication of egotism itself, for egotism is the ground of both psychological and material misery. Again, such a view of the nature of human misery and the method of its eradication is offensive to the modern state, which views human misery as essentially material in nature and proposes political and economic distribution of power as the method of its eradication.

The aspect of Christ's lowliness that in Kierkegaard's view most fundamentally offends those who consider his life rests in the essential relation that is drawn between Christ's life and his suffering and in the practical implications of this relation for human salvation. For Kierkegaard, salvation and suffering are essentially and not accidentally related. Kierkegaard asks, "What then is Christianity? What is it for? One seeks help from it, one is willing to thank it indescribably, and then just the opposite occurs, one has to suffer for its sake—so there does not really seem to be anything to thank for. Here the understanding is brought to a halt by the possibility of offence" (*TC*, 116).[31] Christians in Christendom are not unfamiliar with the concept and experience of suffering as religiously significant. Their ministers are even capable of speaking about suffer-

[30] The idea that sin has a moral content was developed by Kierkegaard in the earlier pseudonymous writings. See my *Being and Existence in Kierkegaard's Pseudonymous Works* (Princeton: Princeton University Press, 1975), pp. 213-22.

[31] Accordingly, "Christianly understood, the real possibility of offence (the possibility of offence which is properly related to becoming a Christian) first emerges . . . in the remedy which Christ recommends as salvation from offence" (*TC*, 113).

ing " 'because of the word', and 'for righteousness' sake' . . ."
(*TC*, 110). What is mistaken is that Christians in Christendom regard "usual human sufferings as if they were the specifically Christian . . ." (*TC*, 110). If one listens closely when the minister speaks about suffering, "one discovers with surprise that these many tribulations are nothing else but illness, financial difficulties, anxiety for the year to come, what one is to eat, or anxiety about 'what one ate last year—and has not paid for', or the fact that one has not become what one desired to be in the world, or other such fatalities. About these things one preaches Christianly, one weeps humanly, and one crazily connects them with Gethsemane" (*TC*, 115). Danish Christians either causally connect these everyday sufferings with the fact that they are Christians or regard them as precisely that evil from which Christianity will deliver them. In Kierkegaard's view, to argue for such a relation is just another example of the way in which the Danes' understanding and practice of Christianity has been reduced to the aesthetic mode of existence.

For Kierkegaard, "The decisive mark of Christian suffering is the fact that it is voluntary, and that it is *the possibility of offence for the sufferer*" (TC, 111; Kierkegaard's italics). The voluntary nature of religious suffering is the key condition, at least formally, of its offensiveness. "For when voluntarily I give up all, choosing danger and adversity, it is not possible to ignore *the offence* . . . which derives from responsibility . . . when they say, 'But why will you expose yourself to this and commence such an understanding, when you could perfectly well leave it alone?' This is specific Christian suffering. It is a whole musical tone deeper than common human suffering" (*TC*, 111; Kierkegaard's italics). This passage is a bit misleading, for it suggests that the Christian chooses "danger and adversity"; in fact, it implies that suffering is the direct object of the ethical and religious choice. The Christian does not choose suffering, however. Rather, Kierkegaard more cor-

219

rectly should have claimed that in choosing the good—
"eternal blessedness," in his words—one chooses suffering
as an unavoidable consequence.

We have already observed that Christ's conception of human misery offends the natural man because it includes the
view that the life of the natural man has sin (egotism) as
its basis and is the real condition of human misery. This
offense is only deepened when Christ claims that eternal
blessedness, which is the highest good, can be understood
from the natural standpoint only as an offense. The natural
man can accept neither Christ's conception of human misery nor his view of the kind of life that offers salvation
from human misery. In our discussion of *Purity of Heart*
and *Works of Love*, we discovered that Kierkegaard conceived of the highest good as existing in a community of
ends that is ethically grounded in every individual's resolve
to love every other as he loves himself.[32] Precisely this view
of human salvation most offends the natural man. Kierkegaard admirably expressed this view of salvation in a passage of *Training in Christianity*: "That is, Christ attaches
infinite importance to entering into life, to eternal blessedness, regarding it as the absolute good. . . . What therefore
really offends is the endless passion with which the eternal
blessedness is conceived. . . . This is precisely what offends
the natural man. Such a conception of the eternal blessedness the natural man does not possess, nor does he desire to
possess it; and hence he does not possess a conception of the
danger of the offence" (*TC*, 113).

The danger of the offense is two-pronged. First, it is dangerous to fail to recognize the offensive nature of Christ, for
it is only through facing the possibility of offense that
"faith comes into existence—if one does not choose instead
to be offended" (*TC*, 122). Either to avoid the offense or to
choose to be offended entails perdition. For Kierkegaard,
only those who through religious faith triumph over the
offense by willing the existence of a community of ends

[32] See Chapter Four, passim.

escape the reality and consequences of perdition. But those who triumph over the offense must also face the reality of suffering as the core of the ethical and religious life. This is the second sense in which the offense is a danger.

One does not will to suffer; on the contrary, one suffers because one resolves to will the existence of a community of ends. And the life of suffering that follows this choice is characterized by physical and psychological deprivation and pain, guilt, and a sense of abandonment. These three modes of suffering can be shown to correspond to Kierkegaard's three stages of existence. In the first case, the suffering that accompanies the ethical resolve to will the existence of a community of ends is aesthetic in nature. The ethical resolve to love others as one loves oneself requires that one treat others as ends. As for oneself, one may only hope that others will also choose to will a community of ends, in which case one also becomes an end. But even though one hopes for this result, it is more reasonable to expect that one will not be so willed. Thus, the psychological desire to become an end will likely go unsatisfied. This aesthetic suffering also possesses a material component in the sense that physical danger and deprivation will accompany those who seek compassionately to challenge social and political structures and conventions that are egotistically grounded. The physical and psychological suffering of Christ is a paradigmatic expression of this aesthetic mode of suffering.

The second mode of suffering that follows from the resolve to will the absolute good is ethical in nature and is to be interpreted as guilt. Nowhere in the second literature does Kierkegaard treat the question of guilt as exhaustively as in the pseudonymous *The Concept of Dread* and *Concluding Unscientific Postscript*.[33] Even so, it is reasonable to assume that the conception of guilt there worked out in terms of the failure of the will within time consistently to

[33] See my *Being and Existence in Kierkegaard's Pseudonymous Works*, pp. 174-90.

will the good applies equally in his later writings. Guilt is the consciousness of the existential disparity between the real and the ideal and characterizes all persons who resolve to will the good. Moreover, guilt is the highest mode of ethical suffering and is a dimension of the life of each person who wills the existence of a community of ends. The struggle between the natural and ethical selves, between egotism and willing the good, is never complete. Suffering is the consciousness of one's failure as a finite human being to win the struggle against the natural and egotistic self.

The third and final mode of suffering is specifically religious in its content. It springs from a sense of having lost oneself and of having been abandoned by others and by God. It emerges out of uncertainty and self-doubt. Christ's weeping over Jerusalem, his sweating blood in the garden before his arrest, and his crying out to God on the cross convey aspects of the religious dimension of Christian suffering. Christ weeps over the city, for he fears that the acts of ethical men and women will not be sufficient to transform the state of nature into a community of ends. Christ sweats blood in the garden prior to his arrest because he fears his own destiny as a man and wants to be relieved of it by some transcendent authority. Yet there is no God who has the power to relieve him of his obligation to himself and to his neighbor. And, finally, Christ cries out on the cross for an explanation of why God has forsaken him. Again, Christ learns that there is no God with the power to deliver him from his suffering and at the same time preserve the possibility of actualizing the community of ends. To relieve Christ of his suffering would be to destroy the possibility of realizing on earth the absolute good. It is, then, Christ's sense of being abandoned to an uncertain destiny that is at the heart of his religious suffering. In the final analysis, defeat, despair, and abandonment dominate the experience of Christ the man. Herein lies the essence of religious suffering.[34]

[34] Dostoevsky's "The Grand Inquisitor" in his great novel *The*

For Kierkegaard, then, this life of suffering is not accidentally related to the Christian life but is in the final analysis the only sign that authenticates that one has genuinely become a Christian. And suffering is the essence of Christ's lowliness and the central reason for its offensiveness.

In concluding this discussion of Kierkegaard's conception of the offense, it is correct to say that this category, along with the category of contemporaneity, constitutes what must, for Kierkegaard, be regarded as central to Christianity in nineteenth-century Denmark. We have seen that this category contains a set of claims that Christ makes about himself, the good life, and suffering. Taken together, these claims set forth a style of life that can in no manner be made compatible with the style of life promoted by nineteenth-century liberalism. Kierkegaard's radical emphasis on the offense as an aspect of the essence of Christianity sets Christianity in uncompromising opposition to Christendom. The theoretical component of the offense appears in Christ's exaltation. God does not appear in human experience through the dialectic of history or in the collective judgments and actions of politically motivated groups of individuals. The presence of God is manifested only in the ethical resolve of an individual to love others as he loves himself. For Kierkegaard, this theoretical judgment is the meaning of the claim that Christ is a man who acts "in a way suggestive of being God" (*TC*, 99). Such a claim can only be an offense to those individuals who in one way or another theoretically identify divine purpose with the power of the state, science, and culture.

If Christ's exaltation prevents theoretical identification of divine purpose and presence with the modern liberal state, Christ's lowliness prevents identification of the Christian life with prudence. It is this practical dimension of the offense related to Christ's lowliness that most interested Kierkegaard. We must not forget that his aim as a writer

---

Brothers Karamazov is an excellent example of Kierkegaard's understanding of suffering.

was always the ethical and religious transformation of individuals. Such a transformation entails an assent to the notion of the good life as one of existing in a community of ends that is grounded in an individual resolve and a readiness to accept suffering as the only certain outcome of any such resolve. If suffering is the practical outcome of Christ's lowliness, it is not difficult to comprehend that the reaction of the prudential individual in the new liberal order will be one of offense. To interpret Christianity as offensive to reason, as Kierkegaard did, is simply to set it in opposition to its acculturation by the phenomenon he called Christendom.

CONTEMPORANEITY AND CHRISTENDOM

In turning our attention to the concept of contemporaneity, we focus on what Kierkegaard called "the central thought of my life" (*AC*, 242).[35] This claim is mildly surprising, given the limited discussion and use of the concept in the later literature. To be sure, it is, along with the concept of offense, the centerpiece of *Training in Christianity* and there receives its fullest development.[36] The concept appears as early as 1844 with the publication of *Philosophical Fragments*. In a chapter entitled "The Case of the Contemporary Disciple,"[37] Kierkegaard argues that one who is immediately (materially) contemporary with Christ is in no way advantaged over the disciple who lives generations later, because there is nothing religiously mediated by the perception of Christ that would lead one to faith. This view is the standard Lutheran position: religious contemporaneity with Christ is a miracle made possible by divine

[35] Cf. *JP*, I, 691.

[36] Kierkegaard insisted that we should take "good heed to this thought of contemporaneousness! And to that end do not fail to make thyself acquainted, if already thou hast not done so, with the book I published in 1850, *Training in Christianity*; for here precisely this thought is stressed" (*AC*, 241).

[37] *PF*, 68-88. Cf. *CUP*, 88, 89n.

grace. Religious contemporaneity appears again two years later in Kierkegaard's discussion of Adler's claim to have experienced a revelation.[38] The alleged revelatory event constituted religious contemporaneity with the divine, according to Kierkegaard, and was for this reason the ground of Adler's faith. But Kierkegaard criticized Adler for making the mistake of attempting rationally to justify his claim to have experienced a revelation. By attempting to ground the revelation in reason, Adler usurped its religious authority.

In both *Philosophical Fragments* and *Authority and Revelation*, the concept of contemporaneity functions polemically as a challenge to the nineteenth-century speculative appeal to reason and history as the justifications for and legitimations of faith. Few of Kierkegaard's journal entries prior to 1848 deal with contemporaneity, but in journal entries from 1848 to 1854, as well as in *Training in Christianity*, the term appears frequently and acquires a meaning much richer and broader in scope than that developed in the earlier works. Once the concept received its full development in *Training in Christianity* in 1850, Kierkegaard turned his attention to other issues and rarely returned to it as a matter for analysis and interpretation (*JFY*, 128, 199ff.). Given the rather provincial status of the term in the second literature, one may wonder why it deserves the exalted status of "central thought" in Kierkegaard's writings.

The centrality of the concept of contemporaneity has to be justified in terms of its conceptual status in the second literature rather than in terms of its actual use. As is the concept of neighbor in Kierkegaard's ethical thought, contemporaneity is an encompassing technical concept without which one cannot fully interpret and interrelate all other key concepts in his religious thought. Contemporaneity, however, includes more, because it embraces the key ethical concept of neighbor as well. Thus, religious concepts like

[38] *AR*, 58-59, 63-64, 66, 155, 157.

Christ, God, offense, imitation, faith, suffering, and grace and ethical concepts like freedom, justice, individuality, duty, reality, and neighbor receive their full intelligibility through the concept of contemporaneity. The concept literally unifies Kierkegaard's ethical and religious thought into a single and coherent position. And given the distinctly religious coloration of his ethics, Kierkegaard can justifiably write that "becoming a Christian in truth comes to mean to become contemporary with Christ" (*TC*, 67).[39] Elsewhere Kierkegaard insisted that "what true Christians there are in each generation are contemporary with Christ . . ." (*TC*, 68). To exist as a Christian is to exist contemporaneously with Christ. What more can one ask of Kierkegaard in the matter of explaining his understanding of Christianity? Our task here is to investigate the comprehensive character of this concept of contemporaneity.

Kierkegaard asserted that being a Christian in Christendom essentially differs from existing contemporaneously with Christ (*TC*, 109). He deliberately set the concepts of Christendom and contemporaneity in an uncompromising struggle for the allegiance of the individual who would take Christianity seriously. As we have seen, Christendom takes it for granted that Christ is God and is constantly reassured in this conviction by theologians like Martensen and Grundtvig and ministers like Mynster. Moreover, it is convinced that modernization is a religious event that is both providentially willed and ethically good. Kierkegaard regarded Christendom's self-deification as paganism and argued that "the simplest means of putting an end to all this sentimental paganism which in Christendom is called Christianity is quite simply to introduce it into the situation of contemporaneousness" (*TC*, 97). In the situation of contemporaneity, the offense and the imitation of Christ— the two hallmarks of essential Christianity—can be introduced into Christendom.

A reader introduced into the situation of contempora-

[39] Cf. *TC*, 84.

neity with Christ, Kierkegaard believed, would unavoidably be offended. In "the situation of contemporaneousness with Christ . . . the Christian is bound to discover the possibility of offence in relation to his own life . . ." (*TC*, 112).[40] And as Kierkegaard works through this idea in *Training in Christianity*, it becomes apparent that the material immediacy so minimized in *Philosophical Fragments* has become an important factor. For it is precisely the immediate or imaginative perception of Christ's lowliness and humiliation that makes the offense possible.

Kierkegaard's problem was how best to introduce the offensive nature of Christ's life, and he found his answer in the concept of contemporaneity. He asked, "would it occur to anybody to deny . . . the possibility of the offence" when he is placed "in the situation of contemporaneousness with that individual man, whose origin one knows all about, whom one recognizes on the street, etc. . . . ?" (*TC*, 102). In fact, existing contemporaneously with Christ requires that individuals imaginatively "go out in the street and perceive that it is God in this horrible procession . . ." (*TC*, 69). Of course, "directly there was nothing to be seen but a lowly man, who . . . continually posited the possibility of offence" (*TC*, 69). Contemporaneity with Christ makes possible the offense when the individual imaginatively encounters a human being who is poor, powerless, and persecuted and yet makes difficult claims not only about himself but also about the nature of human misery and compassion. "A lowly man . . . thus expressed (1) what God understands by compassion . . . and (2) what God understands by man's misery, which in both cases is utterly different from what man's understanding is, and which in every generation until the end of time everyone for his own part must learn from the beginning . . . *practising it in the situation of contemporaneousness*" (*TC*, 69; my italics). Here the situation of contemporaneity possesses not so much

[40] Cf. *TC*, 102, 104.

an aesthetic quality engendered by the imagination as an ethical quality embedded in the practice of compassion.[41]

Existing contemporaneously with Christ means to begin to be able to practice the ethical core of Christianity, which is exemplified in the life of Christ. Indeed, to exist contemporaneously with Christ is to practice the compassion that one sees concretely exemplified in the life of Christ. In order to consider the possibility of becoming a Christian, one must become individually contemporaneous with the actions and words of Christ. For in and through Christ's presence there arises the offense, which challenges the "sentimental paganism" of modern Christendom, which identifies Christ with the established order and maintains that one is a Christian by virtue of one's participation in it. Kierkegaard refused to accept this cultural mediation of the presence of the divine—what he called "world-historical hocus-pocus" (*TC*, 110)—which interprets Western history as a justification of the claim for the divinity of Christ. Contrary to the Danish Hegelians and the Grundtvigians, Kierkegaard argued that only by becoming an individual who is contemporary with Christ is it possible for one to participate in the presence of the divine.

Kierkegaard implied that the divinity of Christ is to be understood ethically, not metaphysically. Christ's nature and actions are commensurate; his divinity logically cannot be divorced from the character of his actions. Moreover, the divinity of Christ is made present to each succeeding generation not through speculative reason, historical progress, or political *praxis* but in the ethical act of compassion toward other human beings. Herein lies the possibility of offense. Kierkegaard's emphasis on contemporaneity directly challenges those who would mediate the presence of the divine through reason and history. For Kierkegaard, the divine is rationally and culturally inaccessible. Indeed, di-

[41] This conception of compassion is closely aligned with the concepts of loving one's neighbor and imitating Christ. The unity of these three terms will be discussed below.

vine presence is mediated only by the act of compassion. Recognition of this fact can only offend the modern Dane who has so thoroughly come to identify Christ and Christendom.

Thus, Kierkegaard sought to throw the Christian existing in Christendom into the situation of contemporaneity, where he is not only *offended* by the powerless and humiliated Christ but also invited to *imitate* the ethical actions of Christ. If the individual is to accept Christ in the situation of contemporaneity, he "must conform to his life" (*JP*, II, 1864). This is so, because "Christ's life here upon earth is the paradigm . . ." (*TC*, 109). Moreover, "In truth Christ did not come to abolish the law—he himself is the fulfillment of the law, and has presented himself as the prototype" (*JP*, II, 1905). Christ is the "Pattern" or prototype that is "oriented to the universally human, of which everyone is capable" (*JP*, II, 1939).[42]

This emphasis on the imitation of Christ is a strong undercurrent running through and governing the course of most of the later literature. The only "true way of being a

[42] Kierkegaard insisted that "everyone must be measured by the Pattern, the ideal. We must get rid of all the bosh about this being said only to the Apostles, and this only to the disciples, and this only to the first Christians, etc. Christ no more desires now than He did then to have admirers (not to say twaddlers), He wants only disciples. The 'disciple' is the standard: imitation and Christ as the Pattern must be introduced" (*JFY*, 207). That Christ exemplifies a pattern that is a genuinely human possibility is reflected in Kierkegaard's description of Christ as one who "sought the kingdom of God, and so expressed the absolute, and that he absolutely related himself to the absolute, or that he was 'spirit' . . ." (*JFY*, 128-29). This formula of absolutely relating to the absolute or becoming spirit is one that Kierkegaard worked out in his pseudonymous writings to describe the ethical ideal of human life. *Concluding Unscientific Postscript* and *The Sickness unto Death* develop this formula in great detail and Kierkegaard picked it up again in *Works of Love*. I have examined Kierkegaard's pseudonymous discussion of this formula in my *Being and Existence in Kierkegaard's Pseudonymous Works*, pp. 29-71. See Chapter Four above for a discussion of this formula for the self as it appears in *Works of Love*.

Christian [is] to be a disciple" (*JFY*, 215). Elsewhere, "imitation is Christianity" (*JP*, II, 1932). This emphasis, Kierkegaard believed, is just the right one for Christendom, and he staunchly maintained that "If Christianity is to be reintroduced into Christendom, it must again be proclaimed unconditionally as imitation, as law . . ." (*JP*, I, 401).[43] Then the disciple will be "construed in accordance with the paradigm—not as in established Christendom," where he is judged a Christian merely by being a Dane (*TC*, 110).

The centrality of the imitation of Christ in medieval Christian life made that age, in Kierkegaard's view, a more advanced one religiously than his own. Its superiority lies in its concepton of Christianity as a commitment "to action, life, the transformation of personal existence" (*JFY*, 201). Religious commitment to the transformation of one's life sets one in an unalterable opposition to the world as one finds it, but Kierkegaard regarded as naive and innocent the medieval view that the monastic and ascetic life provides the best means to this transformation (*JP*, I, 693).[44] The medieval understanding of an existential transforma-

---

[43] This emphasis on the ethical nature of religious salvation strongly contrasts with the view of salvation that predominates in Christendom. Kierkegaard had nothing but contempt and derision for its emphasis on the acceptance of an unmerited grace as a sufficient condition for salvation, and he saw clearly the ideological function that such a religion comes to have. " 'Established Christendom' really dates from the time Christmas was declared the supreme festival (in the Fourth Century). The Savior of the world is now a baby. And why would anyone want to be saved by a baby? Because men thought: Here there can be no question of imitation" (*JP*, II, 1893). "Thus from generation to generation Christianity in the Church has been transformed egotistically into something more and more according to man's interest: the Atonement makes imitation into a nothing, or we completely cheat our way out of imitation. Then Christendom more and more develops a bad conscience, and the thought that to relate oneself to God should mean suffering becomes completely foreign; and the very opposite—success and prosperity—becomes the sign of being related to God—and then Christianity is really abolished" (*JP*, II, 1911).

[44] Cf. *JP*, II, 1385, 1399.

tion requires a denial of temporality, finitude, and bodiness and a commitment to a spiritual ideal that is essentially divorced from the material. For Kierkegaard, this mystical dimension of monasticism represents a fundamental misunderstanding of the nature of the self and its Christian transformation. The proper Christian action is in fact a transformation rather than a denial of the material dimension of the self.[45]

The spirit of Kierkegaard's first and sound literatures emphasizes the transforming power of Christianity in relation to the embodied self. But it has been pointed out that Kierkegaard's final writings, especially *Attack upon Christendom* and, to a lesser extent, *Judge for Yourselves*, contain just this ascetic strain that the body of his works consistently denies.[46] In these two works, Kierkegaard maintains that the Christian is one who hates the world and is willing totally to renounce and die to the world (*JFY*, 179); he must be "absolutely heterogeneous with the world" (*JFY*, 179). Since the world is the arena of illusion, deception, and falsehood, the most Christian of all actions is chastity, by which the Christian contributes to the ending of the world (*AC*, 214). It is not difficult to discern in these worlds a reversal of the religious, ethical, and philosophical direction of Kierkegaard's preceding books. This apparent reversal of thought at the end of Kierkegaard's life is a continuing problem for interpreting the authorship as a whole, and it will be explored in Chapter Seven.

One also finds in these two works the same Protestant emphasis on grace that is present, though muted, in the earlier works in the second literature. Here, as well as in a number of late journal entries, Kierkegaard also justifies imitation of Christ as a means of teaching human fallibility and the need for grace (*JFY*, 207). "Now I understand that

45 Chapter Four, pp. 137-38.

46 See Marie M. Thulstrup, "Kierkegaard's Dialectic of Imitation," in Howard A. Johnson and Niels Thulstrup, eds., *A Kierkegaard Critique* (Chicago: Henry Regnery Company, 1967), pp. 266-85.

imitation . . . is intended to keep order, to teach humility and the need for grace, to put an end to doubt" (*JP*, II, 1903).[47] Christendom has forgotten the genuine subjective conditions that make grace a necessity, and the best way to reestablish those subjective conditions is to emphasize the imitation of Christ as the essence of Christianity. "What Christianity presupposes, namely, the tortures of a contrite conscience, the need of grace, the deeply felt need, all these frightful inward conflicts and sufferings—what Christianity presupposes in order to introduce and apply grace, salvation, the hope of eternal blessedness—all this is not to be found, or is to be found only in burlesque abridgement . . ." in Christendom, because Christians no longer take seriously the imitation of Christ as central to the Christian life (*JFY*, 209).[48] Imitation of Christ here appears to lose its status as a religious end and becomes simply a means to the end of salvation by grace. This distinctly Protestant theme in *Attack upon Christendom* and *Judge for Yourselves*, like the Catholic emphasis on asceticism, appears to attenuate Kierkegaard's major emphasis on the essentially ethical and polemical nature of Christianity.

Whether this world-denying, grace-relying language constitutes a reversal of the direction of the preceding books has not been settled,[49] but at least two possible interpretations should be mentioned here. First, one might simply argue that since there is material in *Judge for Yourselves* and *Attack upon Christendom* that is consistent with the direction of the preceding books, there is only a partial and incomplete, possibly an aborted, departure or reversal of the direction of the earlier books. Second, one might plausibly

---

[47] Cf. *JP*, I, 692, 693, 694.

[48] Cf. *JP*, I, 694, 695; II, 1793, 1862, 1908.

[49] Considering the later works from the point of view of Kierkegaard's own psychological motivations for writing, Josiah Thompson sees them as entirely consistent with the earlier pseudonymous books. Thompson's thesis will be discussed in detail in Chapter Seven. See Josiah Thompson, *Kierkegaard* (New York: Alfred A. Knopf, 1973).

argue that the tension in these last two books between love for God and hatred for the world is latently present throughout the second literature. After all, Kierkegaard distinguished throughout the second literature between the natural man and the ethical-religious man. It is possible that for whatever reasons when writing these last two books Kierkegaard lost sight of the ethical as that which unifies the aesthetic (the natural) and the religious and fell into a more traditional opposition of the religious and the natural. In this case, the ethical ceases to be that which unifies the aesthetic and the religious and becomes merely a transitional stage before the religious stage of life, where one now relies exclusively upon grace for salvation—with an accompanying hatred of the world as the realm of spiritual bondage. Although these two possibilities present themselves as distinct and separate alternatives, a combination of the two seems the most plausible explanation for the tension between these last two and the preceding books in Kierkegaard's second literature, and we shall explore this option in Chapter Seven.[50]

We must now examine the precise nature of the relation between Kierkegaard's concepts of contemporaneity and imitation of Christ. For Kierkegaard, Christ is the embodiment of the law. By this claim, Kierkegaard did not mean that something external constrains Christ to keep the law. On the contrary, Christ is a holy man because he keeps the law out of love. It is in this sense that individuals are to strive to imitate Christ. Moreover, the love that individuals express for Christ is not simply "to appropriate his merit" (*JP*, II, 1858). More fundamentally, it is to enable the individual "to be transformed into likeness [*i Lighed*] to the beloved; otherwise it is merely wanting to profit by the beloved" (*JP*, II, 1870). This strong and persistent rebuttal to the notion in Christendom that one can religiously profit from the suffering and death of Christ is one of the central

---

[50] See Chapter Seven, pp. 292-94.

reasons for Kierkegaard's interpretation of the Christian life as the imitation of Christ.[51]

Corresponding to Christendom's emphasis on the atoning significance of Christ's suffering is its attempt to base religion on the notion of God as father. In Kierkegaard's view, both theological positions are childish and should be replaced by a religion based on the notion of Christ as model or paradigm. "When a person is related only to God, then the relation is like that of a child to a father. When Christ enters into the relationship, the man is treated like an adult. Imitation [Efterfølgelsen] and voluntariness show that the requirement here is higher than for a child" (JP, II, 1875). True or genuine religion is based on love for Christ as an expression of the desire to be changed into his likeness. The most crucial change that such a religion can effect in an individual is to bring him to love the commandment to love, to become "more and more intimate with the commandment, . . . more and more of one with the commandment, which he loves: therefore he is able to speak so mildly, almost as if it had been forgotten that love is the commandment" (WL, 344-45). This internal change, which is brought about by a love for Christ, enables the individual to love his neighbor as he loves himself. Herein we see clearly that Kierkegaard viewed religious love as a necessary condition for the realization of the moral law. Ultimately, one is transformed by that which one loves. To love Christ is to love the ideal, and to persist in a love for Christ is to begin to become like that which one loves.

Inevitably, Kierkegaard's religion always finds its way back into the ethical. Nowhere is this more clear than in his claim that the "only ethical relationship to the great (thus also to Christ) is contemporaneity" (JP, I, 961). In a jour-

---

[51] "[T]o let one person or a few be martyred agonizingly—in order that the others can have it easy [is human villainy]. The animal nature, the bestiality of man really sticks out clearly in this invention" (JP, IV, 4711).

nal passage that could have been lifted directly from Kant, Kierkegaard beautifully makes this point.

> An essentially ethical individual immediately converts greatness to contemporaneity. He says—to himself—this is what I will. Quite possibly I cannot reach it, but this is what I will. If [I] cannot reach it immediately, then I will creep; if in my whole lifetime I cannot do any more than creep along, then I shall creep along my whole life —but this is the direction. He does not let go of it; he is like a pilgrim who perhaps has vowed to walk on his knees to Jerusalem—and he died on the way; but from the point of view of the idea he has reached Jerusalem. And in this way the true ethical individual must reach the highest—he must reach it, if not before, then in eternity. (*JP*, I, 973)

Contemporaneity with Christ is ethical in nature, involving essentially the imitation of Christ as an ethical paradigm. However, contemporaneity possesses an aesthetic or natural determination as well. One is ethically contemporary with Christ by virtue of choosing the good, while at the same time one is naturally or immediately contemporary with the age in which one lives. These two modes of contemporaneity constitute for Kierkegaard the nature of reality for temporally existing human beings: "What thou dost live contemporaneous with is reality—for thee. And thus every man can be contemporary only with the age in which he lives—and then with one thing more: with Christ's life on earth; for Christ's life on earth, sacred history, stands for itself alone outside history" (*TC*, 68).

The claim that one lives contemporaneously with one's personal reality does not imply the idealist notion that to be is to be perceived. Quite to the contrary, Kierkegaard believed that the individual is existentially constituted by that which is present to him. This view of Kierkegaard's has been explored in Chapters Three and Four, where it was seen that individuals seek to work out their identities

235

in terms of their historically and culturally determined private and public relations with their contemporaries. These relations are always egotistic in nature in that each individual both psychologically and materially seeks the realization of his own ends in and through the other. In the journal passage above, Kierkegaard expresses this fact in terms of the category of contemporaneity. A person is always "contemporary . . . with the age in which he lives." Being present to one's own generation is the natural or aesthetic mode of human reality.

According to Kierkegaard, one can be contemporary not only with the other but also with Christ. We have already observed that his emphasis on contemporaneity with Christ was designed polemically to combat or to offend the notion that divine presence can be speculatively and culturally mediated. As a corollary to the polemical or offensive function of the category of contemporaneity, we have also seen its ethical function: to be contemporary with Christ is to imitate Christ as an ethical paradigm. Moreover, by existing contemporaneously with Christ, it is possible to transform the egotistic character of one's contemporaneity with others. Kierkegaard was attempting to enrich the concept of contemporaneity by arguing that one can be present not only to the other, with whom one is necessarily contemporaneous, but also to Christ, with whom one may voluntarily be present. The choice to introduce Christ into the present by imitation results in the ethical transformation of one's natural contemporaneity with the other by converting the other from a means into an end in himself. To be contemporary with Christ is, then, to be a neighbor to the other (*TC*, 62). Put another way, to imitate Christ is to love one's neighbor as one loves oneself.

For Kierkegaard, the normative value of Christ's life is not the product of an arbitrary, capricious, and indefensible decision of blind faith, for it is precisely the human situation that makes the imitation of Christ a reasonable and worthy risk. To refer to Christ as the absolute, as

Kierkegaard does, is of course a choice that each individual is free to make, but it is not a groundless choice, given its theoretical and practical complementarity with the human situation as Kierkegaard understood it. It is important to recognize that for Kierkegaard it is the human situation that must determine the character of what is absolute for human beings. Both the form and the content of the absolute are dialectically determined by the situation that it is intended to resolve. Thus, Kierkegaard was quick to reject the standard candidates for absoluteness in nineteenth-century thought—destiny, thought, and natural rights—because they all fail as possible solutions for the human dilemma. Destiny, the absolute for the Grundtvigians and the Hegelians, is historically accessible but cannot be an absolute, since faith in destiny is powerless to resolve the dilemma of human existence. Thought, championed by Danish Hegelians like Martensen, is speculatively accessible but is also powerless to transform human life. Finally, natural rights, put forward by Danish liberals, are accessible through political *praxis* but also fail as the absolute, since the political attainment of these rights does nothing to purge the human situation of its egotistic basis. Only compassion—love for one's neighbor—can legitimately qualify as the absolute, according to Kierkegaard, since it alone has the transforming power to convert nature into community. Moreover, to claim that "Christ is the absolute" (*TC*, 67) is to claim that the absolute is accessible to us not through faith in destiny, speculative thought, mystical intuition, or political *praxis* but through a personal act by which one affirms the value and worth of the other as an end in himself.

Kierkegaard termed this act compassion in *Training in Christianity* (*TC*, 62-67) and love for one's neighbor in *Works of Love*. Compassion, love, is the content of the absolute, and its form is that of personhood. Compassion and love take the form of one's personal and voluntary commitment to another person. Only a person can express

237

"limitless *abandon* in [his] concern for the sufferer . . ."
(*TC*, 62; Kierkegaard's italics). Only a person can "seriously
seek his society among the poor, live completely with the
humble classes . . ." (*TC*, 62). Only a person can "unconditionally" sacrifice himself for another person (*TC*, 64).
Only a person can repudiate the bounds of class and accept
another person's finitude as intrinsically valuable and
worthy (*TC*, 64). Only a person can express a commitment
to the realization of the freedom of his neighbor, thereby
freeing him from an egotistic enslavement to the other. The
absolute, then, can appear only in and as a person. And
the imitation of Christ is neither more nor less than an
expression of the faith that the absolute can only appear in
human form.

This persistent emphasis in *Training in Christianity* on
the concept of contemporaneity and its accompanying
themes of the offense and the imitation of Christ works
against the notion of Christ as paradox developed earlier in
Philosophical Fragments and *Concluding Unscientific Postscript*. At least this is so to the extent that one gives a metaphysical interpretation to Kierkegaard's use of paradox in
these two earlier books.[52] However, some passages in *Training in Christianity* suggest a similarity between the conception of Christ in this book and the conception of Christ as a
paradox in the earlier works. For example, Christ is "not
at all a merely historical person, since as the Paradox He is
an extremely unhistorical person" (*TC*, 67). Similarly,
"Christ's life on earth, sacred history, stands for itself alone
outside history" (*TC*, 68). Although these passages diverge
widely from earlier claims that Christ is a synthesis of opposites—time and eternity—and is therefore paradoxical, they
nevertheless suggest a kinship with this earlier metaphysical

[52] It seems correct to say that the metaphysical value of the concept of paradox is much greater in *Philosophical Fragments*, where
Kierkegaard describes it as a "metaphysical crotchet" (*PF*, 46-60), than it
is in *Concluding Unscientific Postscript*, where Kierkegaard links the
paradox with his analysis of the claim that subjectivity is truth.

emphasis. But their antihistorical bias reflects not the ahistorical character of Christ's nature but the historically independent character of his presence and power. Kierkegaard insisted that "in its time 1,800 years ago," Christ's life on earth "did not wait, nor does it wait now, for any assistance from the upshot" (*TC*, 68). In other words, the divine presence in history never requires propitious historical circumstances to bring it into being. Moreover, divine presence at one point in history cannot in any way be propitious for its reappearance in history at a later moment. In fact, the appearance of the divine in history depends not upon historical exigencies but upon an individual ethical resolve to be compassionate or to love one's neighbor as one loves oneself. That Kierkegaard intended no metaphysical interpretation of Christ's life is made very clear: "His earthly life accompanies the race, and accompanies every generation in particular, as the eternal history; His earthly life possesses the eternal contemporaneousness" (*TC*, 68). Note that what is eternally present is the possibility of existing contemporaneously with Christ's *earthly life*, which we have described as an ethical model or paradigm of compassion. With the setting aside of the metaphysical Christ in *Training in Christianity*, as well as in the other works in Kierkegaard's second literature, one easily discerns the reasons for Kierkegaard's animosity toward speculative, mystical, and historical interpretations of the presence and power of Christ. The imitation of Christ, understood as an ethical resolve to love one's neighbor as one loves oneself, is alone the way to achieve contemporaneity with Christ.

CONCLUSION

In analyzing Kierkegaard's polemical religion, we have seen that he focused both on extracting Christian categories from their alliance with modernization and on establishing through these resuscitated categories an attack on Christendom. Kierkegaard's task was a difficult one, because he found himself in the position, on the one hand, of having to develop a polemic against the Christianity of Christendom and, on the other hand, of having to show how Christianity is the basis of this polemic. He had to attack the Christianity of Christendom in a Christian manner or from a Christian perspective. Put another way, Christianity had become a double agent in the sense that was serving its original enemy of egotism. Kierkegaard had to seduce the double agent back into its original task of resisting egotism.

It is in this context that Kierkegaard developed the category of contemporaneity. He believed that the speculative and historical interpretations of the nature and power of Christ served up by Martensen and the Grundtvigians both neutralized the subjective power of Christianity and allied it with the triumph of egotism in the form of democratic liberalism. When speculative reason stands between the individual and Christ, the thinker loses touch with those subjective conditions in his own life, such as guilt and despair, that make Christianity a living existential choice. This speculative objectifying of religion as a metaphysical and epistemological problem also obscures the ethical efficacy of the life of Christ. That is, when human history is construed as an effect of the presence and power of the divine, the individual not only loses a sense of personal responsibility for doing God's will but also comes to identify historical events like liberalism with the will of God. The personal identification of the individual with "Christ's life on earth" as the preeminent task of the Christian life becomes a fanatical delusion, a silly quest for an impossible ideal, or a rejection of what is prudentially required for the good life in Christendom. Precisely this is the purpose of Kierkegaard's postulation of the category of contemporaneity: to remove speculative reason, history, and culture as mediators of the presence and power of the divine in Christ.

The concept of contemporaneity includes, as we have seen, the concepts of offense and imitation of Christ. To be contemporaneous with Christ is to encounter Christ as an

240

offense in the sense that Christ's self-exaltation as a media-
tor of divine presence and Christ's lowliness challenge the
notion of Christ developed within Christendom. One cannot live within Christendom and not be offended by the
compassion and suffering of Christ, because we perceive in
Christ's compassion a view of human misery and salvation
that is opposed to the view promoted by Christendom. Furthermore, one perceives in the suffering of Christ the powerlessness of compassion to enforce or to negotiate through
democratic processes the resolution of human suffering and
misery. In short, the offensiveness of the earthly life of
Christ lies in its challenge to nineteenth-century Denmark
and its religious legitimation as Christendom. We have also
seen that Christians in Christendom will inevitably encounter Christ as an offense and that to be offended is a necessary condition for the choice to imitate Christ as an ethical
paradigm for human life. The offense is the shock of recognition that Christendom and Christianity are qualitatively
distinct. Thus, to exist contemporaneously with Christ involves, on the one hand, being offended by the earthly life
of Christ through the recognition of the qualitative difference between Christ and Christendom and, on the other,
setting oneself in opposition to Christendom through the
act of imitating Christ, which is the expression of compassion toward one's neighbor and the acceptance of suffering.

It is also important to notice that once Christianity is
excised from Christendom and is redefined in terms of the
category of contemporaneity, one is able to see not only the
polemical design but also the all-encompassing nature of
the concept. All the categories invoked by Kierkegaard as
essential to an understanding of Christianity are anchored
to the concept of contemporaneity. The offense, the imitation of Christ, love, compassion, the neighbor, faith, suffering, grace—all are given meaning in terms of the concept of
making oneself present to the earthly life of Christ. The
categories properly belonging to Christian discourse are
those that illuminate the subjective and the ethical impli-

241

cations of accepting the demands placed upon those who make themselves present to the earthly life of Christ.

In concluding this discussion of Kierkegaard's understanding of religion, two problems of interpretation deserve brief consideration. The first difficulty concerns the nature of the relation between what we have called Kierkegaard's ethical religion and his polemical religion. The phrases "existing before God" and "imitation of Christ" characterize the foci of these two aspects of Kierkegaard's understanding of religion. In his pseudonymous works, the notion of existing before God is closely linked with what he called the religion of hidden inwardness. In these earlier works, especially in *Concluding Unscientific Postscript*, existing before God involves the individual in a search for self-knowledge, which culminates in the acts of repentance and faith, through which an existential unity of the self as a synthesis of necessity and possibility is achieved.[53] A careful tracing of the self's movement toward self-knowledge discloses that it passes through numerous stages within the larger aesthetic, ethical, and religious horizons of its development. This development is presented as an individuated, private, and inward process that transforms the self internally without necessarily requiring an accompanying external transformation of its material relations with others. Kierkegaard referred to these changes as constituting a religion of hidden inwardness.

Many have noted what Louis Dupré nicely points out, that "over the years, Kierkegaard gradually comes to see the ethics of 'hidden interiority' as a compromise with the world, which all but eliminates the severe demands of Christ."[54] In journal entries from 1850, well after he had turned his attention to the concepts of contemporaneity, the imitation of Christ, and the offense, Kierkegaard seems

[53] See my *Being and Existence in Kierkegaard's Pseudonymous Works*, pp. 243-45.

[54] Louis Dupré, *Kierkegaard as Theologian* (New York: Sheed and Ward, 1963), p. 164.

to disavow hidden inwardness as a religion that "excuses one from all the inconvenience of suffering for the cause of Christianity" (*JP*, II, 2125). He sardonically observed, "If Christianity does not become anything more than . . . extraordinary hidden inwardness, which is about *so viel wie nichts*, then the world pledges itself to tolerate Christianity" (*JP*, II, 2125).[55] Such a strong transition from emphasis on religion as hidden inwardness to emphasis on religion as the imitation of Christ has led many to assume a sharp and substantive discontinuity between Kierkegaard's first and second literatures. Whether this position is warranted is not to be decided here,[56] but it is extremely important to notice the maturation of the concept of existing before God in Kierkegaard's thought.

Clearly, that concept is closely allied with the concept of religion as hidden inwardness in the pseudonymous literature, but it would be mistaken to limit its meaning to this period in Kierkegaard's thought. We have seen that the concept of existing before God played a crucial role in the development of *Works of Love*, which does not set forth an ethics and religion of hidden inwardness. The existential unity of self-love and love for one's neighbor requires as a necessary condition that one exist before God. The egotistic character of all human relations within nature must be grounded in God's love if those relations are to avoid the self-contradicting *telos* of egotism. To exist in a community of ends requires that one will all others as concrete, identifiable, and intrinsically worthy beings. The religious condition or ground that makes such an ethical act of love possible is the individual's experience of himself as both loved by God and obliged by God to love others. In his social relation with God, the individual becomes, as Kierkegaard would say, conscious of himself as a synthesis of necessity and possibility, of reality and ideality, of desire and obliga-

[55] Cf. *JP*, III, 2543.
[56] The relation between Kierkegaard's emphases on inwardness and imitation will be explored in depth in the following chapter.

tion. That is to say, in a relation to God the individual becomes conscious of himself not only as one who desires to be loved as the concrete being that he is by necessity but also as one who is so loved by God. He also becomes conscious of himself as one who is obliged by God to love others, and he recognizes that his loving others, or his willing the existence of a community of ends, is a necessary condition for actually existing himself in such a community. In his relation to God, he comes to know that God's love is a necessary, but not a sufficient, condition for establishing a community of ends. We see, then, that in *Works of Love* an ethics of interiority is retained to the extent that an internal transformation of the self is made possible by the individual's choice to exist before God. The individual's internal transformation then becomes the ethical and religious foundation for the material transformation of nature so that it can become a community of ends. Thus, the concept of existing before God appears to be compatible with Kierkegaard's later and more radical emphasis on the imitation of Christ.

To imitate Christ is, as we have seen, to do neither more nor less than to love one's neighbor as one loves oneself. Christ is a model, paradigm, prototype, pattern for us precisely because he is the perfect exemplification of the willingness to exist before God. It is not inappropriate to claim that for Kierkegaard, Christ is subjectively the connecting link between always ought and always can. In Christ we encounter a model of this unity of ought and can so that we are able to see that what is required of us is indeed possible. To exist before God is to imitate Christ, and to imitate Christ is to exist before God. One cannot accomplish one without the other. And for Kierkegaard, the nature and the destiny of the individual existing before God is nowhere made more vividly apparent than in the life and suffering of the earthly Christ. Christ is the concrete exemplification of the law as love and of the suffering that inevitably accompanies its appearance within nature.

244

As we have seen, Kierkegaard claimed that Christ is a representation of what is universally required and possible for human beings. If this is so, then to perceive Christ essentially and exclusively as an atoner and redeemer is theologically incorrect, for such a view imputes to Christ qualities and powers that are essentially incongruous with our humanness. Christendom, according to Kierkegaard, is the practical outcome of such a theology. It lacks the ethical essence of Christianity, which places the uncompromising and severe demand upon the Christian to take up the life of Christ by a commitment to imitate his earthly life of compassion and his willingness to suffer. Kierkegaard viewed it as his task to make it unequivocally clear to Christians in Christendom that the imitation of Christ is the practical outcome of the religious commitment to exist before God. To love God is to imitate Christ, and to imitate Christ is to love one's neighbor as one loves oneself. Here is the central theme of this ethicist's analysis of Christendom.

The logical unity of the concepts of existing before God and imitation of Christ and their existential unity in the life of the Christian grounds Kierkegaard's understanding of the ethical essence of Christianity. But precisely this understanding of Kierkegaard's conception of Christianity gives rise to the second difficulty of interpretation. If such weight is given to the ethical nature of Christianity, it becomes difficult to include or to account for Kierkegaard's emphasis on the redemptive significance of Christ's life and death. Innumerable passages in his journals and published works lay an unmistakable stress upon the redemptive value of Christ. For example,

> With regard to contemporaneity with Christ, an observation must still be made about making it the criterion for being a Christian.
> What I have developed in various works about contemporaneity as the criterion is poetically, historically, and

245

> ethically absolutely true, has thus its validity and to that extent also its validity with respect to Christ as a historical, actual person.
>
> But Christ is also the dogmatical. Here is the distinction. His death is indeed the atonement.
>
> Here the category takes a qualitative turn. . . . For Christ's death is not a task for imitation but is the atonement—I do not dare regard or consider Christ as a merely historical person. (*JP*, I, 693)[57]

This passage illuminates Kierkegaard's commitment to the redemptive value of Christ in its conjoining of the historical and the dogmatic, the ethical and the redemptive Christs. This conjoining reflects Kierkegaard's refusal to separate the religious concepts of works and grace. Another passage clarifies this point: "Luther rightly arranges it thus: Christ is gift—to this corresponds faith, He is exemplar—to this corresponds imitation. But more accurately one should say: 1) imitation toward decisive action by which the situation originates for becoming a Christian; 2) Christ as gift—faith; 3) imitation as fruit of faith."[58]

The movement in this passage from imitation to faith back to imitation reflects Kierkegaard's general theological method. As early as 1844, he had established the guiding principle of his theological method in *The Concept of Dread*: "Either the whole of existence is locked up in the requirement of ethics, or the condition for its fulfillment must be provided—and with that the whole of life and of existence begins afresh, not through an immanent continuity with the foregoing (which is a contradiction), but by a transcendent fact . . ." (*CDR*, 16n). Kierkegaard's theological method is dialectically established by positing a "transcendent fact" as the condition of the fulfillment of ethics. For Kierkegaard, then, theological discussion cannot

[57] Cf. *JP*, I, 306, 334, 342; II, 1432.
[58] This journal entry is taken from Dupré, *Kierkegaard as Theologian*, p. 171. See *SKP*, X⁴, A 284.

begin dogmatically with scriptural or ecclesiastical authority or with revelation. Nor can the individual who desires
to become a Christian begin with assent to propositions of
faith. Rather, theological discussion must begin with the
question of ethical obligation, and the individual must begin existentially with the ethical imperative to love others
as one loves oneself.[59] Kierkegaard's correction of Luther in
the passage above is a clear reflection of this methodology.
In the subjective experience of one's inadequacy as an ethical agent, the experience of grace becomes possible, and even
then, faith's fruit continues to be imitation. Thus, the grace
of God both grows out of and fulfills the ethical struggle to
imitate Christ. Put another way, the grace of God appears
within the individual's attempt to love his neighbor as he
loves himself, and the fruit of grace is the fulfillment of this
ethical imperative to will the existence of a community of
ends. Thus, theological doctrines about the nature of
Christ's divinity are themselves dependent upon the ethical
essence of Christianity. Remove the ethical imperative to
love one's neighbor as one loves oneself as the ethical
foundation of Christianity, and Christological doctrines
slip back into the aesthetic interpretations popularized by
Christendom's apologists.

For Kierkegaard, then, Christ's life constitutes an ethical
paradigm for all individuals who choose to will the existence of a community of ends. Christ's life and death are
also dogmatically an expression of God's love for human

[59] The ethical state of existence in the earlier pseudonymous works
is presented as the individual's obligation to unify himself as a synthesis
of necessity and possibility. This ethical imperative culminates in the
consciousness of guilt. It is at this point in the development of subjectivity as guilt that Kierkegaard introduces the religious phenomenon
of faith, which then makes possible the completion of the ethical obligation to unify existentially oneself as a synthesis of necessity and possibility. Here faith in Christ grows out of the need to transcend guilt,
whereas in the later works religious faith grows out of the need to
transcend egotism. In both cases, guilt and egotism are existential
impediments to self-realization.

beings. Without such a divine love, human relations are inescapably caught in the net of egotism. It is in this sense that Christ cannot be imitated. Human subjectivity cannot establish the ground of its own salvation, cannot manufacture the love of God. It can only receive his love and be transformed by it. Moreover, it is by means of the liberation of the individual from his egotistic relations with others that the necessary condition for the constitution of a community of ends is established. Without the sort of love that we see in the life and death of Christ, human subjectivity is, in Kierkegaard's view, inextricably bound to nature. Christ is, then, an expression of God's desire that nature be transformed through the wills of human subjects into a community of ends.

CHAPTER SEVEN

Kierkegaard and the Matter of Style

In 1846 Kierkegaard officially acknowledged his responsibility for the pseudonymous works in an addendum, "A First and Last Declaration," to *Concluding Unscientific Postscript* (*CUP*, 551-54). In this short confession, Kierkegaard makes the modest claim that the pseudonyms' significance "does not consist in making any new proposal, any unheard-of discovery, or in forming a new party . . . but, precisely on the contrary, consists in wanting to have no importance, in wanting (at a distance which is the remoteness of double reflection) to read solo the original text of the individual . . . the old text, well known, handed down from the fathers—to read it through yet once more, if possible in a more heartfelt way" (*CUP*, 554). This modesty may well be yet another example of Kierkegaardian irony, given the originality of his reading of the "original text" of human existence. Human existence is subjectivity, and the text of subjectivity must be both communicated and read in a form consistent with its nature. The objective elusiveness of subjectivity makes it incompatible with direct forms of communication.

The originality of the pseudonymous production lies in the maieutic form of its treatment of subjectivity. Louis Mackey is correct in claiming that the style of "Kierkegaard's writings insinuate their content: subjectivity, inwardness, the passionate appropriation of objectivity uncertainty, is the only truth possible for an existing individual."[1] The cultivation of inwardness along the paths of

---

[1] Louis Mackey, *Kierkegaard: A Kind of Poet* (Philadelphia: University of Pennsylvania Press, 1972), p. 255.

pleasure, freedom, anxiety, obligation, faith, love, despair, fear, and trembling requires a mode of discourse that invites the individual into the risks of introspection and self-discovery. Kierkegaard believed that these paths were no longer well traveled by his contemporaries, who, as a result, had forgotten the text of inwardness. Indeed, the individual had ceased to know himself. And just as one does not help a person to overcome the loss of happiness by giving him a philosophical lecture on the nature of happiness, so one cannot reintroduce an individual to the existential realities of freedom, faith, and love by rigorous philosophical system building. Rather, the task is to induce the state of happiness, the choice of freedom, the risk of faith, the experience and responsibilities of love. Thus, the maieutic form of the pseudonymous books and the substance of self-knowledge, inwardness, subjectivity are dialectically and inseparably linked.

There should be no doubt that this unity of form and content is one of the most salient features of the pseudonymous writings and one to which Kierkegaard was strongly committed during this period of his life. That Kierkegaard would abandon the use of the pseudonym for a more direct mode of discourse has posed problems for those who would understand him. These problems are the more acute because one component of the dialectical unity remained central to Kierkegaard's writings after 1846. Although Kierkegaard abandoned the use of the pseudonym after 1846, he nevertheless remained as committed as ever to the cultivation of inwardness as the central goal of his writings.[2] In

2 Kierkegaard did not completely abandon the use of the pseudonym after 1846; Anti-Climacus is the author of *The Sickness unto Death* (1849) and *Training in Christianity* (1850). Both works, however, are edited by Kierkegaard and lack the strictly maieutic character of the earlier pseudonyms, given their "edifying" intention. The other pseudonymously published book, *Crisis in the Life of an Actress* (1848), is signed by Inter et Inter. For an excellent discussion of the circumstances leading to the publication of this pseudonymous work, see

1848, for example, he complained that the "basic flaw of the age is this teaching which leaves a person's inwardness completely secure" (*JP*, I, 646). To counter this teaching, Kierkegaard wrote in 1850, "I have worked to awaken disquietude with the aim of effecting inward change" (*FSE*, 45).[3] And in 1855, in his open attack on the church, he stated, "When the castle door of inwardness has long been shut and finally is opened, it does not move noiselessly like an apartment door which swings on its hinges" (*AC*, 81). In other words, the reawakening of inwardness in Christendom will have external consequences that are disquieting and painful to the established order. The journals indicate a growing awareness that the concept of "hidden inwardness" developed in *Concluding Unscientific Postscript*[4] must be replaced with an understanding of an inwardness whose development will have social and public manifestations and consequences.[5]

While one may detect in these passages new nuances of meaning with respect to the concept of inwardness in the second literature, the concept clearly continues to constitute the thematic content of Kierkegaard's writings. Kierkegaard explicitly announced that *Training in Christianity* aims at the "revival and increase of inwardness" (*TC*, 5). In concluding this book, Kierkegaard promises to leave "it to the reader what use he will make of what he reads, with respect to inward transformation" (*TC*, 251). When in the concluding chapters of *Purity of Heart* Kierkegaard turns

---

Stephen Crites's introduction to *Crisis in the Life of an Actress* (*CLA*, 7-63).

3 Cf. *FSE*, 46: for "disquietude in the direction of inward change I have laboured."

4 *CUP*, 182-85, 216-19.

5 "Everyone who is Christian in such a way that he says: In hidden inwardness or on Sunday in church I evoke these exalted thoughts, but in practical life I know very well things don't go that way, and so in practical life I do just as the practical world does—he plays at Christianity, and he makes a fool of God" (*JP*, I, 561). Cf. *JP*, II, 2118, 2119, 2120, 2121, 2122, 2125, 2127, 2129, 2130, 2136.

to the question of the book's purpose, he reminds the reader that "the talk asks you . . . or you ask yourself by means of the talk, *what kind of life do you live, do you will one thing, and what is this thing?*" (*PH*, 182; Kierkegaard's italics). In *The Gospel of Suffering*, Kierkegaard brings his reader's attention to the significance of suffering in acquiring self-knowledge (*GS*, 49). This emphasis on inwardness extends into Kierkegaard's treatment of Christianity in his second literature. Yet, even the centrality of Christianity in Kierkegaard's vision of earthly life does not deter his commitment to the transforming power of inwardness. Indeed, since "Christianity is inwardness, inward deepening" (*ANOL*, 49), it is "victorious inwardness" (*ANOL*, 51).

The disruption of the dialectical symmetry of form and content, pseudonym and inwardness in the second literature is perplexing given Kierkegaard's continuing interest as a writer in the inward transformation of his reader. This transition to an almost exclusive use of direct discourse was problematic even for Kierkegaard himself. He took enormous pride in his use of the pseudonym as an ingenious way of involving his reader in a subjective analysis of ethical and religious questions (*JP*, V, 5987). Although he abandoned this pseudonymous mode of discourse as his central means of communication, he never completely lost interest in it, as his preoccupation with it up to 1853 evidences. Both his belief in the pedagogical soundness of the pseudonymous writings and his fascination with them as bearing "the birthmarks of my personality"[6] motivated his continuing interest. In addition to these philosophical and psychological considerations, there eventually developed for Kierkegaard a problem concerning the relation of the pseudonymous writings to the numerous nonpseudonymous writings that he began to produce after 1846. By 1847 the

---

[6] *Breve og Akstykker Vedrorende Søren Kierkegaard*, ed. Niels Thulstrup, 2 vols. (Copenhagen: Munksgaard, 1953-54), I, 121. Quoted by Josiah Thompson, *Kierkegaard* (New York: Alfred A. Knopf, 1973), p. 137.

nature of the relation of indirect and direct communication, of pseudonyms and discourses began seriously to agitate him.

We can see from his journal entries for 1846-1848 that Kierkegaard was groping unsteadily toward some sort of compromise between the indirect and direct modes of communication.[7] It is clear that he decided during these years not to return to a consistent use of the pseudonym, but he could not make a similar decision about indirect communication and vacillated over the appropriateness of these two modes of discourse for his purposes as an author. Even without the pseudonyms, he believed that he must maintain a maieutic relation with his reader as long as his central purpose as a writer was to evoke an internal and subjective activity within his reader. At the same time, it was clear to him that a religious writer cannot effectively communicate religious beliefs without resorting to a mode of discourse that in some sense directly addresses the reader.

Kierkegaard arrived at no quick and totally satisfactory resolution of this dilemma. A reading of his journals, however, especially the entries for 1846-1848, and an examination of the posthumously published *The Point of View* and the books published after 1846 will help us to piece together Kierkegaard's uncertain strategy for resolving this pedagogical tension. In analyzing Kierkegaard's dilemma, we shall focus on four related issues: Kierkegaard's reasons for maintaining a form of indirect communication after closing the pseudonymous authorship in 1846; his reasons for claiming that the times require a more direct mode of discourse; his attempt to synthesize key elements of both styles in the Christian discourse; and his direct attack on the established order in the last years of his life.

[7] Dru's method of arranging Kierkegaard's journals chronologically is especially useful at this point. The reader can obtain a clear sense of the chronology of Kierkegaard's struggles with this issue (*SKJ*, 149-78).

253

REASONS FOR MAINTAINING AN INDIRECT MODE OF DISCOURSE

In discussing Kierkegaard's use of indirect communication, it is not my intention to cover the pseudonymous period. Mackey's analysis of Kierkegaard's style in the pseudonymous writings has not been surpassed. My more modest intention here is to focus briefly on the points that Kierkegaard made, primarily in his journals, that have a bearing on his activity as an author after 1845. Most of the reasons Kierkegaard gave to justify the use of indirect communication in this later period are ones he also gave to justify its use in the pseudonymous period. As extensive studies of Kierkegaard's maieutic method of communication are available, we need not do more here than briefly review this issue.[8] More important will be our discussion of Kierkegaard's justification of the use of direct discourse and his attempt to bring direct and indirect communication into a harmonious and consistent usage.

One of Kierkegaard's most persistent defenses of the use of indirect communication was to point out the inadequacies of direct communication in relation to ethics and religion. Direct communication, Kierkegaard argued, presumes to convey propositional knowledge about an object. It presupposes a communicator, a receiver of the communication, an objective fact to be communicated, and the communication itself (*JP*, I, 651). Such presuppositions necessarily deflect the receiver's attention away from himself and in the direction of the objective information being communicated. This kind of pedagogical orientation may be adequate, for example, for mathematics, history of philosophy, and the sciences, but it is deleterious to the ethical and religious life. When the ethical good and religious faith become essentially objects of reflection, the individual tends

[8] See n. 23 below for references to key studies of Kierkegaard's literary style.

to forget to question his own ethical and religious life in his haste to settle abstractly questions about goodness and faith. Kierkegaard recognized the danger that ethics and religion would become part of the knowledge industry: "In a certain sense there is something horrible about contemplating the whole mob of publishers, book-sellers, journalists, authors—all of them working day and night in the service of confusion, because men will not become sober and understand that relatively little knowledge is needed to be truly human—but all the more self-knowledge" (*JP*, I, 649). The deep irony of studying ethics and religion objectively and forgetting oneself in the process was not lost upon Kierkegaard. He saw, moreover, that this objectifying spirit reaches far beyond the philosopher's study and into the lives of common folk, and he took great delight in satirizing the butcher, the baker, and the cobbler who have taken to discussing their professions in terms of German philosophy.

To attempt to communicate both ethics and religion directly may also have the unfortunate consequence of confusing the criterion for knowledge. As we have seen, Hegel believed that a religious truth is known only when it is explained conceptually by philosophical reflection.[9] Thus, the truth of the religious life is known through its direct communication in a philosophical system explaining its nature. This view has the ironical consequence of making it possible for philosophers to know religious truth without being religious. Of course, the philosopher claims that the truth he knows is a philosophical one that in the past has been disguised in religious myth, story, or belief. Kierkegaard repudiated this position outright and countered it with the Socratic conception of knowledge, which states that the only real criterion for knowledge is behavior. One cannot know the good without being good: "Socrates is right: if a man does not do the right, it is because he does

9 See Chapter Two, pp. 52-58.

not understand it; if he understood it, he would do it . . ."
(*JP*, IV, 4297).[10]

Once the idea takes hold that a knowledge of ethics and
religion is simply propositional and that the criterion for
being ethical and religious is an acknowledgment of the
truth of these propositions, then it will follow that the
ethical and religious life can be lived without disturbing
the status quo.[11] Kierkegaard argued that if ethical and religious truth "is communicated in a direct form, then the
point is missed; then the reader is led into misunderstanding—he gets something more to know, that to exist [*at
existere*] also has its meaning, but he receives it as knowledge so that he keeps right on sitting in the *status quo*"
(*JP*, I, 633). Propositional knowledge about ethics and religion is as neutrally related to its social environment as is
any theoretical knowledge. In and of itself, propositional
knowledge of anything does not necessarily compel action
or change within the environment that generates it. While
this attitude may be appropriate for mathematics and the
sciences, it is a perversion of the ethical and religious life,
which is by nature action-oriented. Thus, Kierkegaard
viewed direct communication of the ethical and religious
life as partially responsible for the neutralization of the
action that is central to that life. For this reason, he sought
throughout his life to discover appropriate modes of indirect discourse.[12]

---

[10] Cf. *JP*, IV, 4301: "Socrates would himself understand this in the
same way; for here we see how true and how Socratic was this Socratic
principle: to understand, truly to understand, is to be."

[11] The religious person, unlike the philosopher, does not know
religious truth in its higher philosophical form. While the philosopher
appeals to reason to justify his claim that the philosophically purified
religious proposition is true, the nonphilosopher will appeal to biblical
or ecclesiastical authority to justify his belief that the same proposition
in its protoreligious form is true. For both, however, religious truth
takes a propositional form and requires mental assent.

[12] Kierkegaard referred to this ploy to convert the subjective character
of ethics and religion into an objective problem of knowledge as the

A second reason that Kierkegaard gave for the necessity of communicating indirectly with his readers is that he must speak without authority. This claim to be speaking without authority is a refrain that Kierkegaard's reader repeatedly encounters in the journals, in *The Point of View*, and in the prefaces, introductions, and conclusions of most of his published works.[13] This decision to speak without authority set Kierkegaard in opposition to the religious and philosophical establishment of his day and to the authority of its representatives—pastors, theologians, and philosophers. Pastors clearly represented the ecclesiastical and biblical authority of the Christian tradition. Theologians also basked in this authority, while philosophers enjoyed the authority of reason. In all three cases, authority is neither grounded nor expressed in an existential and subjective appropriation of the ethical-religious life. Rather, it is grounded in or justified by either the church or the reason of philosophical idealism and is expressed, as we have seen above, by communicating religious and ethical truths directly in a propositional form. Moreover, to accept a proposition as true on the authority of either the church or philosophical idealism requires no other activity than mental assent on the part of the receiver. The individual is compelled neither to analyze the claim for himself nor to attempt to reduplicate the truth in his own life.[14] Thus, to speak with authority merely reinforces the subjective neutrality encouraged by the direct communication of truth in a propositional form.

Kierkegaard, then, must communicate with his reader

---

basic "dishonesty" of his age. By making the subjective life essentially an epistemological problem rather than an ethical and religious one, Christendom had become essentially dishonest (*JP*, I, 654).

13 Søren Kierkegaard, *Two Discourses at the Communion on Fridays*, in *For Self-Examination* and *Judge for Yourselves*, trans. with intro. and notes by Walter Lowrie (Princeton: Princeton University Press, 1968), p. 5.

14 For Kierkegaard's extensive development of this point, see the "Redoubling" and "Reduplication" entries in the third volume of *JP*.

not only indirectly but also without authority. Parodying the authority of the philosophical and religious establishment, Kierkegaard claimed that he could not speak with authority because he himself was not a Christian (*JP*, VI, 6511). One's authority in anything is based on one's knowledge of that thing; therefore, one can be an authority on the religious and the ethical only by virtue of one's knowledge of both. And since, Socratically, ethical and religious knowledge must be existentially apprehended, it is impossible for one to speak with authority without existentially having become a Christian.

It is important to note that Kierkegaard rested his case for speaking without authority not only on the epistemological claim that knowledge is the ground of authority but also on his belief that a person's speaking with authority about religion without being existentially religious constitutes a serious threat to the viability of religion. For this reason, Kierkegaard viewed the Danish pastor as one of Christianity's worst enemies. To misrepresent Christianity as does the Danish pastor is a serious enough problem, but when he does it with authority, the problem is more than doubly compounded. Misrepresentation of Christianity under the guise of authority simply reinforces and protects the enfeebled Christianity of the Danish church. The authoritative aura surrounding all direct communication about religion and ethics led Kierkegaard to maintain an indirect mode of discourse that is for epistemological and strategic reasons communicated without authority.[15]

A third reason for employing the method of indirect communication is related to Kierkegaard's perception of the impact of liberalism on the individual's self-understanding. As we have seen in Chapter One, the old feudal and monarchical order of medieval Denmark began to disintegrate in the eighteenth century; by the turn of the century the individual no longer so clearly perceived himself

[15] For a further elaboration of Kierkegaard's views about the Danish pastor, see *AC* and the "Pastor" entries in the third volume of *JP*.

as woven into the fabric of an established order that gave priority to the community over the individual. Increasingly in the nineteenth century, as the political and economic authority of the feudal order diminished and its rigid social stratification cracked, individuals began to acquire an image of themselves as self-determining beings in the political, economic, and social arenas of life. This metaphysical view of the self as a self-determining individual was, as we have seen, cultivated by a constellation of factors, including the emergence of liberalism in the realm of Danish politics and economics, the flowering of romanticism in art and philosophy, and the evangelical emphasis on the conversion of the individual in the Christianity of rural Denmark.

Kierkegaard's journals reflect a keen sensitivity to the impact that the political revolution in Denmark had on the emergence of this new self-understanding. He observed, for example, that because Danes had become so self-reflective, "no individual (king, pope, etc.) can ever again become a tyrant" (*JP*, IV, 4118). In fact, the institution of monarchy was seriously threatened by the subjective reflection engendered by the modern age. Kierkegaard predicted that "it will appear all the more disproportionate for one person to be king" (*JP*, IV, 4143). If one looks carefully, it can be seen that *king* "is actually a common noun, [and] belongs essentially to natural states in which the individual is not reflected in himself . . ." (*JP*, IV, 4143). Referring in 1846 to the institution of the monarchy, Kierkegaard argued that "the political is a dialectical relation between the individual and the community in the representative individual [the king]; but in our time the individual is in the process of becoming far too reflective to be able to be satisfied with merely being *represented*" (*SKJ*, 563).[16] The disappearance of the monarchy and its *representative* king was symptomatic of a more fundamental revolution in human self-consciousness by which the individual was coming to view himself as his own legitimate representative. The no-

16 Cf. *JP*, VI, 6604.

tion that the individual can represent himself politically and economically becomes the spiritual foundation of this radically reflective age. Within this conception of subjectivity, the power and rules for development are politically grounded, while the possibilities and goals of subjective development are economically determined. Thus, we can see clearly that the new order weaves a new conception of subjectivity out of the political and economic fabric of liberalism.

Kierkegaard is often credited with introducing the concept of individual subjectivity into contemporary philosophy in opposition to the objectification of ethics and religion by philosophical idealism. This judgment is only partially correct. Kierkegaard's emphasis on subjectivity was not only a response to idealism but also an attempt to provide an alternative understanding of human subjectivity. Kierkegaard perceived his Denmark as being committed not only to objectifying religion and ethics but also to developing an acquisitive subjectivity. The relation between these two, he believed, is not simply coincidental or accidental, since this secular version of subjectivity can occupy the individual only when its ethical-religious interpretation has been safely removed. Indeed, as we have seen, the old religion can be spruced up and transformed into an ally of this more modern aesthetic version of human subjectivity. "As I have demonstrated on all sides, all modern Christendom is a shifting of the essentially Christian back into the esthetic" (*JP*, VI, 6466). Religion in Denmark is combined not with an ethical interpretation of subjectivity but with an aesthetic interpretation that is provided by the leaders of modernization.

Kierkegaard quickly realized that the introduction of an ethical-religious interpretation of subjectivity in opposition to its aesthetic-religious interpretation must proceed indirectly. Little is to be gained by speaking directly about religion; such speech would immediately be confused with the speech of the pastors and theologians. Since their religious speech is linked with the aesthetic mode of existence and since they are perceived as speaking with authority, the pastors have made it difficult for anyone to employ religious discourse in a conventional manner without being understood as the pastors themselves are understood. Moreover, a direct presentation of an ethical interpretation of subjectivity would remind Danes too much of the past they are trying to escape. Ethical discourse would sound like moralizing to an age infatuated with the glittering promises of the new liberal order. Kierkegaard recognized that the best strategy was to take modern Denmark seriously on its own terms. He must therefore begin with its own aesthetic interpretation of subjectivity.

As we know, Kierkegaard is at his dialectical best in indirectly disclosing the limitations and contradictions in the aesthetic mode of existence. The power of the first volume of *Either/Or* lies in the manner in which Kierkegaard leads the reader indirectly toward an awareness that when life is conceived as essentially the pursuit of pleasure, it can end only in despair. In the second literature, especially in *Works of Love* and *Purity of Heart*, Kierkegaard is anxious to point his reader toward the recognition that an acquisitive society sets each individual at war with all others so that the ends of happiness and self-respect are in fact always either endangered or out of reach. Only when a reader has been lured into personal experience and awareness of these contradictions within the Danish aesthetic interpretation of subjectivity will it be possible for him seriously to consider the ethical alternative. Once the reader has reached the point of being willing to consider the ethical alternative, Kierkegaard recognizes that he must continue to deal with him as a self-determining individual. The age is too reflective for a return to a more authoritarian past in which king and pope govern the secular and religious lives of their subjects. The reflective awakening of the individual to his own subjective power and possibilities has determined once and for all the ground rules according to which the ethical-religious game is to be played. Thus, the reader must be indirectly addressed. Otherwise, the author does not take him seriously and will fail in his bid to bring about an ethical-religious mode of existence.

These three reasons for indirectly addressing his reader about the ethical-religious mode of existence are justified by the historical situation in which Kierkegaard wrote. Kierkegaard believed, as we have seen, that indirect communication should be used as a countermeasure to the tendency of philosophers, theologians, and pastors to address their readers and listeners directly and with authority. Kierkegaard also concluded that any author in Denmark who intended to communicate effectively with his countrymen concerning the life of the spirit could not ignore the reflective and critical character of the age and its exaltation of the individual within the secular and religious sectors of life. Thus, his resorting to indirect modes of communication reflects his decision to take his historical situation seriously.

But Kierkegaard was also prepared to defend the use of indirect discourse on purely philosophical grounds. Beginning, as he does, with the supposition that "all communication of knowledge is direct communication" (*JP*, I, 651), Kierkegaard maneuvered the communication of ethics into a different pedagogical arena with the claim that the "ethical is indifferently related to knowledge . . . (*JP*, I, 649:5). Unlike the sciences and mathematics, Kierkegaard insisted, "It is unconditionally true of the ethical that it cannot be taught. The instructive lecture deals with an object—and ethically there simply is no object . . ." (*JP*, I, 656). Since an ethical communication does not presume the existence of an object independently of the communicator and the receiver, it is logically impossible to convey facts or information about such an object in a directly communicated proposition. Thus, it is mistaken to refer to ethical communication as a communication of knowledge.

Kierkegaard further complicated this position by making

the additional claim that the direct communication of ethics as knowledge is impossible. "The ethical presupposes that every person knows what the ethical is . . ." (*JP*, I, 649:10); thus, communication of the ethical as knowledge is an absurd redundancy. One cannot communicate to a person knowledge that he already possesses. One can infer from these two passages that there is after all a species of knowledge that can be called ethical knowledge, although it is of the sort that every individual already possesses and therefore is not to be learned in the conventional sense of learning.

Kierkegaard, then, denied the possibility of directly communicating ethical knowledge on two grounds: there is no ethical object about which objective knowledge or information can be acquired; and the subject already possesses whatever ethical knowledge there is to be known. Both statements reduce to a single problem concerning the nature of ethical knowledge. What sort of knowledge is, on the one hand, not related to an objective fact existing in some sense independently of the communicator and the receiver and, on the other, is already in every person's possession? Kierkegaard answers, "Insofar as the ethical could be said to have a knowledge in itself, it is 'self-knowledge,' but this is improperly regarded as a knowledge" (*JP*, I, 653:30). Kierkegaard, however, was not intimidated by such an impropriety, for he speaks consistently throughout his writings about self-knowledge and argues as consistently that the task of ethics is to turn "a person out of his delusions" by leading him to self-knowledge (*JP*, I, 649:5). The self is, as we have seen, a triadic unity of necessity (particularity), possibility (universality), and spirit (consciousness). The individual's necessity, which particularizes him, is a historically determined identity; his possibility, which universalizes him, is his ethical obligation to himself and to his neighbor. The action of becoming reflectively conscious of oneself as a synthesis of necessity and possibility is the manner in which the self becomes its own object. As a being

263

with the capacity for self-consciousness, the individual, as spirit, can make himself, as a synthesis of necessity and possibility, an object of consciousness.

Since the self as knower and known are ontologically unified as spirit and the synthesis of possibility and necessity, there also exists an epistemological unity of knower and known. Thus, it is correct to say that the knower already knows what is to be known. Kierkegaard recognized that reflection is required in order to bring this knowledge to the level of reflective self-consciousness. To be sure, the individual is always in a privileged position with respect to self-knowledge, since it is *his* historical identity and *his* ethical obligation that are to be known. Both objects of knowledge are grounded in the ontological constitution of each particular self and are therefore immediately available to him. In the activity of critical self-reflection, the individual brings this immediate knowledge to the level of reflective self-consciousness. He thereby reflectively acquires a knowledge that he already prereflectively possesses; he does not acquire new knowledge about some object existing independently of himself.[17]

Kierkegaard further claimed that since the acquiring of self-knowledge is the *telos* of the ethical life, an age that communicates the ethical as science and scholarship is essentially "dishonest" (*JP*, I, 649:5). "If one begins first of all with a course to instill the ethical into the individual, then the communication never becomes ethical and the relationship is disturbed from the beginning. The communication here implies luring the ethical out of the individual, because it is *in* the individual" (*JP*, I, 649:5; Kierkegaard's italics). Whereas science "probably can be pounded into a person . . . the ethical has to be pounded out of him . . ." (*JP*, I, 649:6). This "luring" and "pounding" of the ethical out of the individual requires a mode of communication

[17] For a more complete discussion of Kierkegaard's ontology and epistemology with respect to the self, review Chapters Four and Five above.

that awakens an active and critical self-reflection within the reader. Kierkegaard described this mode of communication as "art-instruction" (*JP*, I, 650:13) and "communication of capability" (*JP*, I, 651, 653) (*Kunnens Meddelse*), as opposed to the communication of knowledge (*Videns Meddelse*), which is discursive and propositional in nature. With respect to effective communication, the means must be consistent with the ends. Where the active and critical self-reflection of the reader is the end, an artistic mode of discourse must be employed in order to awaken the reader to his own subjective inwardness. The ethical writer must deflect the reader's attention away from the world of objects and toward his own subjective being. This goal can be accomplished only by luring the reader into a world of discourse that both mirrors and provides the means for cultivating his own subjective inwardness. Such a communication seeks not to impose propositional knowledge about objects. Rather, it attempts to stimulate the subjective ethical activity of coming to know and to accept oneself as a being with an ethical obligation to accept and to affirm as good one's own historical identity and the identity and freedom of one's neighbor as well.

Kierkegaard, then, resorted to indirect modes of discourse not only because the historical situation demanded it but also because the ethical *telos* of knowing and choosing oneself requires indirect communication. Thus, for historical and philosophical reasons, Kierkegaard believed that he must employ indirect discourse as long as he as a writer was committed to the cultivation of this ethical *telos* in his reader.

REASONS FOR THE TRANSITION TO DIRECT DISCOURSE

With the publication of *Concluding Unscientific Postscript* in 1846, Kierkegaard not only publicly acknowledged the pseudonyms as his own production but also privately expressed in his journal a sense of satisfaction and comple-

265

tion. "The *Concluding Postscript* is out; the pseudonymity has been acknowledged; one of these days the printing of the 'Literary Review' will begin. Everything is in order; all I have to do now is to keep calm, be silent, depending on *The Corsair* to support the whole enterprise negatively, just as I wish. . . . In itself it was a most capital ideal to make a break with *The Corsair* in order to prevent any direct advances at the very moment I was through with the authorship and, by assuming all the pseudonyms, ran the risk of becoming an authority of sorts" (*JP*, V, 5887). Kierkegaard was delighted that his criticism of *The Corsair* provoked its editor, Meïr Goldschmidt, into an attack on him that was both personal and professional in nature.[18] Kierkegaard regarded this attack as a perfect antidote to the possibility that he might, after having acknowledged his responsibility for the pseudonyms, become in some sense an authority for his age. Since he himself had become an object of ridicule, Kierkegaard believed, each pseudonym would have to be taken seriously on its own terms and could not gain prominence because of his reputation as an author. The *Corsair* affair and Kierkegaard's coming out "polemically against the age" in *A Literary Review* (1846)[19] guaranteed that the maieutic character of the pseudonymous authorship would be protected and maintained.

Having reached this professional plateau, Kierkegaard succumbed to a vocational malaise that troubled him through 1848. Journal entries from the 1846-1848 period reflect Kierkegaard's attempt to resolve this crisis by choosing a new life's work.[20] The struggle had both psychologi-

[18] For the *Corsair* affair, see Chapter Four, n. 26. For a complete picture of this pivotal point in Kierkegaard's life, see Søren Kierkegaard, *The Corsair Affair*, trans. and ed. Howard V. Hong and Edna H. Hong, Vol. XIII of *Kierkegaard's Writings* (Princeton: Princeton University Press, forthcoming).

[19] A portion of this book has been available to the English reader as *The Present Age*. The complete work is now available as *Two Ages*; see Chapter Two, n. 1.

[20] See n. 7 above.

cal and philosophical dimensions. From the psychological perspective, Kierkegaard's problem was to transcend his melancholy, which had found an imaginative outlet in the production of the pseudonyms.[21] His poetic nature was perfectly suited to the pseudonym, but by 1846 his task had become one of surpassing this psychological barrier to self-expression in a more direct manner. The challenge was to cease being a poet, to abandon the life of the imagination and to "touch actuality" in some nonaesthetic life orientation. Thus, Kierkegaard seriously entertained the thought of becoming a rural pastor. He had considered and abandoned this possibility as early as 1843 at the time he published *Either/Or*. In 1846 this choice was once again replaced by another possibility. It occurred to him that something more significant than a rural parsonage lay in his future. He observed that *"the situation here at home is becoming more and more confused"* and that the "question now is, insofar as there is any question about the need for an extraordinary in the literary, social, and political situation . . . whether there is anyone in the kingdom suitable to be that except me" (*JP*, V, 5961; Kierkegaard's italics).

Stephen Crites cogently describes Kierkegaard's conception of the *extraordinarius*: a "prophet or apostle set aside by God for a great and absolutely unique mission, and therefore an exception to any of the normal categories of life. . . . He speaks with authority, without appeal to human wisdom; his categories are transcendent, and therefore his words are inherently and irreducibly paradoxical from the standpoint of any human reflection" (*CLA*, 52). Kierkegaard never succeeded in accomplishing more than a meticulous development of the concept of the *extraordinarius* (*AR*, 32-46). Existentially, the act of actually choosing to become an *extraordinarius* was as elusive as the earlier act

21 One of the virtues of Josiah Thompson's book is its persuasive demonstration, by reference to Kierkegaard's journals, of the psychological motivation of the pseudonymous works. See n. 46 below for my response to Thompson on this point.

of becoming a pastor. Kierkegaard simply could not break the influence his melancholy exerted over him; temperamentally, he was never suited to "touch actuality" as either pastor or *extraordinarius*. Moreover, both roles required the ability to speak with religious authority, and, as we have seen, Kierkegaard believed himself unprepared either to preach a sermon or to deliver an attack against the established order in the name of God.[22] Even his conversion experience of 1848 was not sufficiently strong to transform his poetic nature and enable him to abandon the task of poet for that of pastor or prophet.[23]

[22] In the last years of his life, Kierkegaard directly attacked the established order, taking on, in one sense of the term, a role as *extraordinarius*. See n. 46 below.

[23] It is not my intention here to review the psychological dimensions of Kierkegaard's vocational crisis. This problem has been covered by Lowrie in his early study of Kierkegaard. Lowrie takes the position that the 1848 conversion experience broke the melancholic paralysis of Kierkegard's life, releasing him to write his best and most personal works. Lowrie includes in this list, *The Sickness unto Death, Training in Christianity, For Self-Examination*, and the posthumously published *Judge for Yourselves*. See Walter Lowrie, *Kierkegaard*, 2 vols. (London: Oxford University Press, 1938). More recently, this same material has been covered by Gregor Malantschuk, Stephen Crites, Louis Mackey, and Josiah Thompson. Malantschuk persuasively agrees that Kierkegaard's vocational crisis continually troubled him throughout his writing career and was not limited to the years immediately following his admission concerning the pseudonyms. See Malantschuk's introduction, "Søren Kierkegaard—Poet or Pastor?" in *Armed Neutrality and An Open Letter*. Crites's introduction to the Harper Torchbook edition of *Crisis in the Life of an Actress* gives the reader a fresh perspective on Kierkegaard's dilemma by examining it in the light of his uncertainty and confusion concerning the desirability of pseudonymously publishing an aesthetic work in the midst of the development of his religious works in the second literature (*CLA*, 7-63). Mackey's book on Kierkegaard as a poet is perhaps the best on this subject; Thompson's is the most recent treatment. Thompson offers an excellent example of what Kierkegaard would call a "corrective" in that he successfully argues that the use of the pseudonym cannot be analyzed in pedagogical terms alone; a significant psychological dimension informs their use as well. An interesting study of Kierkegaard's theory of communication

The inner turmoil of this vocational malaise found no outward expression during these years. Kierkegaard continued to write at a rapid pace. In 1847 and 1848 he published *Consider the Lillies, Purity of Heart, Works of Love,* and *Christian Discourses.* During this period he was also at work on his book on Adler. All of these books, as well as the ones that follow, are directly communicated.[24] Behind the publishing scene, in both his journals and the posthumously published *The Point of View,* Kierkegaard was trying to work out the relation between direct and indirect communication. As is frequently the case with Kierkegaard, his retrospective glances on his professional writing career cast an illuminating light on its direction and purpose. Keeping in mind that Kierkegaard sometimes read more into his past than is actually there, we can follow his path toward the adoption of a position concerning the relation of direct and indirect communication.

We have already seen that Kierkegaard used the pseudonymous mode of indirect communication because of uncertainty about the relation of direct discourse and Christianity.[25] In retrospect, Kierkegaard claimed that during

---

is Ronald J. Manheimer, *Kierkegaard as Educator* (Berkeley: University of California Press, 1977).

[24] The one exception is *CLA*; see n. 2 above. Even though *The Sickness unto Death* and *Training in Christianity* are written by Anti-Climacus, they do not qualify as indirect communication, according to Kierkegaard. "*Anti-Climacus is not indirect communication,* inasmuch as there is a forward by me. Indirect communication is a placing together of dialectical contrasts—and then not a single word of a personal understanding. The mitigation in a more direct communication is, among other things, that the communicator has a need to be understood personally, has a fear of being misunderstood. Indirect communication is sheer tension" (*JP*, I, 679; Kierkegaard's italics). Cf. *JP*, VI, 6577.

[25] Kierkegaard had, of course, published eighteen *Edifying Discourses* during his pseudonymous period. The publication of a pseudonymous work was usually accompanied by the publication of one or more religious discourses under his own name. These discourses are concerned with those religious sentiments that are natural to man.

the pseudonymous period he "had been continually un-
clear" about this relation (*JP*, VI, 6248). "I was not myself
clear and basically maintained the connection with indirect communication" (*JP*, VI, 6248). We have already discussed the complex problems confronting Kierkegaard
with regard to the use of direct communication in relation
to Christianity. How could he write directly about Christianity without exposing it to the maw of philosophical
idealism? How could he write directly about Christianity
without appearing to speak with authority? How could he
write directly about Christianity without confusing or of-
fending the reader who is being subjectively developed
within the aesthetic mode of existence by the liberalization
of Denmark? Finally, how could he write directly about
Christianity when it is necessary that the ethical and the
religious be subjectively rather than objectively appropriated? By 1848, however, Kierkegaard's uncertainty seems
to have so thoroughly vanished that he could state that the
direct mode of discourse is the correct one for Christianity
and that "henceforth it will be indefensible to use" the
pseudonymous mode of indirect communication (*JP*, VI,
6248). The mode of direct discourse that he had been developing since 1846 did justice, he believed, to the historical situation, pedagogical theory, and Christianity. An 1850
journal entry strongly conveys this self-assurance about the
transition to direct discourse: "my indirect communication
is on a lower level than the direct, for the indirectness was
due also to my not being clear myself at the beginning and
therefore did not dare speak directly . . ." (*JP*, VI, 6700).
Kierkegaard's claim that his direct mode of communication

This natural religion is discussed in great detail in *Concluding Unscientific Postscript* under the descriptive title "Religiousness A." But
even though these discourses are communicated directly, they are not
direct in any traditional sense, for they are delivered nondidactically
and without authority. For an insightful discussion of the relation of
these early discourses and the pseudonymous books, see Mackey, *Kierkegaard*, pp. 85-132, 256-58.

is superior to his indirect mode will be explored in depth below.[26]

Before we investigate this claim, however, it would be well to notice another key factor in Kierkegaard's understanding of the relation of direct communication and Christianity. Kierkegaard came to believe that Christianity cannot properly be conveyed through the pseudonymous mode of indirect communication as he had developed and used it from 1841 to 1846. Something about Christianity requires a direct mode of communication. "Ethically man as such knows about the ethical, but man as such does not know about the religious in the Christian sense. Here there must be the communication of a little knowledge . . ." (*JP*, I, 650:13). In opposition to ethics, the "maieutic cannot be the final form, because, Christianly understood, the truth doth not lie in the subject (as Socrates understood it), but in a revelation which must be proclaimed" (*JP*, II, 1957). Thus, the element of knowledge associated with the Christian understanding of truth requires a direct mode of communication. Kierkegaard took a long time in discovering how properly to communicate this knowledge to his reader in such a way as to avoid the mistakes and "dishonesty" characterizing the direct communication of Christianity by the philosophers, theologians, and pastors in modern Denmark.

By 1848 Kierkegaard appeared confident that he had developed a mode of direct discourse that he could employ exclusively for the purpose of communicating Christianity. He noted in late 1847 that "along with the pseudonyms there always was direct communication in the guise of the upbuilding or edifying discourses, and the last few years I have used direct communication almost exclusively" (*JP*, I, 656). In a journal entry from that same year he claimed that "In regard to the ethical and the ethical-religious, the genuine communication and instruction is *training* or *upbringing*" (*JP*, I, 650:12; Kierkegaard's italics). In this cru-

26 See pp. 274-92 below.

cial judgment that the directly communicated discourse is the key for religious training and upbringing, we find Kierkegaard's main pedagogical reason for shifting to an exclusive use of direct discourse. Whereas the focus of the pseudonyms had been on reintroducing the reader to the reality of ethical-religious subjectivity, Kierkegaard shifted his focus in the second literature to his reader's upbringing and training within the ethical-religious mode of existence—that is, in Christianity. In other words, just as the earlier pseudonyms lead the reader *toward* Christianity, Kierkegaard in the second literature develops him *as* a Christian. Kierkegaard can thus proceed to deal more directly with the Christian life without giving the impression that it can be directly appropriated. The pseudonyms conveniently stand as a counterweight to this sort of misconstrual of the directly communicated second literature. Put yet another way, once the ethical-religious stage of existence is reached, the mode of discourse designed to lead the reader to this point can be abandoned. Direct discourse, which cultivates and edifies Christian inwardness, must replace the indirect discourse that subjectively develops the reader *toward* the point of becoming inwardly religious.

Nevertheless, even the direct discourse of the second literature must in a sense be indirect. It is not only essential that its directness be counterbalanced by the indirectness of the pseudonymous literature, but it is also crucial to retain a degree of indirection even within an explicitly direct address to the reader. Kierkegaard insisted that the "instruction, the communication, must not be as of a knowledge, but upbringing, practising, art-instruction" (*JP*, I, 650:13). Even though a strictly religious discourse includes a communication of knowledge, it must be communicated indirectly. Thus, the "ethical-religious communication, namely, Christian [communication] . . . is direct-indirect" (*JP*, I, 657). A religious communication, though unlike the ethical in the sense that it contains an element of knowledge and must be stated directly, is nevertheless like the ethical in the sense that it must be a communication of capability and therefore imparted indirectly (*JP*, I, 651). With respect to the ethical-religious life, "The communication is still not essentially of knowledge but a communication of capability. That there is an element of knowledge is particularly true for Christianity; a knowledge of Christianity must certainly be communicated in advance. But it is only a preliminary" (*JP*, I, 653:29). The inward cultivation of an ethical-religious existence requires the active participation of the individual. Just as the *pseudonyms* indirectly lured the reader out of the aesthetic into an ethical-religious mode of subjectivity, so *Kierkegaard himself* seeks to enable the reader actively to cultivate his own ethical-religious inwardness. His mode of writing must become direct, because direct communication is more suitable for religious upbringing and training and because an element of knowledge must be communicated.

Even though these elements of a more direct style become evident in his work after 1846, Kierkegaard never completely abandoned indirect communication, since the individual's religious training requires active and internal appropriation of the religious way of life. Thus, Kierkegaard found himself in the position of having to communicate in a direct-indirect fashion.

For Kierkegaard, religious upbringing essentially involves sharply and clearly focusing the ethical core of the religious life and the God-relationship that grounds it. Toward this end, Kierkegaard, employing his new mode of discourse, engaged four separate yet interrelated tasks: to specify the concrete situation, Christendom, in which religious inwardness must be cultivated; to cultivate the individual's God-relationship as the ground of the religious life; to define concisely the categories of religious inwardness; and to demonstrate the polemical dimension of religious inwardness. These are the specific dimensions of the task of cultivating religious inwardness that Kierkegaard believed required a direct-indirect mode of discourse.

DIRECT-INDIRECT COMMUNICATION

Kierkegaard began to use the term *Christendom* consistently in his journals and published works in 1847. It is significant because Kierkegaard introduced it to describe the concrete historical situation of his reader. Kierkegaard viewed his task after 1848 as leading his reader to understand that his subjective awakening and religious development do not occur in a material vacuum and that his concrete situation in nineteenth-century Denmark will work against his ethical and religious development. In the pseudonymous literature, the reader's situation gradually comes to be defined in terms of German and Danish idealism and its philosophical commitment to the dissolution of the concept of the individual as an ontological reality and the objectification of religion.[27] As early as 1846, as evidenced by the publication of *A Literary Review*, Kierkegaard began to realize that his reader was spiritually ensconced not so much in a philosophical system as in a way of life, which Kierkegaard called Christendom. As we have seen from our discussion of the "natural man" in Chapters Three and Four, Kierkegaard perceived the individual as being situated in a set of determinate social, political, and economic relations in the modern state, which is in turn religiously legitimated by both liberal and orthodox versions of Christianity.

Kierkegaard complained that the individual in Christendom loves nothing "as he loves the secular, his profit, honor, esteem, the community of mutual self-love, etc." (*JP*, I, 383). Christendom "is an attachment to this life and is an understanding of the things of men . . ." (*JP*, I, 387). The individual in Christendom "does not have an essential relationship to God . . . he lets his prudence be in control" (*JP*, I, 656).[28] Moreover, Christianity has been taken over

[27] For a review of my discussion of this situation, see Chapter Two, passim.

[28] In *For Self-Examination* and *Judge for Yourselves*, Kierkegaard

274

by "all too intensely secularized people whose entire life and way of thinking are secular . . ." (*JP*, I, 386). As a result, "The situation is neither more nor less than that Christianity has been abolished in Christendom . . ." (*JP*, I, 383). It functions ideologically in that it "sanctifies all our cherished relationships and our earthly fortune and striving" (*JP*, I, 401) and offers a "consolation served up in the form of human sympathy . . ." (*JP* I, 386). Kierkegaard recognized that the nineteenth-century Dane who eagerly participates in the experiment of modernization sees and feels the need for this religious legitimation and is half-consciously aware of his transformation of Christianity into a religion of culture.[29] "What every religion in which there is any truth aims at, and what Christianity aims at decisively, is a total transformation in a man, to wrest from him through renunciation and self-denial all that . . . to which he *immediately* clings, in which he *immediately* has his life. This sort of religion, as 'man' understands it, is not what he wants. . . . [The priests'] métier is to invert the whole situation, so that what man likes becomes religion. . . . The rest of the community, when one examines the case more closely, are seen to be egotistically interested in upholding the estimation in which the priests are held—for otherwise the falsification cannot succeed" (*AC*, 221).[30] Christendom is this blending of secularization and Christianity (*JP*, I, 407) and constitutes the situation in which the individual must be subjectively awakened and religiously nurtured.

For this purpose, the direct-indirect communication of religious discourse, rather than the indirect communication of pseudonymous discourse, is more suitable. The pseudo-

---

critically discusses the essentially prudential character of human actions that are engendered by the spirit of liberalism.

[29] It is in this sense that Kierkegaard used the concepts of illusion and self-deception when describing the individual in Christendom.

[30] The term *immediately* is italicized in order to remind the reader of the technical meaning of the term as it is used in Chapters Three and Four.

nym wants simply to jolt the individual into an awareness of his subjectivity. This awakening can be accomplished by a variety of pseudonyms, with a corresponding variety of results. An ironist like Johannes the Seducer may awaken the reader to a sense of despair. A humorist like Johannes Climacus may rouse his reader to a sense of guilt. A psychologist like Constantin Constantius may provoke his reader into despairing recognition of the impossibility of repetition. Or a Knight of Infinite Resignation like Johannes de Silentio may terrify his reader into a recognition of the fear and trembling one experiences in standing before God. In all these cases, the individual is awakened to a mode of subjectivity commensurate with the point of view of the author. Supposing that subjectivity is a continuum with beginning and ending points, it is possible for the individual to break into this continuum at any intermediary point. Where the individual enters depends upon his own personality and the particular pseudonym with whom he seriously converses. The religious growth and development of the individual does not enjoy this diversity of beginning points, however. Every individual in Christendom who reaches the point of developing his religious inwardness must begin with the recognition that he is situated in a prudential way of life that is legitimated by an enfeebled version of Christianity. Without this recognition, cultivation of religious inwardness toward becoming a Christian cannot begin.

For the task of engendering this self-recognition, a more direct mode of discourse is required. Thus, a sense of urgency must overtake the playfulness of the pseudonyms, and a sharply focused religious perspective must replace the pseudonyms' multiple points of view. It takes a religiously developed point of view to recognize Christendom for what it is and a sense of urgency to challenge its ethical and religious pretensions. Such requirements are too earnest for the pseudonyms' tastes. This focusing of the individual's situation in Christendom requires, then, a religious point of view, a sense of urgency, and an ethical earnestness that is best expressed through the direct-indirect communication of the ethical-religious discourse.

A second reason for Kierkegaard's shift to direct-indirect communication is that it places him as an author in a better position to cultivate a relationship between the reader's subjectivity and the divine. Contemporary philosophers, scholars, preachers, and theologians, according to Kierkegaard, fail to develop through their speech the individuality, personality, and primitivity of their readers (*JP*, I, 654, 655). Kierkegaard complained, for example, that in his dogmatics Martensen never once refers to his reader as *you* or to himself as *I* (*JP*, I, 673). In fact, "All personal communication and all individuality have disappeared; no one says *I* or speaks to a *you*" (*JP*, I, 673).[31] Contemporary writing smothers personality, whereas discourse in which there is a dialogue "immediately posits: *you* and *I*, and such questions as require: *yes* and *no*" (*JP*, I, 673). Kierkegaard believed that the age required a mode of discourse that would awaken the personality anesthetized by the objectifying discourse of the intellectuals and pastors. "Personality is what we need . . . [and] I have contributed, if possible, to familiarizing the contemporary age again to hearing an *I*, a personal *I* speak . . ." (*JP*, I, 656). The purpose of this first-person mode of discourse is to awaken personality as a necessary condition for or a prelude to the reform of Christendom. In fact, Kierkegaard does not distinguish the awakening of subjectivity and the reform of Christendom. "The concept 'Christendom,' 'established Christendom,' is what has to be reformed (the single individual). What is needed is the maieutic. It is not at all a matter of getting any change in externals . . . it is a matter of men being guided to an awareness that every individual is to seek the primitive God-relationship" (*JP*, VI, 6463). Thus, the awakening of subjectivity and the reform of Christendom lead back to the constitution of "the primitive God-rela-

31 Cf. *JP*, VI, 6440.

tionship." Kierkegaard viewed his role as an author as one of "guiding" his reader to this ethical-religious self-awareness.

Toward this end the pseudonyms are directed. "I regard it as my service that by bringing poeticized personalities who say *I* (my pseudonyms) into the center of life's actuality, I have contributed . . . to familiarizing the contemporary age again to hearing an *I* . . ." (*JP*, I, 656). Kierkegaard added in an apologetic fashion, "The poetic personality always has a something which makes him more bearable for a world which is quite unaccustomed to hearing an *I*. Beyond this I admittedly do not go" (*JP*, I, 656). Each of the pseudonyms enters into a conversation with the reader in a fashion that forces the reader back upon himself. Irony, humor, and ethical counsel, for example, are employed to deflect the reader's attention away from his interlocutor and toward himself. Kierkegaard's reader could not seriously confront the diverse array of pseudonyms without seeing himself reflected in his interlocutor's speech. Moreover, each pseudonym offers a particular reflection that is consistent with its own character. Kierkegaard explained, "The pseudonymous writers are poetic creations, poetically maintained so that everything they say is in character with their poetized individualized personalities . . ." (*JP*, VI, 6786). Thus, the many hues of the spectrum of subjectivity are mirrored in this array of pseudonymous authors. A serious reader cannot avoid being jolted out of the objectifying spirit engendered by nineteenth-century philosophers and politicians. The pseudonyms disclose to the reader, for example, the subjective beginning point of all reflection about human existence. There can be no presuppositionless beginnings. The pseudonyms expose the reader to the abyss of despair underlying the life lived for pleasure. They destroy the illusion of historical necessity and certainty concerning the life of Christ. And they lead the reader to the moment of faith and reveal to him the necessity of choice and risk. There can be no logical or historical certitude re-

278

garding the object of faith. The pseudonyms are at their best in luring their readers into the domain of subjectivity where the individual discovers himself in the ethical-religious stage of existence.

Though each of the pseudonyms is capable of seducing the reader into choosing to enter the ethical-religious stage of life, none is capable of nurturing the God-relationship that is the existential basis of the ethical-religious life. Once Kierkegaard has maieutically generated a relationship between the individual reader and a pseudonymous *I* for the purpose of reopening the domain of subjectivity, it becomes necessary for him to adopt a style of writing through which he can maieutically establish an existential relation between his reader and a divine *I*. No longer is Kierkegaard interested in mediating relationships between his reader and an ironist, a moralist, or a humorist. He came to see his task as one of cultivating a relationship between his reader and God. Through a relationship with the pseudonyms, the individual is guided into the ethical-religious stage of existence. Kierkegaard then seeks to replace the pseudonymous *I* with a divine *I* so that the ethical-religious life can grow in earnestness.

Once Kierkegaard embarked upon this course of action, a return to the pseudonymous mode of publishing seemed difficult, if not impossible. The prospect of pseudonymously publishing *Crisis in the Life of an Actress* in 1848 constituted a serious problem for him. He had "embarked so decisively upon Christianity, [had] presented much of it so strictly and seriously," that he feared a return to pseudonymous publication would confuse his reader.[32] By this time, he had published *Works of Love, Purity of Heart,* and *The Gospel of Suffering* and was at work on *Authority and Revelation* and *Training in Christianity*. All these works are devoted to the nurturing of the religious inwardness of his reader. *Works of Love* and *Purity of Heart* lay out the

[32] See my brief discussion of Crites's treatment of this point in n. 23 above.

full scope of Kierkegaard's ethics, which, as we have seen, is developed within the individual and is grounded in the God-relationship. *Training in Christianity, For Self-Examination,* and the posthumously published *Judge for Yourselves* lay out the polemical nature of the God-relationship. One who develops ethically in terms of *Works of Love* and *Purity of Heart* must certainly establish a polemical relationship to Christendom, which has given the Christian religion its own ideological twist. The ethical and religious development of the individual and the polemical thrust of this development are predicated on the God-relationship and the imitation of Christ. That his writing had taken this direction since 1846 caused Kierkegaard to question the strategic wisdom of returning to the pseudonymous mode of publication. He finally went ahead with the publication of *Crisis in the Life of an Actress,* by Inter et Inter, trusting in providence to use the little book in the best interest of his reader.[33]

Kierkegaard is quite explicit about this particular function of the discourse in his writings. In *Purity of Heart,* he compared himself as an author who writes discourses with a theater prompter who reminds the actors of their lines. The prompter is not himself an actor; he merely facilitates the action. It is the "actor's repetition" of the prompter's words that is of central importance (*PH,* 180-81). Thus, "the speaker is . . . the prompter, and the listener stands openly before God. The listener, if I may say so, is the actor, who in all truth acts before God" (*PH,* 181). The journals make more explicit the character of the relationship between the human and the divine. The relationship is an ethical one in which God plays the role of teacher (*JP,* I, 649). Moreover, the form of the author's communication with his reader must encourage this relation. "The communicator always dares influence only indirectly, (1) because he must always express that he himself is not a master-teacher but an apprentice and that God, on

[33] See Crites's introduction to *CLA,* pp. 7-63.

the other hand, is his and every man's master-teacher . . . because ethically the task is precisely this—that every man comes to stand alone in the God-relationship" (*JP*, I, 649: 20).[34] In this ethical relationship with a divine teacher the individual becomes conscious of himself as an ethical agent with an eternal responsibility toward himself and the other (*PH*, 197).

We have seen in Chapter Five how Kierkegaard argued that existing in a God-relationship is a necessary condition for existing freely as an ethical agent.[35] God, as an ethical teacher, functions Socratically in relation to the apprentice by instructing him in his freedom. The purpose of God's power "is precisely to make free . . . it is only omnipotence that can truly do it" (*CD*, 187n). Human beings, caught as they are in the web of egotistic self-seeking, are ethically incapable of dialectically constituting the freedom of the other; "in the relationship between man and man this cannot be done . . ." (*CD*, 187n). Only a being who is himself not motivated by the desire for self-justification can dialectically enter into a relationship with an individual in order to make him free. Such is the Socratic task of Kierkegaard's God, and it is through the discourse that Kierkegaard sought to mediate this ethical relationship between the divine teacher and his human apprentice.

In *Works of Love*, Kierkegaard goes out of his way to declare that neither art nor the poet—the form and creator of the pseudonyms—is appropriate for praising love. The poet and his art are "related to the accident of talent," while work is related to "the universally human" (*WL*, 330). This observation is significant because it situates love in the context of work and action and not in the artistic imagination. Moreover, the works of love are related to the universally human, which is the subject of the discourse

34 Cf. *JP*, I, 649:16: "In regard to the ethical, one person cannot have authority in relation to another because, ethically, God is the master-teacher and every man is an apprentice."

35 See Chapter Five, pp. 176-79.

(*POV*, 123-24). The poet celebrates "the riddle of life" as well as its blossoming and perishing, but Christian love "cannot be sung about—it must be believed and it must be lived" (*WL*, 26). It is the function of the discourse to cultivate the life of love precisely by "prompting" a relationship in which such a life can be learned. There is "only one intention in our discourse, and that I dare call the highest, there is only one thing it seeks, and that I dare call the highest: by every manner of means to make it forever sure that God is love" (*GS*, 85). This sentiment is clearly echoed in *Works of Love*: "What a human being of himself knows about love is very superficial; he must get to know the deeper love from God . . ." (*WL*, 334). Knowledge of the ethical nature of freedom, which is expressed in the works of love, can only be gained· in a relationship with God, which in turn Kierkegaard sought to "prompt" and cultivate in and through the discourses in his second literature.

In the divine relationship the individual learns not only freedom and love but also the reality and purpose of suffering. *The Gospel of Suffering* "does not seek to admonish anybody how he must go the way of tribulation but it makes for the sufferer the joyful proclamation that tribulation is the 'how,' defining the way of perfection" (*GS*, 97). The aesthetic, ethical, and religious modes of suffering[36] that occur as a consequence of the God-relationship serve to increase the individual's knowledge of himself and of his task of perfecting himself as an individual who exists in the presence of a loving God. The book has the character of a manual in its effort to instruct the reader about the variety of ways in which the suffering that results from existing in the God-relationship can be interpreted as the "way" toward rather than as an obstacle to self-perfection. Finally, one learns in the God-relationship that one should not fear other persons. Kierkegaard deplored "that men as individuals, forgetting their relation to God, in their relations among themselves become afraid of one another" (*GS*,

[36] See Chapter Six, pp. 221-23.

134). Having forgotten God "in our zeal to liberate mankind by overthrowing the dictatorships," Danes had fallen victim to one another in their envy and fear. Thus, in the final analysis, Kierkegaard turned to the discourse in order to cultivate the divine-human relationship (*JP*, IV, 3951, 3953). This relationship maieutically draws from the individual the acknowledgment of his freedom, a recognition of the works of love, and an acceptance of suffering. Herein one sees the texture of religious inwardness and the possibility of genuinely establishing a community of ends.

But without rectification of the category confusion besetting Christianity,[37] Kierkegaard recognized, it would be impossible either to focus his reader's understanding of his situation in Christendom or to cultivate the God-relationship. Both tasks require a clarification of Christian categories, and this conceptual overhauling of the Christian religion constitutes the third task that Kierkegaard attempted to complete in his second literature. He stated explicitly in 1850, "My activity with regard to the essentially Christian . . . is to nail down the Christian qualifications in such a way that no doubt, no reflection, shall be able to get hold of them" (*JP*, I, 522).[38] It would not be possible for the individual to develop inwardly without understanding the appropriate categories on which Christian self-examination and self-understanding are based. The theologians, philosophers, and pastors of Christendom had, in Kierkegaard's view, expropriated Christian terms and concepts for their own purposes; consequently, it had become impossible for the individual to perceive critically either himself or his situation through Christian categories. Kierkegaard's task was to restore the proper meanings to Christian terms and concepts in order to enable his reader to see Christendom for what it is and to begin the inward journey toward becoming genuinely Christian.

Two books in the second literature are particularly de-

37 See Chapter Two, pp. 82-84.
38 Cf. *JP*, I, 661.

voted to clarification of Christian categories, though it would be mistaken to view *Works of Love* and *Training in Christianity* as exclusively devoted to category analysis. Both books also clearly focus on the inward transformation of the individual and undertake a polemical assault on Christendom. In fact, all of the works in the second literature contain category analysis, inward upbuilding or transformation, polemics, and situation analysis.[39] They differ primarily in emphasis and focus. In *Works of Love*, the emphasis shifts toward a clarification of the categories of Christian ethics; in *Training in Christianity*, toward a clarification of the categories of faith. We should also note that Kierkegaard referred to *Works of Love* as a Christian reflection (*Christelige Overveielser*) (*WL*, 19) and to *Training in Christianity* as a poetic (*JP*, VI, 6528) and idealized presentation of the Christian life with which no human being in Christendom favorably compares.

In 1847 Kierkegaard seemed concerned to find a way of distinguishing *Works of Love* from his earlier *Edifying Discourses*. Like these earlier discourses, *Works of Love* was not published pseudonymously; for this reason, it was important to Kierkegaard to make his readers aware of its distinctness. Two strategies occurred to him. First, he appropriately points out that the earlier discourses develop the religion of immanence, or a religious consciousness that is not explicitly Christian; *Works of Love*, on the other hand, attempts to develop a Christian ethics. Second, *Works of Love* is not a discourse; rather, it is a Christian reflection that attempts to clarify the central categories of Christian ethics.

In an important 1847 journal entry, Kierkegaard distinguished between the reflection and the discourse in terms of their presuppositions. "Reflections do not presuppose the qualifying concepts as given and understood; therefore, they must not so much move, mollify, reassure, persuade, as *awaken* and provoke men and sharpen thought. . . . An up-

[39] See *JP*, VI, 6436.

building discourse about love presupposes that men know essentially what love is and seeks to win them to it, to move them. But this is in fact not the case. Therefore the 'reflections' must first fetch them up out of the cellar, call to them, turn their comfortable way of thinking topsy-turvy with the dialectic of truth" (*JP*, I, 641; Kierkegaard's italics). The reflection is designed not simply to clarify category confusion but also to show the reader that his confused way of thinking is rooted in his way of life. Thus, the reflection should *awaken* and *provoke* the reader, lift him out of the "cellar" of life into a more demanding and responsible mode of existence. Howard Hong nicely describes this dual aspect of the reflection: it "moves towards closing escape hatches and running down equivocations and uncovering evasions as it sharpens distinctions . . ." (*WL*, 14).[40] In other words, the reflection presupposes a unity of thought and practice and understands that one cannot be changed without the other.

Kierkegaard's analysis of love in *Works of Love* is a perfect example of the use of the reflection. He strives to draw sharp distinctions between Christian and non-Christian conceptions of love and at the same time to lead the reader to understand that his own blurring of this distinction is a reflection of a desire to legitimate Christianly a non-Christian mode of life. A conceptual clarification of the distinction between *agape* and *eros* must necessarily have one of two practical consequences: Kierkegaard's reader must either admit that he is not a Christian or resist Christendom.

Once the reflection has awakened the reader and clarified and sharpened conceptual distinctions, the discourse can move, mollify, reassure, and persuade. The reflection is a propaedeutic to Christian action in the sense that it provides the necessary categories; the discourse assumes that the reader is clear about category distinctions and urges

40 Douglas Steere makes the same point in his insightful introduction to *Purity of Heart*, pp. 9-24.

him on to action. Again, these distinctions cannot be too sharply made in terms of Kierkegaard's individual works, since all the later writings focus with varying degrees of emphasis upon both tasks.

While *Works of Love* clearly concentrates on sharpening the reader's understanding of the categories of Christian ethics, the concepts of faith and Christ receive the same purification in *Training in Christianity*. Here Kierkegaard adopts a pseudonymous strategy for the purpose of indicating that he himself does not personally approximate the rigorous description of Christianity presented in the book (*JP*, VI, 6528, 6534). He aims to rescue the concept of Christ from its idealist, historical, and middle-class confusions in the thought of Martensen, Grundtvig, and Mynster. His strategy is to link inseparably intellectual clarification with practical activity by combining his description of Christ as an offense with his insistence that imitation of Christ is the chief sign of faith. Kierkegaard hoped to show that the zenith of Christianity must be understood in terms of the ethical rigorousness of imitation of Christ (*JP*, VI, 6445). This conceptual clarification of the ethical nature of Christianity would lead his fellow Danes to admit that they are not Christians in any serious sense of the word. By bringing into focus the key concepts of Christianity, Anti-Climacus will have made it possible for all to see that Christianity does not exist in Christendom.[41] Kierkegaard regarded such a confession as a necessary condition for beginning to develop the religious inwardness of Christian existence.

Just as the self-love of Christendom is confused with the Christian love of *agape*, so the Christ of Christendom is

[41] Through the Anti-Climacus pseudonym, Kierkegaard reflected in 1849, "it was granted to me to illuminate Christianity on a scale greater than I had ever dreamed possible; crucial categories are directly disclosed there" (*JP*, VI, 6361). The categories of sin and faith are directly disclosed in *The Sickness unto Death*. *Training in Christianity* further illuminates the category of faith and directly presents the categories of Christ, the offense, and contemporaneity.

confused with the Christ of faith. In both cases, Kierkegaard believed, a special mode of discourse is required to point out these category and conceptual confusions and to restore their proper meaning in the Christian religion. For this purpose, Kierkegaard sought a mode of discourse in which he no longer conceals his personal understanding of Christianity. If the Christian transformation of inwardness is to occur, then Christendom must be identified, the inward development of each individual must begin, and a polemical assault on the ethical and religious pretensions of Christendom must be launched. All these tasks, which Kierkegaard set out to accomplish in his second literature, require a set of categories that are as clearly developed as possible. Without conceptual clarity, the task of becoming a Christian would languish in the same ambiguities and illusions besetting Christendom. Recognizing the importance of arming his reader with a clearly defined set of Christian categories, Kierkegaard was compelled to resort to a more straightforward and direct mode of discourse.

The fourth and final asset to be gained from the use of a more direct mode of discourse is its capacity for polemical assault on the established order. As early as 1846, Kierkegaard described himself as "advancing polemically against the age" (*JP*, V, 5887), referring no doubt to his attack on *The Corsair* and to his publication of *The Present Age*. Four years later, Kierkegaard claimed that "every religious author is *eo ipso* polemical . . ." (*POV*, 59), and it is clear that his polemical target is Christendom, which, he stated, should be attacked and "proved to be a fable" (*JP*, III, 2803). The polemic must not be a simple provincial attack on the church but must be directed toward the Danish way of life. "It is not church management and the like which ought to be reformed in our time—but the concept: Christendom" (*JP*, I, 592).[42] To concentrate on the external

[42] Cf. *JP*, VI, 6463. Cf. also *JP*, III, 3731: "It is not 'doctrine' which ought to be revised, and it is not 'the Church' which ought to be

reform of ecclesiastical structures as had Rudelbach is mistaken, since the real issue lies with the Danish state's arrogation of ethical and religious qualities (*ANOL*, passim). To participate in the modern Danish state is to participate in a way of life that is regarded as both ethically good and religiously justified. This ethical-religious self-interpretation of the modern state is exemplified, in Kierkegaard's view, by the practice of infant baptism, which implies that to be born a Dane is to be born a Christian. In an illuminating observation, Kierkegaard claimed that "from the moment Christianity conquered *in the worldly sense* and all became Christians in the ridiculous manner which nowadays is jealously guarded by secular-ecclesiastic authorities—so that everyone is baptized as a child—from that moment on the prime polemical target must be the illusion that we are all Christians, and this polemical sighting must be sharper and sharper with each century that 'established Christendom' stands . . ." (*JP*, III, 3196; Kierkegaard's italics).

How better to attack this "monstrous illusion" (*AC*, 139) than to show that there are no Christians in Christendom and to pronounce one's intent to be that of introducing Christianity into Christendom. In 1849 Kierkegaard observed that "it is already rather easy to see that 'the single individual' . . . is also the passage way through which 'Christendom' must go, since the task will continue to be to introduce Christianity into Christendom, which reverses all Christian conceptions, a prodigious illusion, which, if it is to be thoroughly overhauled and raised up must face the task: to introduce Christianity into Christendom" (*JP*, II, 2021).[43] Just as Socrates' point of departure for "disinte-

---

reformed, and so on—. No, it is existences which should be revised. Our whole way of life is stuff and nonsense and lack of character . . ."

[43] A long journal entry from 1848 nicely expresses Kierkegaard's concern to bring forward the ethical-religious mode of life as the proper response to the disintegration of his age into an aesthetic mode of life.

. . . That it was an age of disintegration, an esthetic enervating disintegration, and therefore, before there could be any question of even introducing the religious, the ethically strengthening, *Either/Or* had to precede, so that *maieutically* a beginning might be made with esthetic writings (the pseudonyms) in order if possible to get hold of men, which after all comes first before there can even be any thought of moving them over into the religious, and in this way it was also assured that in the sense of reflection the religious would be employed with dialectical care. That it was an age of disintegration—that "the System" itself signified, not as the systematicians were pleased to understand, that the consummation had been achieved, but that "the System" itself, as an overripe fruit, pointed to decline. That it was an age of disintegration—and consequently not as the politicians were pleased to think, that "government" was the evil, an assumption which would have been a curious contradiction from the standpoint of "the single individual," but that "the crowd," "the public," etc. were the evil, which corresponds consistently with "the single individual." That it was a time of disintegration—that it was not nationalities that should be advanced but Christianity in relation to "the single individual," that no particular group or class could be the issue but "the crowd," and the task: to change it into single individuals. That it was an age of disintegration—all existence as if in the clutch of a dizziness induced and in intensification fed by wanting continually to aid the movement with the momentary, that is, with finite cleverness and with the numerical, which simply feeds the sickness, a dizziness induced and fed by the impatience of the moment demanding to see effects at the moment, whereas what was required was the very opposite: the eternal and "the single individual." That it was an age of disintegration—a crucial age, that history was about to take a turn, that the problem was to have heard correctly, to be in happy rapport with the times and the turn which was supposed to be made: that it was the ethical, the ethical-religious, that should be advanced, but that above all the problem was to watch, with what one could call the self-love of the true or zeal for itself and its heterogeneity, lest the ethical again get garbled up with the old, which meant particularly that it hinged *not on teaching* the ethical but on accentuating the ethical ethically, on again mounting the qualitative force of the ethical—in qualitative contrast to the system, informational instruction, and everything pertaining to them—and at the same time to support it with personal existing, which, however, at the time meant to hide in the circumspect incognito of an idea. This, all of which is implied in "the single individual" as well as in the use made of this category, places the writing into another sphere, for "that single individual" will become an historical *point de vue.* (*JP*, VI, 6255; Kierkegaard's italics)

grating paganism" is the single individual, so Kierkegaard claimed that he would employ the same point of departure for the introduction of Christianity into Christendom (*JP*, IV, 4053).[44] The simple introduction of the individual into Christianity will ironically constitute a major attack on Christendom, since the latter believes in neither the individual nor Christianity.

Recognizing Kierkegaard's strategy for his attack on Christendom enables us to see how every word of his second literature is polemically directed toward the established order. His polemics are not confined to the presentation of an idealized version of Christianity by Anti-Climacus or to the shrill denunciations of the established church in *Attack upon Christendom* but are to be found in those gently persuasive and uncomplicated conversations with his readers through which he tries to cultivate the inwardness of the Christian life. The three tasks of the second literature possess an unmistakable polemical coloration in that they constitute the substance of Kierkegaard's strategy to introduce Christianity into Christianity. Since Christianity is "victorious inwardness" (*ANOL*, 51), it would be contradictory to attempt to introduce Christianity into Christendom by seeking to effect external ecclesiastical and political reform. Reformers like Rudelbach who attempt such measures are, in Kierkegaard's view, deeply mistaken about the proper strategy for changing Christendom. Christendom must pass through the individual, not liberal-minded ecclesiastical and political assemblies, and for this reason Kierkegaard launched an attack against the liberal reformers as well (*JP*, VI, 6710, 6721).

In the place of political action, constitutional reform, and ecclesiastical change, Kierkegaard substituted books written with the purpose of awaking his reader to an awareness that he is not a Christian but a member of Christendom, of developing his reader's inward appropriation of Christianity by cultivating his relationship with the divine,

[44] Cf. *JP*, VI, 6205.

and of conceptually clarifying the categories of Christian self-examination and self-knowledge. This strategy, as we have seen, is meticulously developed and carried forward in *The Present Age*, *Works of Love*, *Purity of Heart*, *The Gospel of Suffering*, *Christian Discourses*, and *Training in Christianity*. Each adopts an indirect method of polemically attacking the established order by maieutically cultivating the reader's sense of himself as an individual who inwardly exists before God. This awareness is Kierkegaard's Trojan horse, for by introducing an ethically and religiously developed individual into Christendom, he adopts the one strategy that Christendom cannot counter. Christendom cannot understand, much less absorb, the individual who claims that his only goal is to attempt religiously to express an absolute and unconditional love for the divine. Such a love is too *ethically individuating* for the established order. *Ethically*, it challenges Christendom by claiming that the content of freedom is fidelity to a moral law and not enjoyment of natural rights. The polemical challenge is deepened by its recognition of the *individual* as possessing a *personal* responsibility for his neighbor. It claims that the good life will be realized in and through a personal commitment to the other and not through political action and constitutional assemblies. This personal commitment, which is religiously grounded in the love for God, leads the individual to love the other in terms of his concrete actuality. The community of ends is one in which each individual is regarded as a worthy being precisely in terms of his concrete and identifiable particularity.[45]

Of course, the progression toward realization of a community of ends can begin only when the individual recognizes and acts upon the ethical character of his freedom. In Kierkegaard's view, such a recognition must be both religiously grounded in a love for God and ethically exemplified in a commitment to imitation of Christ. Finally, it must be pointed out again that this love for God sets the

[45] See Chapter Four, pp. 148-52.

individual along the path of enabling the other also to love God. Kierkegaard believed that the greatest love one can show for another person is to help him to love God (*WL*, 119). This is the supreme ethical action of the ethical-religious life, for only by virtue of a love for God on the part of all persons is it possible for a community of ends to come into existence. Christendom can only view such a life as both quaint and contrary to its own vision of the social nature of human life. Thus, the cultivation of this mode of ethical and religious inwardness is an essentially polemical activity, since it contains within itself a radical challenge to the ethical and religious pretensions of Christendom. We see, then, that it is necessary to perceive Kierkegaard's polemics as of a piece with his intent to introduce Christianity into Christendom through the inward transformation of the individual.

DIRECT COMMUNICATION AS DIRECT ATTACK

One difficulty clouds the claim that Kierkegaard essentially links his polemical strategy with the cultivation of Christian inwardness. *The Present Age, Works of Love, Purity of Heart, The Gospel of Suffering, Christian Discourses,* and *Training in Christianity* are without exception committed to the development of Kierkegaard's three-pronged direct-indirect attack on the established order. But there are difficulties with *For Self-Examination,* the posthumously published *Judge for Yourselves,* and the short attacks on the established church that were initially published in *The Fatherland* and later in *The Instant.* Where the earlier polemical strategy concentrates on directly-indirectly attacking Christendom through the cultivation of inwardness, the later strategy takes the form of a direct attack on the life style of Christendom (*Judge for Yourselves*), on the objectification of ethics and religion (*For Self-Examination*), and on the ecclesiastical structures and policies of the Danish church (*Attack upon Christendom*). Conceptual clarification of Christian categories and cultivation of the divine-human relationship disappear almost completely. Polemical and situation analysis remain, although Kierkegaard's polemics is transformed into a direct critical analysis of the established order of the sort previously found only in his journals. Given the defense of the necessity for indirectly attacking Christendom that is elaborately developed in his journals and the *Open Letter to Rudelbach,* and given Kierkegaard's faithful practice of direct-indirect polemics in all but the last three works, one is entitled to wonder whether Kierkegaard did not make a serious mistake by adopting a polemical strategy that appears to conflict in spirit and substance with his preceding works.

Two possible interpretations of this late change in strategy can be offered. First, it can be argued that the shrill and virulent attack on the Danish way of life is born of Kierkegaard's own impatience and neurosis. This interpretation proposes that he became impatient with the maieutic method and wanted to force the changes that he had earlier attempted to coax his readers into making voluntarily. Or one might agree with Thompson that these last works reflect a world-weariness and the culmination of Kierkegaard's neurotic effort to close himself off from the world.[46]

[46] Thompson, *Kierkegaard,* pp. 215-16. Thompson's book is important because it discloses the extensive influence of Kierkegaard's melancholy on both the style and content of his writings. Thompson relies heavily on Kierkegaard's statements in his journals about the influence his melancholy had on his use of the pseudonym as a way of escaping into image and fantasy in order to avoid actual contact with other persons and events. In Thompson's words, the purpose of the pseudonymous writings is "to shape experience into image" (Thompson, 135). Thompson also draws material from Kierkegaard's post-1846 books and journal entries, which indicate the seriousness with which Kierkegaard claimed in 1855 that "the purpose of life is to be brought to the highest degree of disgust with life" (Thompson, 215). The weakness in this psychological study is Thompson's failure to appreciate that Kierkegaard understood this fact about himself and used it to his advantage as a religious writer. There is insufficient space here to do more than sketch the outline of a defense of this claim.

Kierkegaard understood the category of "the extraordinary" to refer

Second, one may argue that Kierkegaard intended his reader to understand the attack in relation to his preceding emphasis on inwardness. Just as the body of the second literature must be understood in conjunction with the pseudonymous writings, so the direct polemic against the external dimensions of Christendom in the last works must be understood in conjunction with the direct-indirect attack against its lack of inwardness in the main part of the second literature.

---

to one who either attacks the established order with religious authority and in the name of God, as did Luther, or, more modestly, one who criticizes the established order without authority. This latter conception is worked out in detail in *On Authority and Revelation* and more aptly applies to Kierkegaard than does the first. In both cases, the extraordinary is one who exists outside the universally human; that is, the extraordinary does not participate ethically in the public and private social dimensions of life. Kierkegaard was aware of his inability to enter ethically into the universally human but claimed in 1850 that "I have never viewed my heterogeneity as a perfection, but rather as an imperfection on my part . . ." (*JP*, VI, 6577). Moreover, those who have been heterogeneous with the universally human from "an early age and in the most unhappy way . . . felt their difference from others . . ." (*JP*, I, 1081). These persons may recognize that their heterogeneity is the occasion for becoming an extraordinary. Clearly, the extraordinary is not born but develops slowly. "Then comes the time when he takes over his task. And here it is required that he love men to a high degree and be well-intentioned toward them" (*JP*, I, 1091). The extraordinary benefits not at all from living, "but the world has benefit out of their having lived, for they are the ones who introduce what is new" (*JP*, I, 1084). In this sense, Kierkegaard conceived of himself as an extraordinary and could without hesitation so sum up his life: "I can understand my life in this way: that I declare consolation and joy to others while I am myself bound in a pain for which I can see no alleviation . . ." (*JP*, V, 6133).

Before we slip into the cynical position of claiming that Kierkegaard was simply trying to put a complementary interpretation on his inability to enter into the universally human, it is possible to argue that one can support Kierkegaard's view of himself in terms of his own ethical interpretation of Christianity. A more sympathetic interpretation than Thompson's can legitimately be made in terms of Kierkegaard's claim that "Ethically there is nothing extraordinary, for the highest

Kierkegaard's analysis in his last works of his reader's situation in Christendom focuses more explicitly than ever on both its objective and subjective dimensions. The opening pages of *For Self-Examination* are devoted to a discussion of the fortunes of the Bible in Christendom. Ideally, according to Kierkegaard, the Bible is a mirror in which the reader is able to perceive reflectively his own subjective nature and destiny. "God's Word is the mirror—by reading or hearing it I am to see myself in the mirror . . ." (*FSE*,

---

is simply the requirement . . . The 'extraordinary' is not connected with ethical fulfillment of what is commanded but is connected with the singular relationship to God" (*JP*, I, 1090). The ethical requirement is, as we have seen, to love one's neighbor as one loves oneself. To keep this moral law is to enter into the universally human. Kierkegaard cannot enter into the universally human precisely because he cannot love himself. As we have seen in Chapter III, self-love is expressed as a striving to become a concrete, identifiable, and worthy self. But Kierkegaard's early childhood experiences, about which so much has been written, were of such a nature as to make self-love in his case an impossibility. The religious experience of 1848, in which Kierkegaard sensed the grace of God and the forgiveness of sin, is as close as he ever came to self-acceptance, which, as we have also seen, is grounded religiously in the sense of being accepted by God. Even this moment, however, was not sufficiently strong to shatter completely Kierkegaard's melancholy; as a result, he was never able to enter ethically into the universally human. Both the public and private dimensions of the universally human are heterogenous to his deformed and melancholic personality. Nevertheless, Kierkegaard strove to become a Christian. Even though he could not love himself, he could strive to love God for as he insisted, the extraordinary is connected not with the ethical but "with the singular relationship to God." Kierkegaard sought to love God by loving the other, which took the literary form of maieutically communicating with his reader in order to enable him to love God. In spite of the stylistic success of his writings, in spite of his strong effort to love his neighbor, Kierkegaard never fully became a Christian, because he could not fulfill the law that requires not only that he love his neighbor but also that he love himself. It is in this sense that Kierkegaard used his melancholy to his advantage as a religious author. Some light may be shed on this problem by a psychological study of Kierkegaard's personality. See Ib Ostenfeld, *Søren Kierkegaard's Psychology*, trans. and ed. Alastair McKinnon (Ontario: Wilfrid Laurie University Press, 1978).

295

51). This observation makes explicit a practice that Kierke-gaard observed throughout his second literature. By pre-senting his works in the guise of exegeses of biblical pas-sages, he leads the reader to reflect on the divine word, which in turn facilitates his purpose of cultivating the di-vine-human relationship. The individual is able to see him-self reflected in the divine word just as earlier he had seen himself reflected in the words of the pseudonyms.

The ethical-religious mode of subjectivity that is medi-ated by the divine word is at odds with the aesthetic mode of subjectivity that Christendom cultivates. It is the "cun-ning" of Christendom to objectify the Bible by converting it into a problem for scholarship. The reader approaches the Bible not in order to discover himself in the word of the divine but to determine in an objective and scholarly way whether one can claim that such a word is in fact divine. Christendom clouds the divine mirror so that the individual can no longer reflectively perceive his nature and destiny in it. The objectification of the divine word is a necessary condition for Christendom's cultivation of the aesthetic mode of subjectivity. With the disappearance of the subjective relation between the individual and the di-vine, it becomes possible for a more secular and acquisitive mode of subjectivity to develop.

In *Judge for Yourselves*, Kierkegaard analyzes this sub-jective development within Christendom in terms of the concept of sobriety. Traditionally, the term *sobriety* has an ethical-religious meaning: *"to come to oneself in self-knowledge, and before God, as nothing before Him, yet in-finitely, absolutely, under obligation"* (*JFY*, 120; Kierke-gaard's italics). Clearly, Kierkegaard interpreted the term to refer to the subjective life as it develops within the ethi-cal-religious mode of existence. In Christendom, however, it is synonymous with prudence: to be sober is to be prudent. Christendom associates "sobriety with common sense, dis-cretion, shrewdness and all that goes with this . . ." (*JFY*, 115). Kierkegaard carefully describes the prudential style of

life that is cultivated within Christendom by the liberalization of Danish life. With a shrewd and calculating reasoning, one is to guide one's life toward maximization of one's
interests and well-being. Kierkegaard viewed the objectification of the Bible and the emerging prudential understanding of subjectivity as necessarily related components
of the modernization of Denmark. Fully one-half of both
For Self-Examination and *Judge for Yourselves* is devoted
to his clarification of the individual's situation in Christendom.

The polemical element of Kierkegaard's indirect-direct
style of communication remains in the last works, although
there is a decisive shift toward the direct. The preface to
the posthumously published *Judge for Yourselves* singles
out the individual as the intended receiver of this book, describing him as one who is committed "to will to have a conscience" (*JFY*, 109). As we have seen, to have a conscience
is to exist before God.[47] Ostensibly, then, the indirect
polemic continues through the cultivation of the individual's ethical-religious inwardness. But whereas Kierkegaard's
criticisms of Christendom in the earlier works of the second literature are muted and overshadowed by his more
patient strategy of inwardly developing his reader, in *For
Self-Examination* and *Judge for Yourselves* he publicly
states his deepest suspicions about Christendom, referring
to it as selfish, cunning, shrewd, ethically dissolute, without
character, cowardly, worldly, bourgeois, mediocre, and self-
deceived. Kierkegaard pays lip service to the inward development of the individual's conscience but concentrates on
a direct and unambiguous attack on the established order.
This direct polemic is sharper in *Judge for Yourselves* than
in the earlier *For Self-Examination*, and it becomes even
more shrill in the attack on Christendom that followed the
writing of *Judge for Yourselves*.

The emphasis in the earlier works on inward cultivation
of the divine-human relationship is replaced in *For Self-*

[47] See Chapter Five, pp. 170-79.

Examination and *Judge for Yourselves* with an emphasis on the imitation of Christ. If one-half of each book is devoted to situation analysis, the other half admonishes the reader to take up the life of discipleship. "Christ is the Pattern, and to this corresponds imitation. There is only one true way of being a Christian—to be a disciple" (*JFY*, 215). Kierkegaard's style no longer attempts to cultivate an inward relationship between his reader and the divine. It is no longer directed toward the development of an ethical-religious subjectivity. The emphasis on the imitation of Christ is no longer linked with the concept of contemporaneity, as it is in the indirect polemic of *Training in Christianity*. In these two books, Kierkegaard reads more like a fiery pastor admonishing his congregation to take up the life of Christ against a sinful world. Where earlier Kierkegaard allowed his reader to discover for himself his heterogeneity with Christendom as a result of his own inward development, he now states bluntly that the Christian must die to the world and accept the suffering that inevitably follows from such a rejection. There is no subtle coaxing of the reader into opposition with Christendom through inward development; instead, Kierkegaard practically orders his reader to take up opposition to Christendom. Even the subtle polemic latent in the presentation of Christ as an offense in *Training in Christianity* is abandoned. Christ has become more a bludgeon than an offense against Christendom.

Corresponding to this emphasis on discipleship is the atmosphere of embattlement that Kierkegaard generates in these two books. Clearly, Kierkegaard is attempting to launch his readers into an outright ethical conflict with Christendom. The battle cry is taken from Matthew 6:24: "No man can serve two masters: for either he will hate the one and love the other; or else he will hold to the one and despise the other. You cannot serve God and Mammon." (*JFY*, 161).[48] A gnostic tone pervades the later writings as

[48] Cf. *JFY*, 139-40.

Kierkegaard sets his reader against Christendom, good against evil, light against darkness, heaven against earth. This dualism is intended to provoke a sense of ethical urgency, to prepare his reader to accept suffering and, in the final analysis, to hope for divine grace. Ethical rigor against an evil world, a contrite and penitent heart, and acceptance of grace: these are the key elements pervading *For Self-Examination* and *Judge for Yourselves*.

The intensity of Kierkegaard's direct attack in these two books reaches a frenzied pitch in his last attack on Christendom. The short articles published initially in *The Fatherland* and later in *The Instant*, a journal he inaugurated especially for the publication of these polemical articles, continue the direct attack against the established order, taking the analysis of and the polemic against Christendom to a shrill and at times irrational peak.[49] These articles also maintain the emphasis on the Christian life as one of imitating Christ and of ethically combating Christendom. They even introduce the idea of ecclesiastical reform, although Kierkegaard does not in any serious and thorough manner think through this problem. For the church to abandon its practices of paying salaries to its pastors and of baptizing infants hardly constitutes serious reform. It is more important to perceive Kierkegaard's attack on the established church as symbolic of his recognition of the ideological role that it had come to play in modern Denmark.

Pervading all the articles is Kierkegaard's claim that Christendom is an illusion (*AC*, 139), its inhabitants self-deceived (*AC*, 201), and its priests the sophistic servants of this illusion and self-deception. Kierkegaard cast himself in the Socratic role of exposing the illusion and deception and the sophistic priests who nourish and capitalize upon both (*AC*, 283-84). It is ironic that Kierkegaard refers to Socrates in this most unsocratic attack on the established order. Clearly, he is looking back over the history of his own

---

49 For example, Kierkegaard claimed that the noblest act for a Christian is not to have children so as to hasten the end of the world.

writing career when he refers to himself as having carried out the Socratic task of revising "the definition of what it is to be a Christian" (*AC*, 283). To be sure, his redefining of Christian inwardness is executed Socratically by the earlier pseudonyms and in the second literature. But his last three books convert the Socratic cultivation of the inward life into a direct assault on Christendom.

In order to explain this apparent aberration from Kierkegaard's Socratic course of action we must briefly review the central direction and purpose of the second literature. It can be summarily stated in four propositions. (1) To have a conscience is to exist before God. (2) To exist before God is to love one's neighbor as one loves oneself. (3) To love one's neighbor as one loves oneself is to work and hope for the coming of a community of ends. (4) To have faith in Christ is to believe in him as one who perfectly exists before God and is therefore an offense to Christendom. Christ is an offense to Christendom precisely because he represents the perfection of the ethical-religious mode of subjectivity, which conflicts sharply with the aesthetic mode of subjectivity in Christendom. These four propositions represent the subjective scope of the inward ethical transformation that Kierkegaard attempted to achieve through his direct-indirect manner of communicating with his reader. This existential development from an aesthetic to an ethical-religious mode of subjectivity bristles implicitly with opposition to the established order. Initially, the conflict is an inward one in the soul of Kierkegaard's reader. Inevitably, however, this inward transformation must transform the public life of the individual. To have a conscience is to exist before God. To exist before God is to will the other as an end. And to will the other as an end is, as we have seen, to will him materially and spiritually as an end. One cannot will the other as a material and spiritual end without radically disrupting a social order that requires that each will the other as a means to an end.

As we have seen in Chapters Two and Three, Kierkegaard understood political, economic, and social life to have an essentially spiritual foundation in the drive to become a concrete, identifiable, and worthy person. The public and private domains of human existence are inseparable. In Kierkegaard's view, the private is ontologically prior in that the dynamics of the subjective drive for self-respect constitutes the quality and character of public life. Thus, the transformation of this drive from an aesthetic to an ethical-religious mode of subjectivity will inevitably shake the individual's public character. An 1854 journal entry incisively states the practical consequences of this inward transformation. "What the God of Christianity wanted was a world-transformation, but a transformation of the actual, the practical world" (*JP*, I, 561).

It is in this sense that the direct attack on Christendom in *For Self-Examination, Judge for Yourselves*, and *Attack upon Christendom* is neither more nor less than Kierkegaard's explicit acknowledgment of what he had been implicitly cultivating in his reader all along. Although this direct attack may be psychologically motivated, such an explanation is at best incomplete. Ultimately, its rationality is to be judged in terms of its consistency with the works that precede the last three. In addition, the attack is an attempt to make explicit the public implications within Christendom of abandoning an aesthetic for an ethical-religious mode of subjectivity. The only possible misinterpretation that Kierkegaard has to fear is the one which claims that the reform of Christendom hinges upon attacking its external order and structure. Nothing could be further from the truth. Kierkegaard says that the reformation of Christendom must pass through the individual.[50] And he

---

[50] It is an illusion "to believe that corruption comes from a king, an emperor, the Pope, a tyrant, or a national leader; if only he can be toppled, the world will be saved. A reformer now places himself at the head, points to the bearded man on the throne—he is the one. If that were true and not a fantastic illusion, the world would undeniably be an uncommonly wonderful world where one person is

acknowledges Socrates as the only reformer worthy of emu-
lation.[51] The attack is itself a teaching technique, and in
order to prevent a mistaken interpretation of it, Kierkegaard continued to claim to write without authority. As if
to thwart any possible misinterpretation of the character of
the attack he was conducting in *The Instant*, Kierkegaard
returned in the last year of his life to patient direct-indirect
style in *The Unchangeableness of God* (1855). Like all the
preceding discourses, this one appeals to the individual to
establish an inward relationship with God. "But *first* and
foremost, do you also have an understanding with God?
Do you earnestly consider and sincerely strive to understand—and this is God's eternally unchangeable will for
you as for every human being, that you should sincerely
strive to attain this understanding—what God's will for
you may be? Or do you live your life in such a fashion that
this thought has never so much as entered your mind?"
(*JFY*, 231-32; my italics). *First* and *foremost* one must
consider his relationship with the divine. It is *first* in importance because all genuine change occurs initially within
human subjectivity. It is *foremost* in significance because
without such change all other acts are mere appearances
and delusions.

Conclusion

Without accepting the simple-minded conclusion that
Kierkegaard's entire authorship from *The Concept of Irony*

corrupt and all the rest of us are wonderful people. Let us recall a
Socratic question raised in a similar Socratic situation: I wonder if
with respect to horses there is only one who spoils them and everybody
else knows how to ride. *Any reformation which is not aware that fundamentally every single individual needs to be reformed is eo ipso an illusion*" (*JP*, III, 3724; my italics).

[51] "Can there be the slightest doubt that what Christendom needs
is another Socrates, who with the same dialectical cunning simplicity is
able to express ignorance or, as it may be stated in this case: I cannot
understand anything at all about faith, but I do believe" (*JP*, I, 373).

to *The Instant* is predesigned, it is nevertheless possible to see a coherence and direction in the entire authorship. Surely it is not predesigned or prearranged in Kierkegaard's mind at the very beginning, but it can be argued that the authorship unfolds with a logic and rationality that is clearly visible in retrospect. The central course along which the authorship develops is the way followed by Kierkegaard's reader in striving to become a Christian. The pseudonymous authorship awakens the reader from his aesthetic slumber to the possibility of an ethical-religious mode of subjectivity. The second literature, beginning with *The Present Age* and continuing through *Training in Christianity*, is Kierkegaard's attempt to communicate with his reader in such a way as to enable him to cultivate the ethical-religious mode of subjectivity awakened by the pseudonyms. The final stage of the second literature, including *For Self-Examination, Judge for Yourselves*, and *Attack upon Christendom*, attempts to make explicit the public and external consequences of the individual's inward development through his existing before God. Taken as a whole, the authorship is the work of a man who is genuinely committed to the reintroduction of Christianity into Christendom.

A FINAL WORD ABOUT SOCIETY

At the completion of this analysis of Kierkegaard's ethical-religious critique of the modernization of Denmark, an uneasiness may persist concerning Kierkegaard's theory of society. Without a doubt, Kierkegaard found the political activity and social organization of the modern Danish state problematic, and his critique of Christendom brought them into serious question. But exactly what sort of political and social views did Kierkegaard propose to replace those he so thoroughly repudiated in his second literature? This literature presents a reasonably well-developed image of the ethical-religious vision of human association, which we have identified as a community of ends.[1] However, we have yet to see the positive implications of this ethical-religious conception of human association for social-political questions. For example, we may legitimately query Kierkegaard on his views about property, labor, political authority, economic modes of production, distribution, and consumption, as well as the proper form of social organization.

As I stated in the Introduction to this study, Kierkegaard's analysis of the social and political problems of modern Denmark in terms of the individual's desire for an identity does not permit him to develop a social and political philosophy in a standard manner. Given Kierkegaard's perception of the nature of the problem as existing with the individual, he is compelled to address the individual who hopes to find a way of satisfying the desire for identity in the processes and structures of modernization. Thus, Kierkegaard does not fully develop a social and political theory, and those who seek one in his second literature will find

[1] See Chapter Four, pp. 148-52.

only failure and frustration. Beyond this initial reaction, one might claim that Kierkegaard simply failed to carry through fully the key implication of an attack on any existing social and political order. It might be objected that any thinker who takes on the task of radical social criticism must at some point come forward with alternative proposals, that failure to do so is both shortsighted and irresponsible.

Although Kierkegaard's works do not contain an explicit response to such a criticism, it is possible to discern in both the style and content of his second literature a justification for his relative silence on this point. In approaching this problem, it will be useful to remember that Kierkegaard's criticisms of the philosophical dominance of Hegelian idealism are predicated on his belief that this system ignores the importance of the individual's development as an ethical-religious subject. The attention lavished upon the individual by most of the pseudonyms is motivated by their concern over the conceptual and existential absorption of the individual into a philosophical system that anesthetizes him to his ethical-religious destiny. As we have seen, Kierkegaard viewed Christendom as having the identical anesthetizing effect upon the individual as an ethical-religious subject; uncritical and enthusiastic participation in the life of Christendom is a form of ethical-religious amnesia.

Kierkegaard therefore regarded his first responsibility with respect to political and social issues as one of awakening the individual from the ethical-religious slumber that has allowed him to enter into an essentially mistaken political and social order. This tact is predicated on his belief that attainment of an ethical-religious mode of subjectivity is a necessary condition for discussing in a theoretically productive manner the details of social organization and political activity. Individuals who enter into such a discussion must know themselves as individual participants in Christendom and be capable of making category distinctions between social-political and ethical-religious modes of discourse. Given Kierkegaard's perception of Christendom as singularly lacking in both this knowledge and capability, his only strategy could legitimately be one that allows him to address both issues.

Kierkegaard believed that Christendom had lost sight of a fundamental and primitive fact about human life, one that any healthy political and social order must never ignore, namely, that individuals cannot avoid loving themselves. This fact grounds the social dimension of human life, because self-love necessarily expresses itself as a desire for an identity that is publicly recognizable and valued. Satisfaction of this desire essentially requires expression in political, economic, social, and cultural spheres. When this desire is not mediated by an ethical-religious resolve to love one's neighbor as one loves oneself, it takes an egotistical form that sets individuals into private and public networks of instrumental relationships in which they are incapable of generating within themselves any sort of transformative processes. We have referred to this sort of human arrangement as the state of nature, based on Kierkegaard's characterization of the individual in this state as the natural man. The concepts of natural man and egotism provided Kierkegaard with the hermeneutical tools for analyzing the political activities of the modern state, its social organization into economically based classes, and its cultural legitimation in terms of the egotistical mode of self-love. One of the fundamental problems with Christendom, Kierkegaard argued, is that it has permitted the institutionalization of egotism. Indeed, the most primitive fact about Christendom is that it exists within the state of nature. Moreover, this problem is seriously compounded by the individual's ignorance of this fact about himself and the nature of his relation to others within Christendom.

The institutionalization of egotism is theoretically reinforced by the individualistic philosophies dominating political, literary, and religious thought. The philosophical priority of the individual is, of course, the fundamental

306

principle of the liberal political and social theories that grounded the institutional development of modern Denmark. The individual is defined as a being who possesses the natural right always to act with a view to maximizing his own interests. His dependence upon others is only the negative dependence of being legitimately free from their interference so long as he does not infringe upon their enjoyment of this same right. This individualistic conception of human nature is reinforced by the romantic version of the individual as a being whose happiness is teleologically grounded in nature. The romantic literature of Denmark's golden age of literature celebrated the centrality of the individual in the life of nature. Moreover, this priority of the individual's happiness is present not only in nature but also in the heavens, as is reflected in the Grundtvigian and Mynsterian Lutheran conceptions of the individual as one who is essentially a recipient of God's grace. These cultural developments in literature and religion combined with the political and social development of the modern state to institutionalize the egotistical and acquisitive mode of subjectivity.

It is important at this point to remember that when one speaks of a mode of subjectivity, a stage of existence, or a form of life in relation to Kierkegaard's thought, one calls into view a way of being that pervades all thinking, feeling, perceiving, speculating, moralizing, etc. To speak of an egotistical mode of subjectivity is to address not one among many ontological facts about the individual but the only significant fact about the individual and his public and private associations with others in the modern state. Kierkegaard recognized that in order to bring his contemporaries to the point of self-critically reflecting on the egotistical foundation of their social and political structures and activities, it is first necessary to engender a critical self-reflection about the egotistical mode of subjectivity that informs their personal lives.

Ethical-religious mediation of the egotistical mode of

307

subjectivity into which modern Denmark had fallen required a Socratic approach to the individual. Lecturing, preaching, moralizing, theorizing—even revolutionary activity directed toward the destruction of the modern state— are all bound to fail by virtue of their unreflective grounding in an egotistical mode of subjectivity. In Kierkegaard's view, the only way to overcome this problem is to address the individual in such a fashion that he is awakened from his ethical-religious slumber. Such an awakening leads the individual through three stages: coming to perceive the true nature of his subjective constitution with Christendom; choosing to exist before God; and, as a consequence, choosing also to love one's neighbor as one loves oneself. This ethical-religious mediation of egotism is a necessary condition for creatively addressing social and political questions concerning the proper organization of human life.

Nothing is more essential for the individual's completion of this regenerative self-transformation than a mode of discourse that is conceptually precise. Indeed, given the Socratic character of Kierkegaard's undertaking, no tool is more indispensable than language. Through conversation with his reader, Kierkegaard sought to awaken him to a correct self-knowledge. Once the individual attains this self-knowledge, his ethical-religious resolve to love the other as a neighbor involves speaking with him about his nature as a being essentially motivated by self-love and desire. A mode of discourse must be found that allows no possibility of conceptual confusion concerning the individual's nature and his relationship both to God and to other human beings. In addition, the ethical-religious resolve for self-transformation depends upon a mode of discourse that is appropriate for both egotistical and altruistic expressions of self-love.

Kierkegaard believed that the individual's self-recognition in just these terms is seriously weakened by what we have referred to in Chapter Two as a confusion of cate-

308

gories.[2] The religious and ethical categories essential to correct self-knowledge—for example, God, obligation, freedom, equality, the individual—had been absorbed into the philosophical, religious, and political rhetoric of modernization, which had even used them to interpret the individual's participation in this experiment as itself an ethical act. In Kierkegaard's view, these terms must be restored to their proper location in an ethical-religious conception of the individual that on the one hand binds him to God and on the other obligates him to will all persons as ends rather than as means to ends. For example, to be free is not to possess a natural right to pursue one's interests but to be obligated to love others as one already loves oneself; to experience oneself as existing before the moral law legitimately grounds the conception of oneself as free. To clear the conceptual confusion surrounding the category of equality, one must conceive of human equality not in terms of the universality of natural rights but in terms of the existence of every individual before God; one's equality with all other human beings is ethically and religiously, not politically, grounded. Moreover, one must conceive of God as the divine ground not of rights but of the obligation to love one's neighbor as one loves oneself. We have seen in the preceding chapter that one of Kierkegaard's primary motivations for writing both polemics and what he called reflections (*Overveielser*) was to rescue the essential categories of ethical-religious speech from their illegitimate use by the modernizers. Without the linguistic clarification of this confusion of categories, which allows for distinctions between the ethical-religious and the social-political modes of discourse, it would not be possible to enter productively into a theoretical discussion concerning social organization and political activity. Thus, because of the egotistical horizon of all thought and activity on the one hand and the conceptual confusion of the ethical-religious and social-political modes of discourse on the other, Kierkegaard was

2 See Chapter Two, pp. 82-84.

effectively blocked from entering into a discussion of this sort.

From Kierkegaard's uncompromising insistence on the development of a mode of discourse within which the individual can both identify his tendency to egotistical self-love and discover the possibility for self-renewal, one can postulate the corollary that the possibility for ethical renewal lies within the individual and not the modern state. Given Kierkegaard's view that the modern state is an institutionalized extension of the individual's tendency to love himself egotistically, it is not surprising that he entertained no hope that goodness can be derived from it. His suspicions of the optimism of the political reformers of his day, of Grundtvig's well-meaning, though naive, politics of love, and of Mynster's innocent sermonizing to the well-established middle class were based on his belief that these activities are rooted in a critically unreflected self-love that perpetuates an ethical problem of which his contemporaries were not even aware. In Kierkegaard's view, only God can reform men. Hence, the age requires an ethical-religious language that brings its hearers to stand before God.

Kierkegaard concluded that " 'the individual' is the category through which, in a religious respect, this age, all history, the human race as a whole, must pass" (*POV*, 128). Moreover, this category is one "of the spirit, of spiritual awakening, a thing as opposite to politics as well could be thought of" (*POV*, 132). Kierkegaard further claimed that "this category was used only once with decisive dialectical force, and for the first time, by Socrates to dissolve paganism. In Christendom on the other hand it will serve a second time to make men (i.e. Christians) into Christians. It is not the category of the missionary who deals with pagans to whom he proclaims Christianity for the first time; but it is the category of the missionary within Christendom itself, aiming to introduce Christianity into Christendom" (*POV*, 136). To introduce Christianity into the modern Danish state is to introduce the ethical-religious individual into Christendom. Only if Christendom passes through this ethical-religious event and is awakened to the ethical-religious vision of a community of ends will it become possible to enter into a normative discussion about the proper social and political organization of human life. In a very early journal entry, Kierkegaard suggested such a dialectical move for human history: "When the dialectical period (the romantic) has been passed through in world history (a period I could very appropriately call the age of individuality—something which can also be demonstrated historically quite easily), social life must again play its role to the utmost degree, and ideas such as the state (for example, as the Greeks knew it, the Church in the older Catholic meaning of the word) must of necessity return richer and fuller—that is, with all the content that the residual diversity of individuality can give the idea, so that the individual as such means nothing, but all are links in the chain" (*JP*, IV, 4070). The Hegelian undertones of this passage, with its references to "the residual diversity of individuality" and historical demonstrability, may offend the Kierkegaardian ear. But one should not too quickly dismiss it as an example of a subtle Hegelian influence on Kierkegaard's young and experimenting mind. One can plausibly argue that the preceding passages about the category of the individual, which were written by the mature Kierkegaard and posthumously published in *The Point of View of My Work as an Author*, are clearly audible echoes of this early appreciation for the dialectically historical relation between the question of the nature of the individual and the question of the nature of society. It appears perfectly consistent with Kierkegaard's mature thought in both his pseudonymous and second literatures to claim that once the individual is ethically and religiously constituted, one of his key tasks will be to consider the social and political implications of the ethical and religious vision of a community of ends.

But, as we have seen, Kierkegaard must have understood that this investigation must wait for another day. He had

311

to deal first with other problems, the most significant of which is the individual's relation to Christendom. Once the ethical-religious critique of Christendom reaches its conclusion with the recognition that each individual is ethically obliged to will the existence of a community of ends, a new set of questions concerning social and political life can be asked. Obviously, the concept of a community of ends does not offer an easily accessible and conceptually clear political and social program for the future. It is not even clear whether this ethical-religious position entails one rather than a plurality of social and political modes of organization. Given Kierkegaard's emphasis on individuality, one might argue that he has to allow for diversity in political and social forms of organization just as he allows for diversity in the constitution of individuality. It may be the case that a people's history and character are as essential to its political and social destiny as are the history and character of individuals. If so, plurality rather than universality will characterize the social and political organization of the peoples of the earth. Even more fundamentally, it might be possible and necessary to argue that this ethical-religious concept of a community of ends comes into view dialectically as a critical negation of the modern liberal state. It would then be difficult to argue for the immediate universal application of this concept, given the varying stages of development of the plurality of nations and traditions within the world. Perhaps the search for a social and political translation of the ethical-religious concept of a community of ends engages only those peoples who are moving through the experiment initiated in western Europe by the French Revolution.

We could raise other serious and difficult implications of Kierkegaard's ethical-religious vision of a community of ends for the social and political organization of human life. But such an enterprise is not here called for, since the point of raising these questions is to show that difficulties will be encountered by those who search for a viable material expression of the ethical-religious vision of a community of ends.

It is appropriate to conclude the study of any person's thought by focusing upon the range of further problems that it raises. Clearly, we must move from resolving ethically and religiously to will the existence of a community of ends to considering an equally complicated range of issues concerning the social and political incarnation of this choice. This forward motion will not be easy, and it will be made even more complicated, indeed even futile, if we forget that our self-love requires an ethical-religious transformation before it can seek and hope for its social and political expression in an earthly society.

INDEX

319

Library of Congress Cataloging in Publication Data

Elrod, John W   1940-
    Kierkegaard and Christendom.

    Includes bibliographical references and index.
        1.   Kierkegaard, Søren Aabye, 1813-1855.
    2.   Christianity—Philosophy.   3.   Self (Philosophy)
    I.   Title.
    B4378.C5E45   230'.044   80-8547
    ISBN 0-691-07261-2

JOHN W. ELROD is Associate Professor and Chairman of the
Department of Philosophy at Iowa State University and the
author of *Being and Existence in Kierkegaard's Pseudonymous Works* (Princeton).

THE LIBRARY
ST. MARY'S COLLEGE OF MARYLAND
ST. MARY'S CITY, MARYLAND 20686